HEBREW FOR THEOLOGIANS

A Textbook for the Study of Biblical Hebrew in Relation to Hebrew Thinking

Jacques B. Doukhan

UNIVERSITY
PRESS OF
AMERICA

Lanham • New York • London

Copyright © 1993 by
University Press of America®, Inc.
4720 Boston Way
Lanham, Maryland 20706

3 Henrietta Street
London WC2E 8LU England

Library of Congress Cataloging-in-Publication Data
Doukhan, Jacques.
Hebrew for theologians : a textbook for the study of Biblical Hebrew
in relation to Hebrew thinking / Jacques B. Doukhan.
p.   cm.
Includes bibliographical references and index.
1. Hebrew language—Grammar.   2. Bible. O.T.—Language, style.
I. Title.
PJ4567.3.D68   1993   492.4'82421—dc20   93–24506 CIP

ISBN 0–8191–9269–4 (pbk. : alk. paper)

In memory of my teacher André Neher
who taught me the life of Hebrew.

To my students
who taught me how to teach it.

"Hebrew is the source from which springs all theology."

Johannes Reuchlin

CONTENTS

INTRODUCTION

Hebrew for Theologians is primarily designed for ministers, seminary students, and religion students in college, who are interested in the Bible and wish to become familiar with its thought.

This unusual, vast horizon hints already to the conviction underlying this textbook, namely, that the study of Hebrew is indeed pertinent.

The study of Hebrew language is generally considered a difficult, boring, and totally irrelevant requirement. Therefore I shall first outline some of the main reasons which make this enterprise, on the contrary, an exciting and necessary adventure. In this Introduction, I will try then to convince you, to motivate you. I will first argue "positively," because of what Hebrew is, that is, the language of the ancient Israelites, the language of theology, and according to great representative witnesses in history, "the holy language." Then, I will argue "negatively," because of what Hebrew is not, pleading against the biases and myths which surround this language and encumber the minds of many students. Lastly, on the basis of the arguments *justifying* the study of Hebrew (the why?), I will propose a methodology and a pedagogy *guiding* the study of Hebrew (the how?).

I. Hebrew is Relevant

A. The Language of the Ancient Israelites

The study of this language is relevant first of all because it is the language spoken, written, and thought by the Ancient Israelites of the Bible. Along with other traces of the past, the artifacts and the stones uncovered by archaeology, Hebrew language witnesses to that ancient civilization. It is, indeed, facetious to think that it is possible to have an idea of biblical civilization without having an idea of what the biblical language is like. Paradoxically, everyone is aware of this common-sense truth so long as it concerns secular civilization. Who would question the pertinence of learning the English language in order to understand the world of Shakespeare? Or, to be more up-to-date, who would ignore the need for learning English to be able to understand and handle the current intricacies of the political and economical life in America? Yet, when it comes to the Bible, it seems that ignorance is allowed and even recommended. The reason for this paradox lies especially in our "religious" sympathy with the Israel of the Bible, because we identify the God of Ancient Israel with our God. In more simple terms, this means that the claim for a present relationship with the God of Israel makes the study of the antique language irrelevant. This subjective approach overlooks the importance of God's revelation in History. On the other hand, if we believe that our God is the God of Israel, the best way to understand Him will be to understand Him within that very context of Ancient Israel. For about two thousand years, a people have experienced in their flesh the presence of "God with them" and have used the Hebrew language to report this particular experience. If I am interested in the meaning of that experience, I should be compelled to study Hebrew not only because of my personal affinities with Israel, but also because I realize that the Israelite experience is altogether strange to me; we must study it precisely because it is a part of *another* culture which is past, remote and lost[1] for all of us, however valuable our present religious experience may be. *The first reason for studying Hebrew is then historical in nature.*

The Hebrew language did not come from heaven, like magic, but is a natural part of a historical process; it is one of the multiple branches of the Semitic family of languages in the Ancient Near East (cf. Gen 10:21-31).

The Semitic languages are usually distributed, according to their geographical situation, into three main branches, namely 1) North-East Semitic, 2) North-West Semitic, and 3) South Semitic. In the following table we have indicated the distribution of these languages, and provided each of them with some representative documents which attest to them. For the Hebrew language which belongs to the North-West branch, the list of representative documents is more comprehensive than for the other languages.

---

[1] The knowledge of modern Hebrew is, indeed, helpful to understanding biblical Hebrew, as the latter is nothing but the resurrection of the former; a few adjustments are, however, necessary, indicating the fact that something has been lost. For the differences between modern and ancient Hebrew, see Haiim B. Rosen, *Contemporary Hebrew* (The Hague, 1977), 30-37; cf. Eduard Y. Kutscher, *A History of the Hebrew Language*, ed. Raphael Kutscher (Jerusalem, 1982), 196-220.

North-East Semitic:

```
          ┌──Babylonian dialect
          │      • Code of Hammurabi (1750 B.C.?)
Akkadian ⟨     • Enûma Eliš (1400 B.C.?)
          │
          └──Assyrian dialect
               • The Black Obelisk (841 B.C.?)
```

North-West Semitic:

Aramaic • Ezra 4:8-6:18; 7:12-26; Dan 2:4-7:28; Jer 10:11; Gen 31:47;
           (two words)
- The Milqart Stele (9th century B.C.)
- Papyri from Elephantine (495 B.C.)
- The Babylonian Talmud (A.D. 500)
- Targumim (2nd and 5th century A.D.)

Ugaritic • The Legend King Keret (1400 B.C.)

Hebrew • The Hebrew Bible (15 century B.C.-4th Century B.C.)
- The Gezer Calendar (10th century B.C.)
- Inscriptions on Pottery from Samaria (854 B.C.)
- The Siloam Inscription (701 B.C.)
- Letters from Lachish (590 B.C.)
- Seals, Weights, and Coins (9th century B.C.-4th century B.C.)
- Qumran (200 B.C.-A.D. 135)
- The Mishna (3rd century A.D.)
- Midrashim (4th century-12th century A.D.)
- Medieval Poetry and Philosophy (11th century-16th century A.D.)
- Modern Hebrew (since 18th century A.D.)

South Semitic:

Arabic • The Qurʾan (7th century A.D.)

Ethiopic • The Kebra Nagast (14th century A.D.)

B. The Language of Theology

Because Hebrew language is a part of the history of Israel and because this history implies a spiritual experience, it is expected that at least some aspects of that spiritual experience should be reflected in it. It is inconceivable, indeed, that two thousand years of that particular history would have passed without affecting the language in one way or another. On the other hand, the errors and abuses denounced by James Barr[1] should not keep us from recognizing with modern linguistics that there is a connection between language and thought,[2] and that language is, as Noam Chomsky puts it: "the mirror of the mind."[3] This principle is particularly valid in biblical civilization where language plays a most important role,[4] and where an acute awareness of the connection between language and thought (or

[1]See James Barr, *The Semantics of Biblical Language* (London, 1961). In response to James Barr's criticism, see especially Thorleif Boman, "Sprache und Denken: eine Auseinandersetzung mit James Barr," Appendix of the new German edition of his book, *Das hebräische Denken im Vergleich mit dem griechischen* (Göttingen, 1968).

[2]On the connection between language and thought in modern linguistics, see especially John B. Carroll, *Language and Thought* (Englewood Cliffs, NJ, 1964); Samuel I. Hayakawa, *Language in Thought and Action* (New York, 1972); see also Michael K. Tanenhaus, "Psycho Linguistics: An Overview," *Linguistics: The Cambridge Survey*, ed. Frederick J. Newmeyer (Cambridge, England/New York, 1988), 3:1-37.

[3]Noam Chomsky, *Language and Mind* (New York, 1972), x; cf. Ray Past, "When we study language, we are approaching what some might call the 'human essence,' the distinctive qualities of mind that are, so far as we know, unique to man" (*Language as a Lively Art* [Dubuque, IA, 1970], 1).

[4]On the importance of language in the Bible, see especially Moisés Silva, *God, Language, and Scripture: Reading the Bible in the Light of General Linguistics* (Grand Rapids, 1990), 19-40; cf. André Neher, *The Exile of the Word, from the Silence of the Bible to the Silence of Auschwitz* (Philadelphia, 1981).

theology) is clearly attested.[1] *The second reason for studying Hebrew is then theological in nature.*

The Word *dābar.* In Hebrew thought, language is not just an aggregate of sounds, an empty noise. The word expresses a reality. It may be a tangible reality, a thing, an event, or a spiritual truth, a prophetic message. It is significant for instance that the Hebrew word *dābar* means "word," "thing," "history," and "prophecy." The reason for that semantic association is that the word is bound with the reality it intends to refer to. It is one with it. This phenomenon may seem awkward to us in a civilization where the word has lost its significance and its weight. In the Bible, however, this principle vibrates everywhere.

The Giving of the Names. As soon as man was created, his first duty was to give names (Gen 2:19, 23) and thereby participate in the divine Creation. From then on throughout the Bible, the Israelites would give names to designate persons, places, and God. The names were not simply repeated as the product of a mechanical memory, they were supposed to express the inherent reality of what they designated. For instance, the name "Adam" came from the word "ʾadama" which means "earth," because he is of an earthly reality. Likewise Abel which means "vapor" points to the ephemeral destiny of the man who bears that name. Not all the names are explained, but the principle which inspired them is often stated. This is the case for Eve (Gen 3:20), Noah (Gen 5:29), Cain (Gen 4:1), Seth (Gen 4:25), Peleg (Gen 10:25, cf. 1 Chr 1:19), Jacob (Gen 25:26), Abraham (Gen 17:5), Samuel (1 Sam 1:20), Solomon (1 Chr 22:9), Nabal (1 Sam 25:25), Ichabod (1 Sam 4:21), Lo-Ruhamah (Hos 1:6), etc. Likewise, places are named according to the same principle. Babel (Gen 11:9), Beer Sheba (Gen 21:30, 31), Bethel (Gen 35:7, 15), Achor (Josh 7:26), Jezreel (Hos 2:22, 23), Achzib (Mic 1:14), Jehoshaphat (Joel 3:2), etc., are names

---

[1]Regarding the connection between language and thought in the Bible, see L. Alonso-Schökel, "Telogia biblica y linguistica" in *Biblica* XLIII (1962): 217-223; J. P. McIntyre, S.J., "Biblical Theology and Christian Language," in *Sciences ecclésiastiques* XV (1963): 459-466; N. Ridderbos, "Is het hebreeuws één van de bronnen van de openbaring?" in *Gereformeerd Theologisch Tijdschrift* LXIV (1964): 209-229; E. Ullendorff, "Thought Categories in the Hebrew Bible," in *Studies in Rationalism, Judaism and Universalism in memory of Leon Roth*, ed. R. Loewe (London, 1966), 273-288; B. S. Childs, *Biblical Theology in Crisis* (Philadelphia, 1970), especially 70ff. See also Jacques Doukhan, "L'Hébreu en Vie: Langue hébraïque et civilisation prophétique: Etude Structurale" (Ph.D. diss., University of Strasbourg, 1973).

given in relation to what they mean spiritually or historically. The naming process which is a part of the language, works in close relationship with the thought process, suggesting thereby that thought and language are related in biblical civilization.

The Names of Baal. This particular connection shines through in an interesting observation with regards to the use of the name Baal. The word Baal which means in Hebrew "husband," "master," was also used to designate the Hebrew God[1] in the spiritual context of the conjugal covenant where God, *YHWH*, is the husband, and Israel, the wife. Yet, under the Phoenician influence, Israel began to confuse her God, the master, the husband (Baal), and Baal, the Phoenician god of fertility. It is noteworthy that prophets like Amos and Hosea felt the need to react against that confusion on the level of the language. Although Amos knew the conjugal metaphor (3:2; 4:12; 5:2), he never used the term Baal. Likewise Hosea (2:16) warned his people: "And it shall be, in that day, says the Lord, that you will call Me 'My Husband' (*ishi*: my man) and no longer call Me 'My Master' (*baali*: my baal)." On the other hand, names which contain the element of Baal are often changed and the word Baal is replaced by the word *Boshet* (meaning shame). This is the case for Jerubosheth instead of Jerubaal (2 Sam 11:21). This phenomenon is particularly telling in that it shows how aware the Israelites were of the influence of language upon the mind, hence upon religious decision.

Nehemiah's Anger. The acute awareness of the connection between language and thought made Nehemiah angry as he realized that his people were forgetting the Hebrew language: "half of their children . . . could not speak the language of Judah . . . So I contended with them and cursed them, struck some of them and pulled out their hair" (Neh 13:24, 25 NKJV). It is perhaps the same passion which is heard nowadays in the angry speeches and supplications of the Hebrew teacher who dares to think that Nehemiah was right; for he sadly observes that his people are losing their religious identity, and that this tragedy has something to do with their lack of interest in the Hebrew language, because they have lost their Hebrew roots. Certainly the Hebrew teacher will not "pull out their hair," "strike them" or "curse them," but at least—he will write a book.

---

[1]See for instance the name Bealiah (1 Chr 12:5) which means Baal is *YHWH*, or *YHWH* is Baal.

C. The Holy Language

As soon as the Hebrew Scriptures became *"Holy* Scriptures," the language which conveyed them was regarded a "holy" in Jewish as well as in Christian tradition. The quotations we have collected here are not exhaustive, but they are fairly representative of the tendency in both traditions.[1]

1. The Jewish Tradition

For the rabbis of the Talmud and the Midrash, for the Jewish philosophers and mystics of the Middle Ages and the Modern Period, Hebrew was consistently revered and studied as the holy language because it was the language of the Fathers, of the Holy Scriptures, and of God.

The rabbis of the Talmud identify the Hebrew language as the language of God, the first language ever spoken by mankind, even before the division of Babel. The expression "holy language" (*Lashon haqodesh*) specifically designates the Hebrew language.[2] The Scriptures were given in "holy language."[3] This holiness of the Hebrew language is such that it can be used only by special people and on special occasions. Thus, human beings are put on the same level as angels only if they know Hebrew. "They have understanding like the ministering angels, and they walk erect like angels; and they can talk in the holy language like the ministering angels."[4] Furthermore, "it is permitted to discuss secular subjects in the 'holy language,' but it is forbidden to discuss holy subjects in the vernacular."[5] According to the rabbis of the *Jerusalem Talmud*, "one who made it his practice to speak Hebrew would have a share in the afterlife."[6] Playing on the words "one language" in Gen 11:1 which can be read literally

---

[1]See Joshua Kettilby, *The Collection of Testimonies Concerning the Excellency and Great Importance of the Hebrew Sacred Language* (London, 1762), 8ff.

[2]*Sotah*, 32a, 32b, 33a.

[3]*Sanhedrin*, 216.

[4]*Hagigah*, 16a.

[5]*Abodah Zarah*, 16a (trans. I. Epstein).

[6]T. J. Shab, 1.2; Shek, 3.4; cf. Geoffrey Wigoder, ed. *The Encyclopedia of Judaism* (New York, 1983), 331.

"language (of) unique," they infer that it is the language of the Unique, that is of God.[1]

The Midrash observes that Heber, the father of Peleg, survived the confusion of languages. Therefore the word "Hebrew" which is derived from Heber attests to the antiquity of the language, and Hebrew is the original language before Peleg which means "division."[2]

Among the rationalist writers of the Middle Ages, *Yehuda Halevi* (1081-1141) is the one who most emphasized the beauty and the value of the Hebrew language. "It is the most important language . . . the language God spoke with Adam and Eve."[3] Hebrew is then identified as a "divine language created by God"[4] for which "the angels have most consideration, the only one to which they are sensitive."[5] Halevi justifies his position on the basis of three arguments: 1) the antiquity of the Hebrew language which is attested in the etymology of the first men (Adam, Eve, Cain, Noah, etc.);[6] 2) the use of the Hebrew language to convey prophecy[7] and to transmit the *Torah*;[8] and 3) the linguistic characteristics of the language.[9]

It is in *Jewish mysticism*, especially in the so-called Kabbalistic movement, that "the unusually positive"[10] attitude towards Hebrew language as "the holy tongue" reaches its climax. As Gershom Scholem observes: "Language in its present form, that is Hebrew, according to the Kabbalist, reflects the fundamental spiritual nature of the world; in other words, it has a mystical value."[11] In the *Zohar* which is the classic of medieval mystical literature, Hebrew has become a category of revelation. The word of God is not only expressed in the Hebrew language, it is identified with the Hebrew

[1]*J. Meg I* (Talmud de Jérusalem, ed Moïse Schwab), 211.

[2]*Gen R* 37:10; *Yalkut*, Gen §62.

[3]*The Kozari*, Vol. II, §7, 152 (our trans. from the original Hebrew).

[4]Ibid., Vol. II, §68, 153.

[5]Ibid., Vol. IV, §25, 90.

[6]Ibid., Vol. II, §68, 153-155; cf. Vol. I, §46, 69ff.

[7]Ibid., §68, 157.

[8]Ibid., Vol. II, §68, 158.

[9]Ibid., Vol. IV, §25, 90-91; Vol. II, §72, 162-163; Vol. IV, §25, 91-92.

[10]Gershom G. Scholem, *Major Trends in Jewish Mysticism* (Jerusalem, 1941), 12.

[11]Ibid.

language itself. "All the words of Torah are sublime words, sublime secrets."[1]

In the Modern Period, the philosopher *Martin Buber* (1878-1965) who worked at a translation of the Hebrew Bible, came to the conclusion that the message of the Bible was inherent in the language of the Bible. The how (*wie*) was related to the what (*was*). "Contrary to the ore from which it is possible to extract the metal, it would be vain to try to separate the content of the Bible from its recipient, every idea is one with the word which expresses it; it is an indissoluble totality."[2] "With regards to the Bible, any attempt to dissociate the content from the form would be artificial and pertain to a pseudoanalysis."[3] "The alliterations, assonances, the repetition of the words, the structure of phrases, are not to be understood as esthetical categories, but rather as a part of the content of the message itself."[4]

Nowadays the same sensitivity towards the holiness of the language has been beautifully expressed by Abraham Heschel: "The Bible is holiness in words."[5]

2. The Christian Tradition

Here also the Hebrew language enjoyed the high status of "holy language." The New Testament, Church Fathers, Reformers, and modern theologians, have emphasized the value of this language.

In the New Testament, the presence of Hebrew is felt everywhere: important key concepts (covenant, creation, kingdom of God, etc.) inherited from the Old Testament; the great number of references to the Old Testament; Hebrew names of persons and places (Matthew, John, James, Jerusalem, Bethany, Bethlehem, etc.); Hebrew words throughout the text (Sabbath, Abbah, Messiah, rabbi, Hosanna, Alleluia, qorban, amen, etc.). Furthermore, the way the Hebrew language is referred to suggests a "holy language." It is indeed noteworthy that most of God's statements in the New Testament are expressed in Hebrew. This is the case for the giving of the names of

---

[1] *Zohar, the Book of Enlightenment*, with an Introduction, and trans. by Daniel Chanan Matt (New York, 1983), 42.
[2] Martin Buber, *Schriften zur Bibel*, 1112 (our translation).
[3] Ibid.
[4] Ibid., 1122, 1131.
[5] Abraham J. Heschel, *The Insecurity of Freedom* (New York, 1966), 172.

Jesus (Luke 1:31) and John the Baptist (Luke 1:13); this is also the case for the naming of the last battle Armageddon (Rev 16:16). And these prophetic names are not only given in Hebrew but are also explained within Hebrew etymology according to the ancient Old Testament principles. It is in Hebrew that Jesus pronounces the last words on the cross (Matt 27:46; Mark 15:35); and it is also in Hebrew that God calls Paul and reveals himself to him (Acts 26:14). The Hebrew language in the New Testament is not just the historical language of its background, it is also the favorite language of revelation.

Recent research has revealed ancient documents attesting to the profound reverence of the early Christians towards Hebrew language; they regarded it as "the language of Christ and the prophets," in which "the true gospel has also been written" and therefore went so far as to censure "the Christians for their apostasy from this language."[1] The church father *Epiphanius* (310-403) writes that the *"Nazoraioi"* a Jewish Christian sect "carefully cherished the Hebrew language"[2] in which they read both the Old Testament and the Gospel of Matthew.[3]

For *Saint Augustine* (354-430), Hebrew was "The originally universal language," a language "which has the prestige of being not only used in the everyday use of the Patriarchs and Prophets, but in the writing of Holy Scripture." Augustine argues even that the preservation of this language among the people of God was a sign of her holiness. "The penalty involved in the change of language did not fall on those who continued to speak the original language . . . it was continued in the family of the man from whom the language got the name Hebrew [Heber], and that it is a clear sign of the holiness of the family that it was not punished in the way all other nations were punished when they suffered a change of language."[4] Besides Augustine, a number of Church Fathers praised the merits of the

[1]Shlomo Pines, *The Jewish Christians of the Early Centuries of Christianity According to a New Source*, Proceedings of the Israel Academy of Sciences and Humanities, February 13, 1966 (Jerusalem, 1966).

[2]*Panarion*, 1.29.7, 9.

[3]Cf. Pinchas E. Lapide, *Hebrew in the Church*, trans. Erroll E. Rhodes (Grand Rapids, 1984), 2.

[4]Aurelius Augustinus, *The City of God*, Book XVI, vol. 2, trans. Gerald G. Walsh and Grace Monahan (New York, 1954), 510-511.

Hebrew language;[1] *Jerome* (331-420) stressed and demonstrated the value of Hebrew essentially because it preserved the *Hebraica Veritas* (the Hebrew Truth).[2]

Then follows a period of silence in which Hebrew will not be recognized as a value any more. Pinchas Lapide explains the phenomenon:

> The rarity of Hebrew scholarship in Christendom during the millennium from Jerome to Johann Reuchlin is all the more astonishing. The Christian Middle Ages certainly acknowledged a (platonic) respect for Hebrew, but when the Latin Vulgate was recognized as the official standard text of the Bible, interest in the original Hebrew and Greek texts naturally waned. Further, even before Jerome the "language of the Jews" had come to be regarded increasingly by theologians as a symbol of the alien, the sinister, and the hostile.[3]

Only in the wake of the currents of the Renaissance and the Reformation was Hebrew rediscovered and studied again as the holy language, the language of theology. Thus, in the introduction to the first Hebrew grammar ever written in Christendom, *De rudimentis hebraicis* (1505), the humanist *Reuchlin* (1455-1522) points out that "the usual boredom of historical interpretation will disappear when the Bible of the Old Testament will be read and understood in its original language, namely in Hebrew . . . For this is the source from which springs all theology."[4]

The same opinion was shared and confirmed by the great Reformer *Martin Luther* (1483-1546) who stated:

[1]See for instance St. Cyril of Alexandria (378-444) *Interpreter of the Old Testament* (Rome, 1952), by Alexander Kerrigan, 254.

[2]J. N. D. Kelly, *Jerome, His Life, Writings, and Controversies* (London, 1975), 156, 160.

[3]Lapide, *Hebrew in the Church*, 3. According to Jerome Friedman, "no more than a few dozen Christians from 500 to 1500 could read Hebrew at all and perhaps a quarter of that number could use Hebrew in any constructive sense," *The Most Ancient Testimony: Sixteenth-Century Christian-Hebraica in the Age of Renaissance Nostalgia* (Athens, 1983), 13-14).

[4]Johannes Reuchlin, *De rudimentis hebraicis libri III* (New York, 1974), 1-2.

The Hebrew tongue is altogether despised because of impiety or, perhaps, because people despair of learning it. . . Without this language there can be no understanding of Scripture, for the New Testament although written in Greek, is full of Hebraisms. It is rightly said that the Hebrews drink from the fountains, the Greeks from the streams and the Latins from the pools.[1]

In the nineteenth century, *Ellen G. White* (1827-1915) who also played the role of a reformer, emphasized the importance of Hebrew which she called "the most sacred tongue in the world."[2]

Modern theologians of our time have also expressed the same enthusiasm towards the Hebrew language which is still considered as a "special language" deserving a special place in the curriculum of theology students.

For the New Testament theologian *Wilhelm Vischer* (1895-1989), Hebrew is "the holy language" and "the source of Christian theology; thus it is not only a necessity but also a great privilege for a theologian to learn Hebrew . . . Hebrew is the source of theology because God has wanted to use this language as a means of communication with us. In learning the language of their Lord . . . men learn to understand Him and to obey Him."[3] "The plenitude of the eternal Word which has been made flesh, is unfolded before us through the very study of the Hebrew language. Therefore the Christian theologian must undertake this study with a joyful zeal."[4]

For the biblical theologian *Gerhard von Rad* (1901-1971) the Hebrew language is the fruit of the covenant between Israel and God. For "Israel's world was exposed in all its parts to God. Her language is appropriate to such a world. It can therefore be said that when God began to reveal Himself to her in history, he also gave her her language. For the peculiar thing is that in conversation with her God, Israel learned to know and name her world, i.e., to know and name her world in history. This is the origin of the extremely specific linguistic and conceptual tool, a specific form of naming which exactly

---

[1]Martin Luther, *Conversations with Luther*, trans. and ed. Preserved Smith and Herbert P. Gallinger (Boston, New York, 1915), 181-182.

[2]Ellen G. White, *Fundamentals of Christian Education* (Nashville, 1923), 97.

[3]Wilhelm Vischer, "La langue sainte, source de Théologie," in *Etudes Théologiques et Religieuses* IV (1946), 1325.

[4]Ibid., 326.

corresponded to the peculiar nature of Israel's encounter with her God."[1]

More recently, the Old Testament theologian *Edmond Jacob* responding to James Barr's criticism, affirmed that "language remains the adequate expression of thought and the fact that the authors of the Old Testament used it . . . in the etymological argument legitimizes its use in theology."[2]

Also the Old Testament scholar *André Lacocque* is not afraid to define Hebrew "the priestly language of the holy."[3] For in biblical civilization "there was no dissociation between the thought and its expression"[4]; and Lacocque explains "when God and his mandatory (priest, prophet) speaks, he draws from his 'back,' from his innermost, the exposition of his identity."[5]

Whether they are Jewish rabbis, mystics or philosophers, Church Fathers, Reformers or biblical theologians, these great men of God bear from the earliest stages to our days the same powerful testimony in history on behalf of the Hebrew language, and therefore convey the same appeal—powerful incentive indeed for those who still doubt or hesitate about the value of spending some time studying Hebrew.

II. Biases and Myths Concerning Hebrew Language

The example of the prestigious forefathers will remain inefficient, however, and will not convince, as long as biases and fables dwell in the minds of theology students. We have collected here some of the most frequent misconceptions and prejudices which serve, consciously or not, either as mere pretexts or as "holy" excuses.

A. Hebrew is Difficult

In fact, Hebrew is one of the easiest languages of the world. In comparison to other ancient languages contemporary to the biblical times,

---

[1]Gerhard von Rad, *Old Testament Theology*, trans. D. M. G. Stalker, vol. 2 (New York, 1965), 353.
[2]Edmond Jacob, *Théologie de l'AT* (Neuchâtel, 1968), VI.
[3]André Lacocque, *But As For Me* (Atlanta, 1979), 75, 76, cf. 51.
[4]Ibid., 75.
[5]Ibid., 75.

such as Sumerian, Akkadian, or even to Greek, or to any modern language, Hebrew displays a more simple grammar and vocabulary. There are no declensions to learn in opposition to Sumerian, Akkadian, Greek, German, etc. There is very little vocabulary: only about 225 words are used more than 200 times in the Bible; they constitute the basic vocabulary. The remaining words are either made up of etymologically related words, or are rare words. Also, many words have entered our own vocabulary (alleluia, hosanna, amen, rabbi, etc.); some display even a common etymology (e.g., ᵓ*ayin* = eye; German: *Augen*; French *œil*; etc.). In the same way, the grammatical structure is familiar to us, as it is basically made of the same elements (nouns, prepositions, adjectives, verbs, sentences, etc.). The fundamentals of grammar can be apprehended in 15 hours. The main obstacle which confronts the student is the deciphering of the Hebrew signs. Actually, the ancient Hebrew alphabet is the father of our Latin alphabet, via Phoenician and Greek, and the reading of the letters can be mastered in five hours of good practice.

B. Hebrew is Not a Christian Language

This statement will rarely be pronounced nowadays as it was in the past, especially during the Middle Ages (see above). This opinion betrays clear anti-Semitic biases and is derived from the old Marcionite heresy that opposed the Old Testament to the New Testament and deemed the former as being inferior to the latter.

In fact, Hebrew was the first language of the Christians and the language of their holy writings; it is, for that matter, a part of the Christian heritage, not only because of the Old Testament but also because of the New Testament. If the Christian is seeking a Christian truth apart from Hebrew, he will discover a truth that is not biblical and therefore not Christian.

C. Hebrew is Not Useful

Only those who never studied Hebrew or did not learn it correctly, may think that Hebrew is not useful.

The study of the Hebrew language provides a *rich material for sermons*. Almost every Hebrew word through its meaning(s) and ramifications could inspire a beautiful and substantial sermon. (See Appendix.)

The study of the Hebrew language will help the minister to *understand the biblical truth*, and therefore to tune himself and his parish to the way of thinking of the ancient Israelites. The identity of the Church as the "spiritual" heir of Israel is here at stake.

D. There are Other Priorities

This is certainly the argument that is mostly advanced. One may concede that the study of Hebrew may provide with interesting information, but "there are other priorities." For the minister must face the living reality of the community, and the psychological, moral and social needs of its members are indeed overwhelming. Thus, the study of Hebrew appears to be a luxury. The minister needs rather practical and efficient tools and techniques to help him cope with the daily problems of his ministry. Thus little by little, instead of complementing the "what," the "how" tends to replace it, and the people are starving for substantial food. In this context, the study of the Bible and, by implication, its language, has become secondary. More important is socializing, counseling, entertaining, organizing, etc. Sadly, Abraham Heschel had observed this shift of values: "In biblical days prophets were astir while the world was asleep; today the world is astir while church and synagogue are busy with trivialities."[1] It is indeed a matter of priority.

E. We Can Rely on Good Translations and Scholarly Studies

Truth, and especially "religious" truth implies a personal choice and commitment. I should therefore be able to personally check the various opinions, and have direct access to the original biblical text; I should not be solely dependant on secondary sources. At any rate, a minimum knowledge of Hebrew language is necessary to understand and even evaluate what is written about the biblical verse or word. Besides, translations, however valuable they may be, are potentially subjective and may express a particular bias or a theological opinion; they also depend on each other so that mistakes may be transmitted from one translation to another. Also, the passage from one language to another (here from biblical Hebrew to modern English) does not convey all the richness or the particular nuance of the original text. For as the Italian proverb goes, "*Traduttore tradittore*," "Translations are treacherous."

---

[1]Abraham J. Heschel, *I Asked for Wonder: A Spiritual Anthology*, with an Introduction, and ed. by Samuel H. Dresner (New York, 1983), 78.

F. My Knowledge of Hebrew Will Never be Sufficient Anyway

It is true that I will never be able to achieve a perfect knowledge of Hebrew as if I were a native. Although a proficient knowledge of modern Hebrew is of great help, it still remains a language in many respects different from the one spoken in biblical times. The relative evolution of the language and the important difference of the historical context should prevent us from the "romantic" illusion that we need to be born in the Israel of today and speak Hebrew since childhood, to be able to reach an acceptable level in biblical Hebrew. Knowledge of modern Hebrew may even sometimes lead us in the wrong direction.

In fact, a total acquisition of biblical Hebrew as it should ideally be is impossible, not only because we do not belong to the ancient biblical civilization, but also because we have not written the Bible. Only the Hebrew man of that time, and more precisely the Hebrew author of the text, would possess the full knowledge. The remoteness of the goal should therefore not discourage us. It is the same for everyone. To be sure, some study of Hebrew will not give us the final solution to all the problems, but it will at least help us to move in the right direction.

III. A New Method

The destination of this book (seminary students, ministers, Bible students, etc.), the nature of Hebrew language (a language embedded in religious life), and the pedagogical concern of this writer have determined the following method:

A. Both Deductive and Inductive

A merely deductive approach (most Hebrew textbooks) is dry, boring, and appeals strictly to the cognitive faculty of the mind. It is, I believe, this approach which has made Hebrew language a dead language and killed it a second time.[1]

Furthermore, rules which have been taught apart from the biblical text and apart from a reference to the religious dimension, hence apart from what essentially motivates the student of biblical Hebrew, will hardly be

---

[1]Cf. Frank Michaeli, "Grammaire hébraïque et théologie biblique," in *Hommage à Wilhelm Vischer* (Montpellier, 1960), 145.

grasped and memorized. Not to mention the fact that this artificial and abstract systematization of the language does not do justice to the complex life of the language or to the biblical text. The student may succeed, but in many cases he will not be able to cope with the reality of the text and apply the rules he has learned.

A merely inductive approach (few textbooks under the influence of modern linguists) is discouraging. To study the text without any previous knowledge of the rules, and to study the rules from complex and sometimes exceptional cases occurring in the text, is very confusing. Only the teacher knows where he is going; the student is lost from the very beginning of the course. Every word, every letter will stop him. Without any system the student has no point of reference. He may be a good student, able to recite by heart the little details he has gathered along the way, but he will never be able to relate them and to synthesize them; he will forget very quickly most of the material he learned so painfully.

Our approach will be both deductive and inductive. Our first step will be essentially deductive; we shall present the most basic rules with examples taken mostly from the biblical texts we will study later. Our second step will be essentially inductive: we shall study and analyze word by word three biblical texts (Gen 22:1-19, Ps 23, Mic 4:1-4); we will then apply the rules already learned in theory and illustrated with examples reappearing now in their context; we will also draw new rules on the basis of new cases encountered in the text. Thus our approach can be described as follows: deductive, inductive, then back and forth between deductive and inductive in a dialogical manner.

B. In Relation to Hebrew Thinking

Hebrew grammar just as Hebrew vocabulary will be taught in relation to Hebrew thought. The main reason for that method of teaching is the essential motivation of students of biblical Hebrew. Those students are generally not interested in philology *per se*, they are not grammarians, but they are first of all "theologians" especially interested in the spiritual message of the Bible. Teaching only rules of phonetics, comparative linguistics and the intricacies of Hebrew syntax without any reference to what has in fact motivated these students to come to the Hebrew language is a pedagogical mistake, and may cause great frustration. This method is also consistent with the principle we have already pointed out, namely, the relationship between language and thought. Just as the thought of a people cannot be apprehended without reference to its language, the language of a people cannot be learned without reference to the thought of this people. And this is especially true in regard to biblical civilization.

Some of course may criticize this approach as they consider it somewhat speculative. However, it is supported both by the specific nature of the Hebrew language and the way the Bible itself proceeds with Hebrew language. At any rate, as far as possible we have limited our diverse references to Hebrew thought to elements which are generally recognized in biblical scholarship. Furthermore the various traits of Hebrew thought have been inferred from the observation of language only as far as they are also reflected elsewhere in the biblical testimony (in biblical stories, statements, principles, etc.). Indeed to be valid, the connection between language and thought has to be supported by the cultural and literary context. Therefore, the spiritual lessons of the language will be indicated in two ways: first "inductively," from the linguistic and syntactic data; secondly "deductively," in a systematic manner as a synthetic essay at the end of the book.

C. An Effort of Simplification and Synthesis

Instead of getting lost in the tiny details from an analytical point of view, we have preferred to emphasize the great principles of the language and the thought from a synthetic perspective. Too often, Hebrew grammars have gone too far in the little details of the language so that the student, being too much absorbed in them, is unable to get an overall picture of the language. The trees hide the forest. Besides, several grammars are already available which provide a comprehensive and detailed treatment of the Hebrew language (see especially *Gesenius Hebrew Grammar* by Emil Kautzsch; *Introduction to Biblical Hebrew*, by Thomas O. Lambdin; *An Introduction to Biblical Hebrew Syntax*, by Bruce K. Waltke and M. O'Connor; for more information on recent studies of Hebrew language, see Nahum M. Waldman, *The Recent Study of Hebrew, A Survey of the Literature with Selected Bibliography*.

This book is meant essentially as an introduction which exposes the student to the fundamentals of the Hebrew language. Since most of our students are not specialists in linguistics and since most of them will not go beyond a mere introduction, we have focused on the essentials.

* * *

Acknowledgments

Like an offering, a Hebrew textbook cannot go without thanksgiving. First of all, to the God of the Hebrews who chose Hebrew to speak to us.

To my friend Dr. Richard Davidson who shares with me this particular sensitivity towards *Lashon haqodesh*, and provided this bold enterprise with support, encouragement, and even good advice.

To my friend Dr. Bjornar Storfjell who, on short notice, accepted to proofread the entire book, and invested hours of his precious time to promote a better history through a better word(!)

Lastly a special thanks to Mrs. Dorothy Show for her utmost diligence and her valuable work; in the best tradition of the ancient scribes, she joined high qualities of patience and commitment to make the English and Hebrew letters blossom and become alive.

HOW TO USE *HEBREW FOR THEOLOGIANS*

Hebrew for Theologians has been written with diversity of class and students in mind. Therefore the book implies several levels of study, which allows great flexibility. The minimum required to achieve a decent elementary apprehension of the language is indicated along the way. This minimum is to be mastered by all; the rest is manageable depending on the teacher, the class, or the student. While applying this principle throughout the book, the student is invited to use this book in four ways.

A. Reading

Read the *whole* book with *attention and sympathy*. It is a book to be read from the beginning to the end, like a novel (why not?), and not only a book to be learned and consulted. Read also the conclusions and excursus at the end of the chapters, as they bring out a flashback reflection on the language.

B. Memorizing

Tables and paradigms are to be learned. They appear along the way, either following the logic of the grammar (deductively), or the accidents of the text (inductively). The basic material to be memorized (ten tables, one paradigm, two vocabulary lists) has been marked by an asterisk. At the end of the book, a sketch of the minimum of rules and tables is again provided to help the review. Make sure this minimum is well memorized and really mastered. Those who wish to go further are advised to learn the other tables, and eventually the supplementary information and explanation indicated in the text. Pay also close *attention to the examples*; they are mostly taken from the three texts (especially Gen 22:1-19) and will already prepare the ground for the study of the texts even before these appear on the scene.

C. Practicing

A minimum of *twenty exercises* (out of 65) are to be done. They appear at the end of each chapter and are singled out by an asterisk. These exercises follow the progression of the book and refer directly to the grammatical points thereby exposed. Those who wish to go further can work on the other exercises.

D. A Step by Step Progression

I suggest the following steps (nine to fourteen weeks):

FIRST STEP (1 week): learn to read and write.

Read and learn Chapter I:

1) Memorize the alphabet and their phonetic values, and the vowels and their phonetic values (Tables 1.1 and 1.2)—Exercises.

2) Practice reading and writing with the help of the reading book and the tape—Exercises.

3) Read aloud two verses from the Hebrew Bible every day (during the whole session).

4) First cursory reading of the section on Hebrew Thought (Chapter VI).

SECOND STEP (3-4 weeks): learn to analyze.

Read and learn Chapter II.

1) Memorize (back and forth: Hebrew-English-Hebrew) the 40 Hebrew words occurring more than 1,000 times (see vocabulary list, pp. 65-67)—Exercises.

2) Memorize the personal pronouns (Table 2.5)—Exercises.

3) Memorize the Perfect (Table 2.6) and the Imperfect (Table 2.7)—Exercises.

4) Memorize the names of the seven verbal forms, and the vowels of the prefixes (*atynty*) in the Imperfect (see the Menorah of the Verbs, p. 53).

5) Learn to parse the verbs—Exercises.

THIRD STEP (1-2 weeks): learn the vocabulary.

Read and learn Chapter III.

1) Review the 40 words occurring more than 1,000 times (back and forth), and this time pay attention to the indications in parenthesis—Exercises.

2) Memorize (only one way: Hebrew-English) the 175 words occurring more than 200 times (see vocabulary list, pp. 67-72) —Exercises.

3) Second reading of the section on Hebrew Thought (Chapter VI).

FOURTH STEP (3-5 weeks): learn in and from the text.

Read and learn Chapter IV.

Prepare the text with the help of the textbook: analyze each word, and learn the vocabulary.

1) Gen 22:1-19 (3 weeks)—Exercises.

2) Ps 23 (1 week)—Exercises.

3) Mic 4:1-4 (1 week)—Exercises.

At the end of each passage the student should be able to translate the text and parse every verb by himself.

FIFTH STEP (2 days-1 week): learn to be sensitive to the life of the text.

Read and learn Chapter V—Exercises.

1) Memorize the name of the three most important disjunctive accents and conjunctive accents—Exercises.

2) Learn to distinguish a disjunctive accent from a conjunctive accent—Exercises.

3) Learn to recognize the various functions of *vav*—Exercises.

SIXTH STEP (2 days-1 week): learn and understand the principles of Hebrew thought.   Read carefully and consult the biblical references in parenthesis—Exercises.

REVIEW: See Summary at the end of the book.

FURTHER STEPS: Advanced Hebrew, exegesis, word studies, sermon: see our guidelines in the Appendix.

CHAPTER I

SIGNS

This first chapter introduces us into the world of Hebrew signs. Yet, in prelude to the grammatical or even "spiritual" explanation/interpretation of those signs, the Reading of the Signs and the accompanying tape[1] will help us to become familiarized with them, with their shapes and with their sounds. Thus the Hebrew signs, especially the consonants and the vowels will be alive in our eyes and in our mouth before they become meaningful in our mind—suggesting already at this elementary stage the process of Hebrew thinking.

The Reading of the Signs

A solid basis in reading is necessary to ensure good roots in the Hebrew language. This manual and the accompanying tape will help you to learn to read Hebrew correctly and fluently, yet easily. All the peculiarities of Hebrew reading have been sampled and organized in a progressive manner.

Note that reading (and writing) Hebrew runs from right to left; so we begin our Hebrew book where our English books normally end. Note also that we use the Sephardic (see note 1, p. 18) pronunciation which has been adopted nowadays in Israel.

[1]For more information concerning the ordering of the companion tape, see the last page of the book.

We suggest the following guidelines:

1. Learn the alphabet and the names of the vowels by heart (pages 13, 17).

2. Learn to recognize the letters (consonants) and the vowels (page 13-17).

3. Read carefully page by page aloud: first listen to each word and repeat, then reread each page twice without the tape (if you hesitate, check with the tape). Before moving to the next page, make sure that all the signs of the current page are well mastered. In *one week* you will be able to cover the section "Reading of the Signs" (an average of two pages per session).

4. After you have completed this requirement, reread the whole "Reading of the Signs" at least once every day for *two weeks*.

5. During the *fourth and fifth* weeks, read, with the help of the tape, in the Hebrew Bible, Gen 22:1-19, Ps 23, Mic 4:1-4. Read three verses every day.

6. Listen to and enjoy the chanting of these three texts[1] (side two of the tape) while following in the Hebrew Bible.

7. *From now on* read aloud every day two verses from anywhere in your Hebrew Bible.

[1]The chanting of the Masoretic cantillation is performed by the author in a Sephardic tradition.

The Hebrew Alphabet
(See page 13.)

א ב ג ד ה ו

ז ח ט י כ ל

מ נ ס ע פ צ

ק ר ש שׂ ת

Letters That Look Alike

ב כ, ד ר, ה ח, ו ז, ח ת,

ט מ, ם ס, ן ו, ע צ

Naming and Reading of the Vowels
(See page 17.)

אָ אוּ אִ אֹ אַ אָ אֶ אֵ אֲ אֳ

Alef = אָ

אָ אַ אֶ אֵ אִ אָ א

אֻ אָ אֲ אֶ אֵ א

אֵי אִי אוֹ אוּ

אוּ אוֹ אֵי אוֹ אִי

Vet = בַ   Bet = בּ

(See page 14.)

בָ בַ בֵ בָ בֶ בִי בוֹ בִי

בָ בּ בָ בָ בִי בֵי בוּ בּוֹ

אַבָּא בָּאוּ בּוּ אָבוֹ

Shin = שׁ

שָׁ שַׁ שֵׁ שֶׁ שָׁ שׁ שׁ שׁוּ שׁ שׂ שֵׁ שׁוֹ שִׁי שׁוּ שֶׁ

אֵשׁ אִישׁ שׁוּב בּוּשׁ אֶשֵׁב שֵׁשׁ אָשׁוּ

Het = חַ

חָ חַ חֵ חֶ חֵ חֹ חִי חֹ חוּ חָ חֹ חֶ

אָחִי חִישׁוּ אָח חָשַׁב חָבִיב

Lamed = ל

לָ לֹ לֵ לִי לֹ לוּ לִי לֹ לָא לִילִי

אֵלִי אַל ל לֵ לוּ

חֶבֶל חָלָב שָׁלִישׁ לִבִּי שֶׁלִּי

Hey = ה

הֵ הָ הִי הֹ הֵ הָ הֹ הָ הִ

הָה הַב הֶהּ הָא הָאָ הָאָח הֶאָח!

הִיא בֹהוּ הוּא הוֹשִׁיב

Compound Sheva (Hatef)
(See page 18.)

חֵ חֶ אֶ אֱ אֲ הֲ הֵי הָ

הֲלֹא אֱלוֹהִי אֲחִיאֵל חֲלִי

Resh = ר

רִ רֶ רֵ רָ רֳ רֶ רֵ כ כֶ רִ

הַר כַּה כָּה רָה רָה רָא רוּ רוּ

אֲשֶׁר רֹאשׁ בָּרָא שִׁיר

בְּרוּחִי רְאוּ

Mem = מ(ם)

מֶ מֹ מָ מָ מֹ מִי מְ מֵ מַ

שֵׁם רָם וֹם וֹם

מְשָׁלוּ חֲמוֹר חֲמוֹרִים הַלֶּחֶם

Nun = נ(ן)

נוֹ נִי נֹ נְ נָ

אֵין בֵּן נוּן וֹן וּן

מִן אֲנַחֶם נְשָׁמָה נָחָה

Khaf = (ך)כ   Kaf = כּ

(See page 14.)

דֿ דּ כֿ כּ

כֹה כְ כוּ כֹו כֵּ כִּי כָ

חָכָם אָנֹכִי הַכֹּהֵן הַכֹּב כּוֹכָב שָׁכַב כַּלָה

Tav = ת

תֶ תוּ תַ תַה תוֹ תְּ תִּי תְּ תֵ תֹּ תָ תַ תּ

תֶּן תֵּל חַת רוּת מֵת בֵּית

הַשַׁבָּת בְּרֵאשִׁית תּוֹרָה כָּתַב

Dalet = ד   Gimel = ג

גִּ גֵּ גָּ דּ דֿ ד

גוֹ גוּ גִי גָּה גֵי גַ גִּ

גָּדוּד דָּלֶת דָּה דֵי דוּ הֿ דָ דֹ

Fey = (פ)ף   Pey = פ

(See page 14.)

פָּ כָּ ף

פִּי פֶּה פֹה פֶּ פָּ פוּ

דַּף פַּר פֶּן פַּח פַּת נָפַל גּוּף

Zayin = ז

זֹ זֶ זַ

זָ זִי זוּ זֶ זִ הַזֶּה הַזֶּן הַזֹּאת

Ayin = ע   Vav = ו   Yod = י

יָ יַ ו ֻ עָ עֶ עִ

עֶבֶד עוּר עָה עִי עוֹ עֶה

נַ וְ ווֹ נַה וְה הַנֶּלֶד

יִ יְ יוּ יֶה יָה יוֹד וַיֹּאמֶר הָעֵינַיִם

Tsade = (ץ)צ **Samekh** = ס **Sin** = שׂ

שָׂ סָ צָ צֶ ץ

צְ צַ צָ צֵ צִ צֵא צֶא עֵץ

סָ סַ סֶ סִי סוֹ סוּס חֶסֶד

שָׂ שַׂ שְׂ שׂוֹ שׂוּ שֵׂ שְׂ שִׂין יִשְׂרָאֵל

Tet = ט **Qof** = ק

קַ קָ קֶ קֵ ט

קָ קְ קוּ קוֹ קֶה קֵה קָה קוֹף

טָהוֹר טָמֵא טַל נָטַר טֵית

Final Yod

כִּי חַי יָדַי וְרַגְלַי נָשַׁי אַזַּי

דִּבְרֵי דְּבָרַי אֵילֵי אֵילֵי שִׁירַי

בָּנוּי כָּרָאוּי נָטוּי גָּלוּי

Ending AV, IV = יו

בָּנָיו נָשָׁיו סְפָרָיו מְלָכָיו
נְעָרָיו אֱלֹהָיו עֵינָיו רְאִיתָיו אָבִיו

Furtive Patah
(See page 19.)

רֵיחַ נִחוֹחַ רוּחַ נֹחַ יָרֵחַ
מִזְבֵּחַ כֹּחַ לוּחַ תַּפּוּחַ שׁוּחַ
יְשׁוּעָה שְׁמוּעָה תְּעוּדָה נְטִיעָה
מִזְבֵּחַ אֲבָנִים תַּעֲשֶׂה לִי.
עַד קַרְנוֹת הַמִּזְבֵּחַ.
יָדוּעַ וְהִנֵּה מִצְרַיִם נֹסֵעַ אַחֲרֵיהֶם.
וַיִּקְרָא מֹשֶׁה אֶל הוֹשֵׁעַ בִּן־נוּן יְהוֹשֻׁעַ.

Short Qametz
(See page 18.)

אָם חָכְ אָכְ

אָמְנָם חָכְמָה לְאָכְלָה אָזְנוּ חָדְשֵׁי הַשָּׁנָה

נָתָּקָם בְּעוֹד לַיְלָה.　　וַתָּרָץ.

וַיָּקָם אַבְרָהָם.　　וַתָּמָת שָׂרָה.

Names

אָדָם וְחַנָּה.　　קַיִן וְהֶבֶל.　　נֹחַ

שֵׁם חָם וָיָפֶת.　　אַבְרָהָם יִצְחָק

וְיַעֲקֹב.　　שָׂרָה וְרִבְקָה רָחֵל

וְלֵאָה.　　רְאוּבֵן שִׁמְעוֹן לֵוִי

יְהוּדָה יִשָּׂשכָר זְבוּלֻן דָּן.

נַפְתָּלִי גָּד וְאָשֵׁר יוֹסֵף וּבִנְיָמִין.

מֹשֶׁה וְאַהֲרֹן.　　דָּוִד וּשְׁלֹמֹה.

שָׁאוּל שְׁמוּאֵל דָּנִיֵּאל.

אֲדֹנָי אֱלֹהִים יְהֹוָה.

The Grammar of the Signs

In Hebrew, the "sign signifies." Consonants, vowels, and accents are not only signs to be read; along with their phonetic value (sounds) Hebrew signs convey a semantic message (meaning), which has been invented by the founders of the language, and enriched by folklore and tradition. This "spiritual" sensitivity and this memory will inspire our pedagogy.

I. Consonants

The Hebrew alphabet consists of 22 consonants (no vowels). Each consonant bears a name that indicates the sound through its first letter (*b* of bet[1]; *g* of gimel; *d* of dalet, etc.). This principle is known as "acrophony." The same names seem also to have been used as pictorial representations (the form of the letter *alef* is an oxhead, the form of *bet* is a house, etc.). This principle is known as "pictography."

Note:

1. Hebrew is read and written right to left (instead of the usual manner).

2. Letters that look alike: Note the differences between ג and נ (only one slight stroke), ב and כ, ד and ר, ו and ז, ך and ן, מ and ס, ע and צ.

---

[1]For convenience purposes, frequently used grammatical terms (names of the letters, sheva, vav, etc.) are transcribed in a simplified manner and following the modern Hebrew pronunciation (cf. note 1, p. 18). Transliterations of Hebrew words with a *vav* will use the traditional *w* (see table 1.1).

*Table 1.1: The Hebrew Alphabet

Print and Numerical Value		Name	Pronunciation and Transliteration		Block	Cursive	Meaning
א	1	alef	Arm	ɔ	א	Ic	oxhead
בּ ב	2	bet	**Book** **Veal**	b b̲	בּ ב	ュ	house
ג (ג)	3	gimel	**Good**	g (ḡ)	ג	ረ	camel
ד (ד)	4	dalet	**Door**	d (d̲)	ד	ꟼ	door
ה	5	hey	**He**	h	ה	ꜧ	window
ו	6	vav	**Van**	w	ו	ǀ	hook
ז	7	zayin	**Zoo**	z	ז	ر	weapon
ח	8	het	**Bach**	ḥ	ח	ח	hedge
ט	9	tet	**Tear**	ṭ	ט	ﻟ	snake
י	10	yod	**Yet**	y	י	ı	hand
כּ (ך) כ	20	kaf	**Kiss** **Khan (Bach)**	k k̲	כּ (ך) כ	(ק)כ	palm
ל	30	lamed	**Land**	l	ל	ſ	goad
מ (ם)	40	mem	**Make**	m	מ (ם)	(ρ)N	water
נ (ן)	50	nun	**No**	n	נ (ן)	(l) ﻟ	fish
ס	60	samekh	**Support**	s	ס	O	support
ע	70	ayin	**Eye**	ᶜ	ע	ⴋ	eye
פּ (ף) פ	80	pey	**Pear** **Fear**	p p̄ (f)	פ (ף) פ	(ʃ)ᴑ	mouth
צ (ץ)	90	tsade	**Tsar**	ṣ	צ (ץ)	ʃ ʒ	arrow
ק	100	qof	**Question**	q	ק	ρ	needle
ר	200	resh	**Rabbit**	r	ר	ꓱ	head
שׁ שׁ	300	sin shin	**Sin** **Share**	ś š	שׂ שׁ	ꞓ ꞓ	tooth
ת (ת)	400	tav	**Table**	t (t̲)	ת	ɲ	sign

*All the tables marked with an asterisk are to be memorized.

A. Letters with Various Forms and Sounds

1. Final Letters

Five letters assume different forms at the end of a word: כ(ך);
מ(ם); נ(ן); פ(ף); צ(ץ). They can be more easily remembered by this
mnemotechnic word: כמנפץ (**KaMeNaPeTZ** = as the breaker).

2. Dagesh and Mappiq

a. Six letters: בגדכפת (mnemotechnic word: **BeGeDKeFeT**),
receive a dot (weak *Dagesh* or *Dagesh qal*), when that letter
commences a syllable; but this affects their sound in only three
letters (ב, כ, פ). The phonetic value of the pronunciation is
indicated in the following:

ב = v		בּ = b	
כ = kh (or "ch" in Bach)		כּ = k	
פ = f		פּ = p	

b. For some reason other letters may also receive a dot
(strong *Dagesh* or *Dagesh hazaq*), signifying the doubling of that
letter. There is an exception, however, for the gutturals ע, ח, ה,
א, and the palatal ר which sounds like a guttural, precisely because
these letters cannot be doubled phonetically.

וַיֹּאמֶר	=	*wayyŏᵓmer* ("and he said," Gen 22:1)
הָאֵלֶּה	=	*haᵓēlle* ("these," Gen 22:1)
מִצִּיּוֹן	=	*miṣṣyyon* ("from Zion," Micah 4:2)

c. One letter, the final ה may receive a dot (*mappiq*) to
indicate that it must be pronounced. Thus we have נִסָּה (*nissa*, "he
tested," Gen 22:1) with the ה not pronounced, but גָּבַהּ (*gabah*,
"he has been exalted," 2 Chr 26:16) with the ה pronounced
(transliteration: *h*).

d. Quiescent letters. In many instances, final ה and א
(usually at the end of a syllable) are unpronounced.

B. Alphabetical Order

The order of the sequence of the Hebrew alphabet can be perceived on a lexical level, and is also attested in biblical poetry. On a lexical level it has been noticed that some words which are related in meaning are made up with letters which are neighbors in the sequence of the alphabet (see chapter on "Vocabulary"). The explanation of this phenomenon is not easy; either the alphabetical order has inspired the creation of words, or the words themselves have inspired the alphabetical order. This connection between meaning and letters suggests at least that the alphabetical order is not just the result of phonetic accidents.

In biblical poetry, the alphabetical order is attested in a number of chapters where the verses are arranged in alphabetical order (acrostic). Each verse or group of verses begins with a letter of the alphabet. See Ps 9, 10, 25, 34, 37, 111, 112, 119; Lam 1-4; Prov 31:10-31). The fact that this order serves literary purposes in the saved texts may indicate a "spiritual" motivation beyond the mere linguistic explanation. Examples of the Midrashic practice of the order of the alphabet can be found in the Bible. For instance, in Jer 25:26; 51:41 the Hebrew word שֵׁשַׁךְ (*sheshaq*) is the cryptic name of בָּבֶל (*Babel*):

> שׁ 2nd letter from the end :: בּ 2nd letter from the beginning
> שׁ 2nd letter from the end :: בּ 2nd letter from the beginning
> ךְ 12th letter from the end :: ל 12th letter from the beginning

Later, perhaps under the influence of Pythagorean speculations, ancient Jewish interpreters developed a method of exegesis which took into account the order of the letters and their respective numerical value (see Table 1). Thus the name of God יְהוָה (*YHWH*) = 26, was related to אַהֲבָה (love) + אֶחָד (one) = 26. The word נָחָשׁ (serpent) = 358, was related to the word מָשִׁיחַ (Messiah) = 358. Indeed, the order of the letters in the Hebrew alphabet cannot be explained only by reference to the blind laws of phonetics; it seems that the alphabetical order also implies specific intentions on the semantic level. It has even been argued that the order of the letters was based on didactic principles and was designed to teach the pupils the "ways of God."[1]

---

[1]N. H. Tur-Sinai, הלשון והספר, vol. II (Jerusalem, 1954-1959), 150.

The Hebrew alphabet is more than the testimony of sounds and more than phonetics; perhaps it also witnesses to a spiritual value of the sacred letters. Popular stories abound that reflect the tradition of this conscious- ness. To a student who has forgotten the words of his prayer, the witty rabbi wisely advises "just recite the alphabet; this will be enough! The angels in heaven will arrange the letters and compose a new and wonderful prayer."[1] Hear also this pathetic declaration of the martyr Rabbi Hanania ben Teradyon (2nd century A.D.) while wrapped in a Torah and set afire: "The parchment is burning, but the letters are flying free."[2]

II. Vowels

The vowels are signs made of dots and dashes generally put beneath the consonants. They are not letters (except for one) and their function is, so to speak, to animate letters (consonants). They have, therefore, been compared in Jewish mysticism to the soul of the letters, with the letters themselves compared to the body.[3]

A. The Names of the Vowels

Like the names of the consonants, the names of the vowels are meaningful; they not only indicate the sound of the vowel, but also hint at its shape.

[1]Michael L. Munk, *The Wisdom in the Hebrew Alphabet* (Brooklyn, NY, 1983), 38.

[2]Av Zar., 17b-18; Sif. Dt., 307.

[3]This comparison is taken from the Zohar: "All the letters are body without soul; then come the vowels, and the body becomes alive . . . at the very moment when the letters came out of the supreme secret . . . at the very moment when they materialized like the form of the first man, the vowels appeared and breathed into them the breath of life; then the letters were in reality, like man, who *thanks* to the breath of life, stands on foot." (From *Zohar on the Song of Songs*, Aramaic text and Hebrew trans. by R. J. Aschlag, vol. 21 [Jerusalem, 1945-1955], §603, 634). Or according to the linguist's words, "the consonants are carriers of the primary semantic distinction . . . the vowels play the role of modifiers" (Kutscher, *A History of the Hebrew Language*, 5).

*Table 1.2: Vowels

Sign	Transliteration	Name	Meaning	Pronunciation
אַ	a	patah	opening	as in "that"
אָ	ā	qametz	contraction	as in "father"
אִ	i	hireq	gnashing of the teeth	as in "pin" (unique)
אֵ	ē	tsere	splitting	as in "they"
אֶ	e	segol	grape cluster	as in "bed"
אֻ	u	qibbutz	gathering	as in "bull"
אוּ	û	shurek	whistling	as in "flute"
א and אוֹ	ô	holem	strong	as in "goal"

In addition to these eight vowels, a ninth sign is to be noted, the *sheva* בְּ. The name "*sheva*" means "nothingness." It is generally pronounced as a silent "*e*" (*sheva naḥ* = quiet *sheva*), as the *e* in "horse," and is not transliterated. However, at the beginning of a syllable (at the beginning of the word, after a closed syllable, after a long vowel), it becomes difficult not to pronounce it. Therefore the *sheva* (*shevah na^c^* = mobile *sheva*) is partially sounded (also called "vocal *sheva*") as the *o* in "occur" and transliterated "e."

B. Long and Short Vowels

The vowels can be long or short:

5 Long Vowels

qametz (אָ) = *ā* (as in "father")
holem (א, וֹ) = *ô* (as in "goal")
shurek (וּ) = *û* (as in "flute")
hireq - yod (חִי) = *î* (as in "machine")
tsere (אֵ) = *ē* (as in "they")

5 Short Vowels

patah (אַ) *a* (as in "that")
short *qametz* (אָ) in a closed syllable = *o* (as in "dog")[1]
qibbutz (אֻ) = *u* (as in "bull")
hireq (אִ) = *i* (as in "pin")
segol (אֶ) = *e* (as in "bed")

Rule: *The vowel is generally long in an open (accented) syllable,* i.e., a syllable which ends with the sound of a vowel (*ba, be, bo*). *The vowel is generally short in a closed (unaccented) syllable*, i.e., a syllable which ends with the sound of a consonant (*ab, eb, ob*).

C. Compound *Sheva*

The *sheva* can be compound (or half vowel). This affects the throat-sounds, or gutturals ע, ח, ה, א when the grammar entitles them to *sheva*. Since these letters would become quite inaudible with the *sheva* alone, a *patah*, a *segol*, or a *qametz* are added to the *sheva*, depending on the preceding vowel. These vowels are to be pronounced hurriedly, and are therefore called "*hatef*" (hurried) vowels.

---

[1]The pronunciation of the *qametz* is one of the major distinctions between the Ashkenazic pronunciation (Jews of Germany, Eastern Europe), and the Sephardic pronunciation (Jews of Holland, Spain, Italy, North Africa, Iraq, Egypt, etc.). In the Sephardic system, a distinction is made between *qametz* in an open or accented syllable (*a*, as in "far") and the *qametz* in a closed unaccented syllable (*o*, as in "dog"). We have chosen to use the Sephardic system for several reasons: 1) It is the closest pronunciation to "the one prevalent in Jerusalem and in Judah in general before the destruction of the temple" (Kutscher, *A History of the Hebrew Language*, 28); 2) It is the one which has been adopted in Israel, the only living witness to the Hebrew language. This choice does not mean, however, that the Sephardic pronunciation is to be considered as the purest one over against the Ashkenazic one. There are several phonetic variations in each of these pronunciations, just as there were in the time of the Bible. Therefore the question which is sometimes raised about the most correct pronunciation is as William Chomsky puts it, "totally meaningless and irrelevant" (*Hebrew: The Eternal Language* [Philadelphia, 1957], 114).

א *hatef patah:* הַמַּאֲכֶלֶת *ha-maᵓakelet* ("knife," Gen 22:6)
א *hatef segol:* נֶאֱחַז *neᵓeḥaz* ("caught," Gen 22:13)
א *hatef qametz:* אָהֳלִי *ᵓoholî* ("my tent," Job 29:4)

D. Furtive *Patah*

When a *patah* comes under a final ה with *mappiq* (הּ) or a final ח, it is "furtive." The vowel is then to be pronounced before the consonant ה or ח. For example: הַמִּזְבֵּחַ *ha-mizbeaḥ* and not *ha-mizbeḥa* ("altar," Gen 22:9)

*Table 1.3: Transliteration of Vowels

אַ אֲ		= a	אֹ וֹ	= ô	אֶ אֱ אֵ (vocal)	= e
אָ		= ā	אֻ	= u	אֵ	= ē
הָ אָ		= â	וּ	= û	אֵי אֶי	= ê
אֳ אָ (short)	= o			אִ	= i
					אִי	= î

III. Accents

As the Hebrew name for accents (טְעָמִים *taamim* = "taste") suggests, the accents give the biblical texts its spiritual savor. Accents make the text meaningful according to three specific functions. The *phonetic function* by which they indicate the phonetic accent (stress) of the word; the *logico-syntactical function* by which they situate the word in the phrase; and finally the *esthetic function* by which they regulate the cantillation. In this chapter, we shall deal only with the phonetic function. The logico-syntactical and the esthetic functions will be treated in due course, respectively in the chapter on Syntax and the chapter on Style.

The phonetic function of the accents comes from the fact that they show the position of the stress in a word. In Hebrew the stress is mostly found on the last syllable (called מִלְרַע *milraᶜ* = "from below"), ex: אַבְרָהָם ("Abraham," Gen 22:1). In some cases the stress is sounded on the syllable before the last (called מִלְעֵיל *milᶜêl*: "from above"), ex: וְנָשׁוּבָה *wenašubâ* ("and we shall return," Gen 22:5). This distinction is particularly helpful for detecting the correct root in words made up of the same letters, and therefore has an important bearing on the interpretation of the word. See for example these two words made up of שׁב:

the *milᶜēl*: וְנָשׁוּבָה (Gen 22:5) has the root שׁוּב ("to return")
the milraᶜ : שָׁבוּ (Gen 34:29) has the root שָׁבָה ("to take captive").

IV. Excursus

Before starting to read the text the student must be aware of its peculiarities; for mechanical reading has hardly its place here. The text has been transmitted through religious channels; therefore, it must be met on a religious level. The features of the consonantal text and the division of the Masoretic text appeal to that approach.

A. The Consonantal Text

In order to read, the student must combine the consonant with the vowel, and stress the right syllable: בַּ reads "ba", בִּ reads "bi," אַבְרָהָם reads "Ab̲ra*ham*" (with a stress on *ham*), etc. In addition to this effort of deciphering the student will have to face two other tasks.

The first task has to do with the fact that sometimes what is written in the Masoretic text is not necessarily what should be read. This phenomenon is referred to as *Qere* ("it is read") and *Ketib* ("it is written"). Usually the reader is warned by a small circle (˚) in the text, referring to the marginal note, where the *Qere* (the correct reading) is indicated. One of the most striking uses of *Qere* is the Divine name יְהוָה which should not be read as it is written, that is *Ye Ho Wa H* (*Ketib*), but *Adonay* (*Qere*), the vowels "e-o-a" have been borrowed from the word *AeDoNaY* (my Lord), and have been artificially added to the consonants of the divine name *YHWH*. This deliberate change is due to the fact that the Divine name was considered too sacred to be pronounced. The combination of the vowels of *Adonay* with the consonants of *YHWH* has produced the artificial form *YeHoWaH*, or *Jehovah*. It is noteworthy that a theological consideration, the reverence to God, has from very ancient times[1] affected the reading of these letters. Another similar example is found in the misvocalization of the name of the pagan God *Molech*. The consonants מֶלֶךְ ("king") have

---

[1]The device of substitution is already found in the Qumran scroll of Isaiah (2nd century B.C.).

been maintained, but the vowels "o" and "e" of בֹּשֶׁת (shame) have been inserted. These examples show again that even mechanical reading is governed by theological presuppositions.

The second task has to do with the very nature of the Hebrew Scriptures which originally were made up of consonants only. As Hebrew speech passed out of daily use, it became necessary to introduce some form of vocal distinction for a correct reading and explanation of the sacred texts. The process already started in biblical times with the so-called *matres lectionis* "mothers of reading," that is, the letters ה, ו, י which were used to indicate the long vowels.

ה	in	עֹלָה	ʿolâ	("offering," Gen 22:2)
ו	in	בְּנוֹ	benô	("his son," Gen 22:3)
י	in	בְּנִי	benî	("my son," Gen 22:7)

After the close of the canon, devices of vocalization had to be created in order to respect the injunction not to change the sacred consonantal text. Vowels are indeed a late addition and do not belong to the original text. They are instead the work of the Masoretes of the 7th century A.D., the grammatical writers who transmitted the *Massora* (traditional reading). Thus the vowels witness to a specific reading, a tradition of interpretation, and do not necessarily reflect the original situation of the holy word. Perhaps it is this consciousness that is behind the requirement in the synagogue to read even today the Hebrew scrolls of the Pentateuch without vowel-signs. The latter characteristic gives the text a potential of interpretation that goes beyond the strict boundaries of the Masoretic Text. A word like אַל *al* ("do not!" Gen 22:12) could be read אֶל *el* ("to," Gen 22:2). Only the context can determine the choice of the right vocalization hence the right translation. Again we find here the same principle we already noticed. In Hebrew, the context with all its dynamics must be solicited. Just to decipher the letter, the reader must make reference to the spiritual world, whether it is discovered in the immediate consonantal context, or conveyed in the vocal tradition.

B. The Masoretic Text

We shall consider the divisions of the Hebrew Bible as they apply to the different books which compose it, and to the course of the Hebrew text.

1. The Books

The Hebrew Bible or Masoretic Text (from *massora* = "tradition")[1] is divided into three sections and is called **TaNaKh**, a word formed with the initial letters of *Torah* (Pentateuch), *Nebiᵓim* (Prophets), *Ketubim* (Writings). Two editions are commonly used, slightly different in order in the third section (*Ketubim*). The edition of the Rabbinic Bible (*Miqraoth Gdoloth*) is traditionally used in Judaism and has also been adopted by the British and Foreign Bible Society (Norman H. Snaith, ed.). It follows Jacob ben Chayyim's edition, printed by Daniel Bomberg in Venice (1524/25) on the basis of late medieval manuscripts. The other edition is the *Biblia Hebraica Stuttgartensia* (*BHS*). It is traditionally used in Universities, and follows the oldest surviving manuscript of the complete Bible (presently in the St. Petersburg Public Library). It was copied in A.D. 1008 from exemplars written by the last member of the Ben Asher Family.[2]

---

[1]The Masoretic Bible has been transmitted to us with all kinds of information compiled by the Masoretes in the margin of each page (*Massora magna* or "big *massora*," and *Massora parva* or "small *massora*") and at the end of each book (*Massora finalis*). For the meaning of the Masoretic language see Israel Yeivin, *Introduction to the Tiberian Masorah*, trans. E. J. Revell (Missoula, MT, 1979), 77-120; and Ernst Würthwein, *The Text of the Old Testament: An Introduction to the Biblica Hebraica*, trans. Erroll F. Rhodes (London, 1980), 27-29.

[2]Probably a Karaite family who played a leading part in the Masoretic work at Tiberias.

Order of the Books in the Hebrew Bible (*Tanakh*)

TORAH
תּוֹרָה

Genesis	בְּרֵאשִׁית
Exodus	שְׁמוֹת
Leviticus	וַיִּקְרָא
Numbers	בְּמִדְבָּר
Deuteronomy	דְּבָרִים

NEBIᴼIM
נְבִיאִם

Former Prophets:

Joshua	יְהוֹשֻׁעַ
Judges	שֹׁפְטִים
Samuel (1st and 2nd)	שְׁמוּאֵל
Kings (1st and 2nd)	מְלָכִים

Latter prophets:

Isaiah	יְשַׁעְיָה
Jeremiah	יִרְמְיָה
Ezekiel	יְחֶזְקֵאל
Hosea	הוֹשֵׁעַ
Joel	יוֹאֵל
Amos	עָמוֹס
Obadiah	עֹבַדְיָה
Jonah	יוֹנָה
Micah	מִיכָה
Nahum	נַחוּם
Habakkuk	חֲבַקּוּק
Zephaniah	צְפַנְיָה
Haggai	חַגַּי
Zechariah	זְכַרְיָה
Malachi	מַלְאָכִי

KETÛBÎM
כְּתוּבִים

Rabbinic Bible (Snaith, ed.)		BHS	
Psalms	תְּהִלִּים	Psalms	תְּהִלִּים
Proverbs	מִשְׁלֵי	Job	אִיּוֹב
Job	אִיּוֹב	Proverbs	מִשְׁלֵי
Song of Songs	שִׁיר הַשִּׁירִים	Ruth	רוּת
Ruth	רוּת	Song of Songs	שִׁיר הַשִּׁירִים
Lamentations	אֵיכָה	Ecclesiastes	קֹהֶלֶת
Ecclesiastes	קֹהֶלֶת	Lamentations	אֵיכָה
Esther	אֶסְתֵּר	Esther	אֶסְתֵּר
Daniel	דָּנִיֵּאל	Daniel	דָּנִיֵּאל
Ezra	עֶזְרָא	Ezra	עֶזְרָא
Nehemiah	נְחֶמְיָה	Nehemiah	נְחֶמְיָה
Chronicles	דִּבְרֵי הַיָּמִים	Chronicles	דִּבְרֵי הַיָּמִים

2. *The Text*

Besides the general division into books the Hebrew Bible knows a
further division into verses, chapters, and liturgical paragraphs. The
verse division already known in the Talmudic period (A.D. fourth-sixth
centuries) is indicated by the sign: : (*soph pasuq* = "end of the verse").
The chapter division introduced since the 14th century is indicated by
numbers or (and) Hebrew letters, according to their numerical value:[1]
א = Ch 1, ב = Ch 2, or יא = Ch 11, יב = Ch 12; but טו = Ch 15,
טז = Ch 16.[2] The liturgical division was already known to a certain
extent since the second century B.C. Different systems are found:

    a. A division into "open" and "closed" paragraphs of the entire
Hebrew Bible (except for the Psalms). The open paragraph (indicated
by פ, from פָּתוּחַ = "open") marks a new paragraph after an empty

---

[1]The same procedure is used for verses in Jewish editions as well.

[2]To avoid the use of יה or יו which are both abbreviations of the Divine
name יהוה.

or incomplete line. The closed paragraph (indicated by ס, from
סְתוּמָה = "closed") makes a new paragraph after a short space within
the same line.

b. A division into 452 *Sedarim* (סָדָר = "sequence, order") of the
entire Hebrew Bible, 167 of which are for the Pentateuch, according
to the three-year reading cycle (Palestinian usage). The beginning of
a *Seder* is indicated by the sign ס (See Gen 22:1 which starts the 19th
Seder).

c. A division into 54 *parashot* (from פָּרַשׁ = "to explain, to
comment, to divide") is found only in the Pentateuch (in addition to
the two other divisions), according to the one-year reading cycle
(Babylonian usage); the beginning of a *Parasha* is indicated by the
word פרשׁ.

It is noteworthy that the primary function of these biblical divisions
is not so much to provide the reader with landmarks as to regulate the
religious reading of the Bible. The words are not just words to be
consulted for information or used for polemics; they are essentially
words to be read and learned within a religious frame--as a prayer.

V. Exercises (Signs)

*1. Gen 22:1-3: Name all the consonants and vowels; point out letters that
   look alike.

*2. a) Practice reading in the reading manual with the help of the tape; b)
   Write one line of each letter of the alphabet.

*3. Write Gen 22:1 in block letters, in transliteration; learn to read
   fluently.

*4. Write Gen 22:2-3 in block letters, in transliteration; learn to read
   fluently.

5. Write Gen 22:4-7 in block letters, in transliteration; learn to read
   fluently.

6.   Write Gen 22:8-12 in block letters, in transliteration; learn to read fluently.

7.   Write Gen 22:13-19 in cursive letters, in transliteration; learn to read fluently.

*8.   Read aloud two verses from the Hebrew Bible every day; hand over a report at the beginning of each week (14 verses with their reference, the date and the time of reading). At the end of each week, time your reading and indicate it on the weekly report.

CHAPTER II

MORPHOLOGY

As far as morphology, i.e., the forms of the words, is concerned, we shall limit ourselves here to the main three categories of words, namely,[1] 1) the inseparable words, 2) the nouns, 3) the verbs.

I. The Inseparable Words

Inseparable words are single letters: the definite article הַ, the interrogative הֲ, the prepositions בְּ, כְּ, לְ, מִ, and the conjunction וְ. They do not have a separate existence and are attached to the word they govern. By being so attached to the word they govern, these inseparable words create new words (grammatically speaking). In Hebrew, the relationship affects the identity. Indeed, nothing or no one remains the same as soon as it (he/she) is in relationship with something (someone) else. The idea of totality and of unity so specific to Hebrew thought is here suggested.

A. The Article

Only one form for all genders and numbers, הַ, is always attached to the noun; the first letter of the noun then receives a *dagesh*.[2]

For example: הַנַּעַר   "the lad," Gen 22:12

                        הַיָּמִים   "the days," Mic 4:1

---

[1]Adverbs, numerals, conjunctions, etc., will be considered along the way in our treatment of the biblical texts (see Chapter IV).

[2]Probably because of the original ל (of the old form הל like in Arabic) which has been assimilated.

27

Since the gutturals א, ה, ח, ע, ר, cannot receive a *dagesh*, by compensation the *patah* under the article הַ is lengthened as can be seen in the following:

הָאֱלֹהִים   "the God," Gen 22:3
הָאָרֶץ   "the earth," Gen 22:18

Note, however, that this lengthening of the vowel of the article is not regular; it varies depending on the guttural and its vowel:

thus before ה, ח, it remains הַ,
but before א, ע, ר, we have הָ,
and before הָ, חָ, עָ, we have הֶ.

B. The Interrogative

The particle הֲ is prefixed to the noun it governs and generally takes *hatef patah*. Note the following:

הֲשֹׁמֵר אָחִי אָנֹכִי   "am I my brother's keeper?" Gen 4:9

Here also the vowel of the ה interrogative varies when it comes before a guttural:

thus before א, ה, ח, ע, we have הַ,
and before אָ, הָ, חָ, עָ, we have הֶ.

C. The Prepositions

The following prepositions: בְּ ("in, with, by"), כְּ ("as, like"), לְ ("to, for") are normally pointed with *sheva*; the prepositions are prefixed to the word.

Examples: בְּהַר   "in mountain," Gen 22:14
           כְּכוֹכְבֵי   "like stars of," Gen 22:17
           לְדָוִד   "to David," Ps 23:1

The preposition מִן may also be prefixed to the word and will then become מִ with a *dagesh* into the next letter (the first letter of the word), indicating the assimilation of the נ. This phenomenon is seen below:

מִצִּיּוֹן   "from Zion," Mic 4:2

מִגְּבָעוֹת   "from hills," Mic 4:1

but מֵרָחֹק "from far" (Gen 22:4), where the assimilation of the נ causes the *hireq* to become *tsere*, due to the impossibility of putting a *dagesh* in the guttural.

When the prepositions בְּ, כְּ, or לְ are prefixed to a word beginning with a *sheva*, there is collision between the two *shevas*, and as a result the *sheva* under the preposition becomes *hireq*:

לִשְׁחֹט   "to slay," Gen 22:10

בִּנְאוֹת   "in the pastures," Ps 23:2

When the prepositions בְּ, כְּ, or לְ, join a word with an article, the letter ה of the article disappears, leaving however the two other signs of the article: the vowel which is normally under the article shifts under the preposition, and the *dagesh* remains in the first letter of the word.

בַּסְּבַךְ (בְּהַסְּבַךְ) "in the bush," Gen 22:13

D. The Conjunctions

The conjunction ו (and) is always inseparable, and is usually written וְ (with a *sheva*), but וּ (with a *shureq*) before a *sheva* and the consonants בומפ (mnemotechnic "bumf").

וְלֹא   "and no," Gen 22:12

וּמִשְׁעַנְתֶּךָ "and your staff," Ps 23:4

Note:

All these inseparable words occur more than 1,000 times in the Bible. At this stage, we recommend that the student learn beyond these seven words, the 40 words which occur more than 1,000 times (see "Important Hebrew Words" in Chapter III). These 40 words must be memorized back and forth (Hebrew-English-Hebrew); ignore for the moment the indications in parenthesis. By knowing these words, the student will not only have a first hand feeling for the Hebrew words (to prepare him for the next step), but will also be able to practice further exercises.

II. Nouns and Pronouns

In Hebrew, things are expressed in an absolute way (*absolute state*), or in relation to something else (*construct state*). For example, if I say "The donkey," I refer to the "donkey" in an *absolute* way; the word "donkey" is independent. If I say the "donkey of the lad," I refer to the donkey in *relation* to the lad; the word "donkey" is dependent, and is said to be in the *construct state*. Since the *construct* form expresses the idea of belonging or the genitive (possessive case), this form is also used with the *pronominal suffix* to express personal possession ("my donkey," literally "the donkey of I"). Thus we know in Hebrew three kinds of nouns: the noun in *absolute state*, the noun in *construct state* and the noun with *pronominal suffix*.

A. The Noun in Absolute State

Since this noun is independent, its form remains complete whether it is masculine or feminine (gender), singular or plural (number), alone or qualified (adjective).

1. Gender

The noun can be masculine or feminine, never neuter. The masculine noun ends generally with the sound of a consonant.

מַלְאַךְ   "angel," Gen 22:11
הָאַיִל   "the ram," Gen 22:13

The feminine is usually indicated by the ending ת or the vocal sound הָ (*ah*).

הַמַּאֲכֶלֶת   "the knife," Gen 22:6
מְאוּמָה   "anything," Gen 22:12

2. Number

The noun knows two forms of plural.
    a. The usual plural is indicated by the ending םִי◌ (*îm*) for the masculine like in הָעֵצִים ("the woods," Gen 22:9), עַמִּים ("peoples,"

Mic 4:1) or the ending וֹת (*ot*) for the feminine like in מִגְּבָעוֹת ("from hills," Mic 4:1).

b. The dual number is indicated by the ending ַיִם (*ayim*) for both genders; this plural is used for two objects which form an inseparable unity, like in עֵינַיִם "two eyes," Gen 20:16.

*Table 2.4: Number and Gender

Feminine	Masculine		
חֲמוֹרָה	חֲמוֹר	(donkey)	Singular
חֲמוֹרוֹת	חֲמוֹרִים	(donkeys)	Plural
	חֲמוֹרַיִם	(two donkeys)	Dual

3. *The Adjective*

In order to qualify the noun, sometimes an adjective[1] is used; it normally comes after the noun and agrees with it in gender and number.

גּוֹיִם עֲצָמִים   "strong nations," Mic 4:3

a. When the noun and the adjective are both definite, the adjective is used attributively (in English this adjective comes *before* the noun).

הַגּוֹיִם הָעֲצָמִים   "the strong nations," cf. Mic 4:3

b. When the noun is definite and the adjective indefinite, the adjective is used predicatively (in English this adjective comes *after* the noun and a verb like be, seem, look).

הַגּוֹיִם עֲצָמִים "the nations (are) strong," cf. Mic 4:3

---

[1]Adjectives are rare in Hebrew.

B. The Noun in Construct State

Since this noun is dependent, it does not exist by itself, but only in relation to another word. This is another expression of the Hebrew idea of totality; the phrase "donkey of Abraham" is viewed as a global and indivisible unity.

1. It always *precedes the word* upon which it depends, and nothing can be put between the two words, e.g.:

מַלְאַךְ יְהֹוָה   "angel of *YHWH*," Gen 22:11

2. It has *no article*, but takes the benefit of the article of the second word upon which it depends. e.g.:

אֶרֶץ הַמֹּרִיָּה   "country of the Moriah," Gen 22:2
הַר הַקֹּדֶשׁ   "mount of holiness," i.e., the holy mountain, Jer 31:23   (This is another way of expressing qualification).

3. It tends to be *abbreviated* in order to articulate it closely to the following word (hence its name: "construct"). The word in *construct state* tends to lose its phonetic weight: the ending of the word as well as its vowels may be shortened.

a. The Ending

The ending of the word changes in feminine singular and in masculine plural. If the word is feminine, the long vocal הָ becomes the short תַ (ה is replaced by ת).

שְׂפַת הַיָּם   "the lip (shore) of the sea," Gen 22:17.
(**Note:** שָׂפָה has become שְׂפַת.)

If the word is masculine plural the final ִים drops and the hireq becomes tsere.

עֲצֵי הָעֹלָה   "wood of the offering," Gen 22:6
(**Note:** עֵצִים has become עֲצֵי.)

אֱלֹהֵי יַעֲקֹב   "the God of Jacob," Mic 4:2
(**Note:** אֱלֹהִים has become אֱלֹהֵי.)

b. The Vowels

Often the vowels of the construct noun are changed depending on the specific class that noun belongs to. The following illustrates the vocal changes in the inflections of the nouns:

1) First syllable:

דָּבָר ← דְּבַר   (word → word of)
דְּבָרִים ← דִּבְרֵי   (words → words of)
אֶרֶץ ← אַרְצִי   (land → my land)
שֶׁמֶשׁ ← שִׁמְשִׁי   (sun → my sun)

2) Last syllable:

שֶׂה ← שֵׂה   (lamb → lamb of)
דָּבָר ← דְּבַר   (word → word of)
חֲמוֹרָה ← חֲמוֹרַת   (she donkey → she donkey of)
עַיִן ← עֵין   (eye, eye of)
חֹק ← חָק ← חֻקִּי   (law, law of, my law)

C. The Noun with Pronominal Suffix

In Hebrew, the words "my donkey" will be rendered by attaching to the word donkey (חֲמוֹר) a suffix taken from the correspondent personal pronoun. Thus from the personal pronoun אֲנִי (*I*), the ending י (*i*) is added to the construct form of the noun; note, however, that the form of the "construct" with the pronominal suffix is not always identical with the form of the construct with another noun; thus חֲמוֹרִי (my donkey) or דְּבָרִי (my word), but מַלְכִּי (my king), cf. מֶלֶךְ־ (king of . . .).

Again, the same Hebrew concern for unity shines through this construction. The suffixes are united to the noun, to form a single word expressing the totality of the idea.

*Table 2.5

Personal Pronouns		Noun with Pronominal Suffix	
אֲנִי/אָנֹכִי	I	כּוֹסִי חֲמוֹרִי	my cup, donkey
אַתָּה	you (m.s.)	כּוֹסְךָ חֲמוֹרְךָ	your (m.s.) cup, donkey
אַתְּ	you (f.s.)	כּוֹסֵךְ חֲמוֹרֵךְ	your (f.s.) cup, donkey
הוּא	he	כּוֹסוֹ חֲמוֹרוֹ	his cup, donkey
הִיא	she	כּוֹסָהּ חֲמוֹרָהּ	her cup, donkey
אֲנַחְנוּ	we	כּוֹסֵנוּ חֲמוֹרֵנוּ	our cup, donkey
אַתֶּם	you (m.p.)	כּוֹסְכֶם חֲמוֹרְכֶם	your (m.p.) cup, donkey
אַתֶּן	you (f.p.)	כּוֹסְכֶן חֲמוֹרְכֶן	your (f.p.) cup, donkey
הֵם/הֵמָּה	they (m.p.)	כּוֹסָם חֲמוֹרָם	their (m.p.) cup, donkey
הֵן/הֵנָּה	they (f.p.)	כּוֹסָן חֲמוֹרָן	their (f.p.) cup, donkey

Examples:

בְּנִי	"my son," Gen 22:7
כּוֹסִי	"my cup," Ps 23:5
יְחִידְךָ	"your unique," Gen 22:2
יָדוֹ	"his hand," Gen 22:10

In plural, the pronominal suffix is separated from the noun by the *yod* (י) mark of the plural, except for the first person singular where the combination of the two *yods* (the first person and the plural) produces the sound *ay*.

Examples:

נְעָרָיו	"his lads," Gen 22:3
שְׁנֵיהֶם	"their two, the two of them," Gen 22:8
יָדַי	"my hands," Ps 18:21

III. The Verbs

Since the verbs express action, Hebrew grammarians have called the verb, פֹּעַל (*Poal*), which means action. Three features characterize Hebrew conjugation: the root, two tenses, and seven forms. Also the Hebrew verb has two unconjugated "impersonal" moods.

Another particularity of the Hebrew verb is that all these aspects of the verb are always expressed through a single word. The form of that word will change, prefixes or suffixes will be added to it, but there will always be only one word. When in other languages people would need 5 or 6 separated words to express a phrase (examples in English: he has acted with intensity, he will cause you to act, he has acted himself, etc. . . .), Hebrew will be able to do it with only one word conveying the totality of the action.

A. The Root

1. The Basic Idea

The root carries the basic idea of the verb. Most Hebrew roots have three consonants and are therefore called *triliterals*.[1]

אָהַב	"(idea of) love," Gen 22:2
אָמַר	"(idea of) saying," Gen 22:1
שָׁלַח	"(idea of) sending," Gen 22:10
יָדַע	"(idea of) knowing," Gen 22:12

2. Irregular Verbs

The verb is said to be irregular if its root is composed with letters which do not function regularly.[2] Such letters are either guttural letters (ר, ע, ח, ה, א) because they cannot receive *sheva* or *dagesh*, or weak letters because they tend to drop (י, ו, ה, א) or assimilate (נ, ל).

In order to classify the different types of irregular verbs, the three letters of the word פָּעַל (to act) are employed. Thus, the first letter of the root is indicated as its פ, the second letter of the root as its ע, and the third letter of the root as its ל.

---

[1]Words from bi-literal roots (two consonants) are also found in Hebrew. Example: אֵם, mother; רַב, great; גֵּר, stranger; לֵב, heart; קָם, he rose, etc.

[2]In this chapter, only the conjugation of regular verbs (also called "strong verbs") will be learned (see Paradigm A, pages 54-55); the conjugation of irregular verbs (also called "weak verbs") will be learned later in Chapter IV: Texts (see Paradigms B-E, pages 168-175).

> פ stands for the first letter of the root
> ע stands for the second letter of the root
> ל stands for the third letter of the root

Since the first letter of חבש is the guttural ח, we say that חבש is a פ guttural verb.

Since the second letter of צחק is the guttural ח, we say that צחק is an ע guttural verb.

Since the third letter of שמע is the guttural ע, we say that שמע is a ל guttural verb.

Since the first letter of אמר is א, we say that אמר is a פ"א verb.

Examples:	חבש	(to saddle), Gen 22:3, is a פ guttural verb
	צחק	(to laugh), Gen 22:2, is a ע guttural verb
	שמע	(to hear), Gen 22:18, is a ל guttural verb
	אמר	(to say), Gen 22:1, is a פ"א verb
	הלך	(to go), Gen 22:2, is a פ"ה verb
	ידע	(to know), Gen 22:12, is a פ"י verb
	נשא	(to lift), Gen 22:13, is a פ"נ verb
	קום	(to raise), Gen 22:3, is a ע"ו verb

B. Two Tenses

Like in other Semitic languages, Hebrew knows two tenses, the *Perfect* and the *Imperfect*.[1] These tenses do not express, like in our languages, categories of time (past and future), but rather categories of action. The Perfect expresses the idea of an accomplished action; the Imperfect expresses the idea of an unaccomplished action (in becoming). Thus Perfect corresponds more or less to our Past, and Imperfect to our Future. Another striking peculiarity of the Hebrew tense is the use of the Perfect to express a future and the use of the Imperfect to express a past event. This permutation is generally possible by prefixing to the extant form a *vav*

---

[1]There is no present tense in Hebrew; this explains why the Imperfect form in the name of God in Exod 3:14 has been translated with a present by the Septuagint ("I am who I am"). In fact, this rendering is both right and wrong since the Hebrew Imperfect encompasses present and future; but rather than expressing a specific time, the Imperfect expresses a perspective, in this instance, the eternal perspective of the God of Hope.

(called "consecutive" or "conversive"). This form is not just used to indicate the idea of the consecutive, it also has a *real* conversive effect.[1] Besides the historical explanation which is sometimes given to that linguistic phenomenon, one may also interpret that phenomenon, on another level, as an expression of Hebrew thought. Past and Future are actualized not only because the people of today is "one" with the people of yesterday and of tomorrow (idea of corporate personality), but also because of God who can see past and future at the same time (prophecy).

1. The Perfect

The Perfect tense has three forms:

a. The **simple Perfect** is made of the root of the verb (form a-a) with a suffix (afformative) taken from the correspondent personal pronoun. Thus for the verb שׁמע, to listen (Gen 22:18):

---

[1]The strict interpretation of this *vav* as only "consecutive" stumbles on two observations. 1) In many instances the form is used isolated, not within a sequence and therefore without the consecutive idea. (See Gen 22:1 for the Imperfect form, and Mic 4:1 for the Perfect form.) 2) The fact that we find Imperfect forms with *vav* outside of the Bible (the Mesha inscription, etc.) with the meaning of a past, confirms that the Imperfect form was originally the only existing form with all functions (hence the qualification of omnimodal or omnitemporal, see F. R. Blake, "The Hebrew *waw* Conversive," *JBL* LXIII [1944]: 271-295). This evidence does not explain, however, the phenomenon of the Perfect with *vav* which remains a unique feature of the Hebrew language. If this form has been invented in Hebrew by a sort of analogy with the Imperfect, why did the same phenomenon not happen elsewhere? This shows, at least, that this way of expression, whatever the "historical" reconstruction may be, corresponds to the specific Hebrew frame of mind.

*Table 2.6: Simple Perfect

I heard (m.f.)	שָׁמַעְתִּי	from אֲנִי
You heard (m.)	שָׁמַעְתָּ	אַתָּה
You heard (f.)	שָׁמַעְתְּ	אַתְּ
He heard	שָׁמַע	הוּא
She heard	שָׁמְעָה	הִיא
We heard	שָׁמַעְנוּ	אֲנַחְנוּ
You heard (m.)	שְׁמַעְתֶּם	אַתֶּם
You heard (f.)	שְׁמַעְתֶּן	אַתֶּן
They heard (m.f.)	שָׁמְעוּ	הֵם הֵן

Examples: שָׁמַעְתָּ   you heard, Gen 22:18
               חָשַׂכְתָּ   you withheld, Gen 22:16
               יָדַעְתִּי   I knew, Gen 22:12

b. The **Perfect with "consecutive-conversive"** *vav* is made of
the same form as the simple Perfect attached to the regular conjunction "*vav*" (and).

Examples: וְהָלְכוּ   and they will go (not "they went") Mic 4:2
               וְשָׁפַט   and he will judge (not "he has judged")
                         Mic 4:3

c. The *perfectum propheticum* is a simple Perfect which refers
to a future event.[1]

Example: דִּשַּׁנְתָּ   You applied oil, Ps 23:5

[1]Only the context and especially the presence of Imperfect forms indicate the
future sense of this form.

2. The Imperfect

The Imperfect has three forms.

a. The **simple Imperfect** is made of the root of the verb (form e-o) with a prefix (preformative), also more or less taken from the corresponding personal pronoun. The prefixes are the letters אתינתי (mnemotechnic word: *atynty*), punctuated with *hireq* (except for the guttural א which has *segol*). Thus from the verb רדף, to follow (Ps 23:6):

*Table 2.7: Imperfect

I shall follow	אֶרְדֹּף	אֲנִי
You will follow (m.)	תִּרְדֹּף	אַתָּה
You will follow (f.)	תִּרְדְּפִי	אַתְּ
He will follow	יִרְדֹּף	הוּא
She will follow	תִּרְדֹּף	הִיא
We shall follow	נִרְדֹּף	אֲנַחְנוּ
You will follow (m.)	תִּרְדְּפוּ	אַתֶּם
You will follow (f.)	תִּרְדֹּפְנָה	אַתֶּן
They will follow (m.)	יִרְדְּפוּ	הֵם
They will follow(f.)	תִּרְדֹּפְנָה	הֵן

NOTE: in the singular, 3rd feminine and 2nd masculine are identical; in the plural, 3rd feminine and 2nd feminine are identical.

b. The **Imperfect with "consecutive-conversive"** *vav* is made of the same form attached to the conjunction *vav*, this time punctuated with a *patah* and a strong *dagesh* in the "*atynty*" (the pronominal prefix or preformative letter): וַיּ.

Examples: וַיֹּאמֶר he said (not "and he will say") Gen 22:1

                   וַיַּשְׁכֵּם he rose early (not "and he will rise early"), Gen 22:3

                   וַיִּקְרָא he called (not "and he will call") Gen 22:14

c. The **"volitive" Imperfect** comes in three forms depending on the person.

1) For the first person (singular and plural) a lengthened form of the Imperfect is used, characterized by the addition of the ending ה (*Cohortative*).

Example: אֶרְדְּפָה   let me pursue, I am determined to pursue, 2 Sam 22:38

2) For the second person a shortened form of the Imperfect is used, characterized by the dropping of the preformatives (*Imperative*).[1]

Example: שְׁלַח send!   Exod 4:4 (compare with תִּשְׁלַח, "You will send," in Gen 22:12)

3) For the third person (and also sometimes the second person, see "Negation" on page 41) the same consonant body is used as for the single Imperfect; only the last vowel is shortened (*Jussive*).

Example: יְהִי   let it be,   Gen 1:3, 6, 14; 30:34, etc. (Instead of יִהְיֶה; see Mic 4:1.)

---

[1]We include the Imperative under the Imperfect not only because it displays the same form as the Imperfect, but also because it expresses like the Imperfect a non-accomplished action.

3. Negation

The negation is expressed by the two adverbs לֹא and אַל before the verb. לֹא is generally used with the Perfect;

Example: לֹא חָשַׂכְתָּ you did not withhold, Gen 22:12

and also with the Imperfect when it applies to a permanent prohibition, or a future situation.

Example: לֹא תִגְנֹב thou shalt not steal, Exod 20:15
לֹא אֶחְסָר I will not lack (anything), Ps 23:1

אַל is generally used with the *Jussive* of the second person when it applies to an immediate prohibition (negation of the Imperative).

Example: אַל תַּעַשׂ don't do! Gen 22:12

C. Seven Forms

Like a piece of dough cast into different molds producing different forms of the same dough, so the Hebrew root is cast into seven different molds producing seven different forms (בִּנְיָנִים *binyanim*: constructions). If we take the root פָּעַל (basic idea of action) and cast this root into the seven molds of the verb, we obtain seven forms of the same material. The root, i.e., the three letters פעל, remains the same but with a different form. Thus, the basic meaning "action" is presented in seven ways or aspects.

1. Names of the Forms

Traditionally, Hebrew grammarians have named the seven forms after the third person masculine singular of the verb פעל in the Perfect tense. Thus the seven forms are called: *paal, niphal, piel, pual, hiphil, hophal, hitpael.*[1]

---

[1]Those seven forms do not appear in all the verbs. In fact only seven verbs have all the seven forms (בָּקַע, break; גָּלָה, uncover; חָלָה, be sick; יָדַע, know; יָלַד, beget; פָּקַד, visit).

1) פָּעַל *Paal* = he acted,[1] (Simple form - active)
2) נִפְעַל *Niphal* = he was acted (Simple form - passive)
3) פִּעֵל *Piel* = he has acted with intensity (Intensive - active)
4) פֻּעַל *Pual* = he has been acted with intensity (Intensive - passive)
5) הִפְעִיל *Hiphil* = he has caused to act (Causative - active)
6) הָפְעַל *Hophal* = he has been caused to act (Causative - passive)
7) הִתְפַּעֵל *Hitpael* = he acted himself (Simple/Intensive - reflexive)

2. *Characteristics of Each Form*

1) פָּעַל *Paal* = the most simple form (hence its other name *qal* = simple). We have already learned its conjugation in Perfect and in Imperfect; vowel of *atynty*: *hireq* (אִ)
2) נִפְעַל *Niphal* = נ before the root; vowel of *atynty*: *hireq* (אִ)
3) פִּעֵל *Piel* = *dagesh* in the second letter of the root, and the *hireq* (.) under the first letter of the root; vowel of *atynty*: *sheva* (אְ in the first person singular)
4) פֻּעַל *Pual* = *dagesh* in the second letter of the root, and the *qibbutz* (ֻ) under the first letter of the root; vowel of *atynty*: *sheva* (אְ in the first person singular)
5) הִפְעִיל *Hiphil* = הִ before the root, and ִי before the last letter of the root; vowel of *atynty*: *patah* everywhere
6) הָפְעַל *Hophal* = הָ before the root; vowel of *atynty*: short *qametz* everywhere
7) הִתְפַּעֵל *Hitpael* = הִת before the root and *dagesh* in the second letter; vowel of *atynty*: *hireq* (אִ in the first person singular)

---

[1]The *Paal* knows also verbs which express physical or mental states of being; they are called "stative verbs." They may show some characteristic forms of inflection: a form פָּעֵל or פָּעוֹל in the Perfect (Ex: כָּבֵד, he was heavy, or קָטוֹן, he was small); and a form יִפְעַל in the Imperfect (Ex: אֶחְסָר, I shall need). But as a whole, the stative verbs tend to become verbs of action in their meaning and in their vocalization.

*Note that *piel*, *pual*, *hitpael* (intensive forms) receive a *dagesh* in the second letter of the root. The *dagesh* does not appear here because the ע being a guttural cannot receive *dagesh*.

3. The Form of the Perfect

The Perfect is made of the form (*paal*, *niphal*, etc.) with the suffixes of the Perfect, depending on the persons. Examples of Forms in Perfect:

Paal	חָשַׂכְתָּ	You have withheld, Gen 22:12
Niphal	נִשְׁבַּעְתִּי	I have sworn, Gen 22:16
Piel	דִּשַּׁנְתָּ	You have anointed, Ps 23:5
Pual	דֻּשַּׁנְתָּ	You have been anointed
Hiphil	הִשְׁלַכְתָּ	You have thrown, 2 Kgs 14:9
Hophal	הָשְׁלַכְתָּ	You are thrown out, Isa 14:19
Hitpael	וְהִתְבָּרֲכוּ	And they will be blessed, Gen 22:18; (Perfect with consecutive-conversive *vav*; notice that the *dagesh* is not in the ר because it is a guttural).

4. The Form of the Imperfect

The Imperfect is made of the form (*paal*, *niphal*, etc.) with the prefixes of the Imperfect (*atynty*).

Note:

a. The letters (ה, נ) prefixed to the forms drop before the preformative. The dropping of the נ brings by compensation a *dagesh* in the first letter of the root.

b. The preformatives (*atynty*) are vocalized according to the different forms. (See the *Menorah* of the Verbs, page 53.) Examples of forms in Imperfect:

Paal	אֶחְסָר	I shall need, Ps 23:1
Niphal	יֵאָמֵר	It will be said, Gen 22:14; note the *tsere* instead of hireq by compensation to the impossible *dagesh* (נ assimilated) in guttural.

Piel	אֲבָרֶךְ	I shall bless, Gen 22:17; note the *qametz* instead of *patah* by compensation to the impossible *dagesh* (form *Piel*) in the ר.
Pual	תְּדֻשַּׁן	She will be made fat, Prov 11:25
Hiphil	יַרְבִּיץ	He will make lie, Ps 23:22
Hophal	יֻשְׁלְכוּ	They will be thrown, Isa 34:3; note that often the *qibbutz* comes in the first syllable, instead of the *qametz*.
Hitpael	יִתְבָּרֶךְ	He shall be blessed, Isa 65:16

D. Two Impersonal Moods

The Participle and the Infinitive are two impersonal moods (no conjugated form) which behave like nouns as far as the expression of gender and number is concerned.

1. The Participle

Each form has its own participles.

   a. The participle of פָּעַל is: active participle = פּוֹעֵל (acting); passive participle = פָּעוּל (acted).
   b. The participle of נִפְעַל is נִפְעָל (being acted). Note the difference: ָ (Participle) versus ַ (Perfect) under the second letter of the root (ע).
   c. The participle of פִּעֵל is מְפַעֵל (acting with intensity); prefix מ with the vowel of the *atynty* (מְ).
   d. The participle of פֻּעַל is מְפֻעָל (being acted with intensity); prefix מ with the vowel of the *atynty* (מְ).
   e. The participle of הִפְעִיל is מַפְעִיל (causing to act); prefix מ with the vowel of the *atynty* (מַ).
   f. The participle of הֻפְעַל is מֻפְעָל (being caused to act); prefix of with the vowel of the *atynty* (מֻ).
   g. The participle of הִתְפַּעֵל is מִתְפַּעֵל (acting oneself); prefix מ with the vowel of the *atynty* (מִ).

> Except for the *paal* and the *niphal* which
> keep about the same form, all the forms
> receive the prefix מ with the vowel of the
> *atynty* (preformative).

2. The Infinitive

Each form has its own Infinitive. In most cases the Infinitive is
prefixed with the preposition לְ (like in the English infinitive: to . . .).

a. The Infinitive of פָּעַל is לִפְעֹל (to act) Imperfect without
atynty.

Example: לִשְׁחֹט to slay, Gen 22:10

b. The Infinitive of נִפְעַל is לְהִפָּעֵל (to be acted) Imperfect
without *atynty*, yet a ה instead, with the vowel of the *atynty*.
c. The Infinitive of פִּעֵל is לְפַעֵל (to act with intensity) Imperfect without *atynty*.
d. The Infinitive of פֻּעַל is לְפֻעַל (to be acted with intensity)
Imperfect without *atynty*.
e. The Infinitive of הִפְעִיל is לְהַפְעִיל (to cause to act) Imperfect
without *atynty*, yet a ה instead, with the vowel of the *atynty*.
f. The Infinitive of הָפְעַל is לְהָפְעַל (to be caused to act)
Imperfect without *atynty*, yet a ה instead with the vowel of the
atynty.
g. The Infinitive of הִתְפַּעֵל is לְהִתְפַּעֵל (to act oneself) Imperfect without *atynty*, yet a ה instead with the vowel of the *atynty*.

> All forms are like the Imperfect without
> the *atynty* (hence like the Imperative); note
> that the forms which ordinarily have a
> prefix נ or ה loose it and receive instead a
> ה with the vowel of the *atynty*.

N.B. Another more rare Infinitive is to be noted, the Infinitive
Absolute, so called because it is used without preposition (in absolute).

The Infinitive Absolute usually comes before the Imperfect to express emphasis.

Example: בָּרֵךְ אֲבָרֶכְךָ   I will indeed bless you, Gen 22:17

3. The Negation

The negation is expressed by the adverb אֵין (construct form from the absolute אַיִן "there is not") which is commonly used before the noun.

Examples: אֵין מַחֲרִיד   no one making afraid, Mic 4:4
            אֵין לַעֲבֹד   there is not (one) to work, Gen 2:5

E. The Parsing Game

Once the student has learned by heart, 1) the two conjugations (Perfect and Imperfect) of the *Paal*, 2) the name of the seven forms, 3) the vowels of the preformatives of the Imperfect in each form, he is able to recognize and indicate:

1. tense
2. person
3. form
4. root
5. translation

Examples:

אָהַבְתָּ (Gen 22:2)
   1) The verb has an afformative → tense: Perfect.
   2) The suffix is תָּ (reminds אַתָּה) → person: second person masculine singular.
   3) The form is (a-a) ַ ַ (reminds פָּעַל) → form: *Paal* (or *qal*).
   4) Remove added letters (here only the suffix) → root: אהב to love.
   5) Translation: You loved.

וְאָמְרוּ (Mic 4:4)
   1) The verb has an afformative and is prefixed by a *vav* → Perfect with consecutive-conversive *vav*.

2) The afformative is ו → person: third masculine plural.
3) The forms is ְ_ → form: *Paal* (or *qal*).
4) Remove added letters (here the *vav* and the suffix ו) → root: אמר to say.
5) Translation: They will say.

יַרְבִּיץ (Ps 23:2)
1) The verb has a preformative → tense: Imperfect.
2) The preformative is י → person: third masculine singular.
3) The form has a י before the last letter, and *patah* under the preformative → form: *Hiphil*.
4) Remove added letters (here the two *yods*) → root: רבץ to lie down.
5) Translation: he will cause to lie.

לִשְׁחֹט (Gen 22:10)
1) The verb has neither preformative nor afformative, but preceded by the preposition לְ → infinitive construct.
2) root: שחט to slay.

IV. Excursus

At this stage, the student is more or less able to recognize the forms of the Hebrew words, as inseparable words, nouns or verbs. This tripartite classification is convenient and helpful. This traditional organization[1] is, however, to a certain extent deceitful and artificial.

Among the inseparable words we count many words which may be analyzed as nouns in construct state. The prepositions, for example, are shortened forms derived from an original "substantive in construct state."[2] And reversely, verbs may behave like nouns.

Example: תְּחִלַּת דִּבֶּר   In the beginning of the "he spoke" (of the Lord), Hos 1:2

[1]Kutscher, *A History of the Hebrew Language*, 8-10, 35-43.
[2]See Moshe H. Goshen-Gottstein's *Grammar* (Tel Aviv, 1966), 98, 150, 152.

Also within the verb itself the classification is not easy. Past and Future are expressed by both the Perfect and the Imperfect.[1] The boundaries between the two times are erased making possible a back and forth movement between them. From a linguistic point of view, this phenomenon suggests the existence of a single verbal form which has usually been recognized as the Imperfect.[2] In Hebrew, the verb seems to have preceded the noun. This observation has, of course, some implications in regards to the syntax; but it also tells us something about the mechanism of Hebrew thinking: the dynamics of the action prevails over the deliberations of the designation, making the grammatical classification difficult and above all artificial.

Thus Hebrew morphology is not just the result of a mechanical grammatical process, it is also the product of the dynamics of the thinking, a spiritual process.

V. Exercises (Morphology)

Inseparable Words

* 9. Circle all the 13 articles in Gen 22:1-5; point out the 5 articles before gutturals and the 2 articles in prepositions.

*10. Circle the 8 *vavs*, conjunction of coordination, in Gen 22:1-5.

*11. Circle the prepositions בְּ (2), לְ (3), מִ (1) in Gen 22:1-5.

Adjectives

12. Translate the following sentences into Hebrew.[3]

1) Good is the word, 1 Kgs 2:42

---

[1]See Marcel S. R. Cohen, *Le système verbal sémitique et l'expression du temps* (Paris, 1924), 17. (Cf. Hans Bauer and Pontus Leander, *Historische Grammatik der hebräischen Sprache des Alten Testamentes* [Halle and Hildesheim, 1962], 169-170.)

[2]Ibid.

[3]The vocabulary required in these exercises of translation is made of words occurring more than 1,000 times; for the checking of the translations, see the respective texts *only afterwards*.

2) The good land, Deut 1:35
3) Weak (רָפֶה) hands, Job 4:3
4) To a bad (רַע) thing, Ps 141:4
5) Like this big (גָּדוֹל) thing, Deut 4:32
6) In a bad thing, Eccl 8:3
7) Good words, Zech 1:13

Construct State

*13. Find the six words in construct state in Gen 22:1-6 and indicate their number and gender.

*14. Translate the following sentences:

1) and the word of the Lord (is), Isa 2:3
2) The words of the days, 2 Kgs 1:18
3) In the laws of the Lord, 2 Kgs 10:31
4) father of peoples, Gen 17:4
5) the land of Moriah, Gen 22:2
6) the queen of Sheba and the wisdom (חָכְמָה) of Solomon, 1 Kgs 10:4

Pronominal Suffix

*15. Find the 13 words with pronominal suffixes in Gen 22:1-5.

16. Translate the following sentences:

1) I and my house, Josh 24:15
2) She (is) the wife (אִשָּׁה) of your son, Lev 18:15
3) From our hand, Judg 13:23
4) Her feast (חַג), and her Sabbath, Hos 2:13
5) in their (masculine) hand, Josh 21:42
6) Their (feminine) children (יֶלֶד), Gen 33:2

Verbs

*17. Indicate the 15 Imperfect forms and the 3 Perfect forms in Gen 22:1-5.

18. Classify all the verbs of Gen 22:1-10 according to the composition of their root.

    Example: נסה Gen 22:1 ל"ה.

*19. Parse the following verbs (the basic meaning of the root is indicated in parenthesis):

    1) תַּסְתִּיר (hide), Ps 13:2
    2) נִסְתְּרָה (hide), Isa 40:27
    3) לְהִסָּתֵר (hide), Job 34:22
    4) אֶסָּתֵר (hide), Gen 4:14
    5) יִסָּתֵר (hide), Jer 23:24
    6) אֲקַבֵּץ (gather), Isa 56:8
    7) בָּרוּךְ (bless), Ps 135:21
    8) הָמְלַךְ (reign), Dan 9:1

20. Parse the following verbs (taken from Gen 22:1-19):

    1) וַיַּשְׁכֵּם (rise early), Gen 22:3
    2) וַיְבַקַּע (split), Gen 22:3
    3) אָמַר (say), Gen 22:3
    4) יִרְאֶה (see), Gen 22:8
    5) לִשְׁחֹט (slay), Gen 22:10
    6) אַל תִּשְׁלַח (send), Gen 22:12
    7) יָדַעְתִּי (know), Gen 22:12
    8) נִשְׁבַּעְתִּי (swear), Gen 22:16
    9) וְהִתְבָּרְכוּ (to bless), Gen 22:18
    10) שָׁמַעְתָּ (hear), Gen 22:18

21. Perfect—Translate the following sentences:

    1) your voice (קוֹל) I have heard, Gen 3:10
    2) and you have heard, Deut 9:2
    3) Haven't you (feminine singular) heard? 1 Kgs 1:11
    4) With our ears (אֹזֶן) we have heard, Ps 44:2
    5) you (masculine plural) have not heard my words, Jer 25:8
    6) The Lord has heard my supplication (תְּחִנָּה), Ps 6:10
    7) She heard all (כֹּל) the words of the Lord, Josh 24:27
    8) Our fathers have not heard, 2 Kgs 22:13

9) He let you hear His voice, Deut 4:36
10) The voice of the turtledove (תּוֹר) is heard in our land, Song of Songs 2:12

22. Imperfect—Translate the following sentences:

1) you (masculine singular) have said, I will not hear, Jer 22:21
2) You shall not hear (masculine singular) the words of the prophet (נָבִיא), Deut 13:4
3) He will hear, Prov 15:29
4) The earth (feminine) will hear, Isa 34:1
5) we shall do and we shall hear, Exod 24:7
6) don't listen (masculine plural), 2 Kgs 18:32
7) your (masculine singular) ears will hear, Isa 30:21
8) The words will be heard, 1 Sam 17:31
9) I will make you hear the word of God, 1 Sam 9:27
10) All the people will hear, Deut 17:13

23. Imperative—Translate the following sentences:

1) Earth, hear the word of the Lord, Jer 22:29
2) Let there be light (אוֹר), Gen 1:3
3) keep (masculine singular) (שְׁמַר) my commandments, (מִצְוָה), Prov 4:4
4) keep (masculine singular) (שְׁמַר) and seek (masculine singular) (דְּרַשׁ) all the commandments of the Lord, 1 Chr 28:8
5) Be kept from passing (עָבַר) this place, 2 Kgs 6:9
6) cause to hear (masculine plural) and say, Jer 4:5
7) Speak to Pharaoh king of Egypt, Exod 6:29

24. Participle—Translate the following sentences:

1) Like these words that you (masculine singular) are saying, Neh 6:8
2) They are saying: the Lord is not seeing us, Ezek 8:12
3) They are speaking and I will listen to them, Isa 65:24
4) forsaken (עָזֻב), Prov 27:10
5) The king who is making him reign, Ezek 17:16
6) Am I being the keeper of my brother, Gen 4:9

25. Infinitive—Translate the following sentences:

    1) To cause to hear your voice, Isa 58:4
    2) keep (Infinitive Absolute) the day of the Sabbath to sanctify it (קָדַשׁ *Piel*), Deut 5:12
    3) When was heard (Literally: in the "to be heard" of) the word of the king, Esth 2:8
    4) To hear, Judg 2:17

26. Different Forms (*binyan*)—Translate the following sentences:

    1) a voice was heard, Gen 45:16
    2) the joy (שִׂמְחָה) of Jerusalem will be heard from far, Neh 12:43
    3) All the nations of the earth will be blessed, Gen 22:18
    4) And you will (Prophetic Perfect) expulse it, 1 Sam 6:8
    5) Here I am expulsing you from the surface of the earth, Jer 28:16
    6) Don't make your voice heard, Josh 6:10
    7) And the Lord spoke (Imperfect *vav* consecutive) to Moses to say, Lev 4:1
    8) The men were expulsed, Gen 44:3
    9) And we shall cause to reign a king, Isa 7:6

*The Menorah of the Verbs

†These forms receive *dag-esh* in the second letter of the root (if not guttural).

*Paradigm A: The Strong
קָשַׁר, Bind;

		Person	Simple Form	
			Paal (bind)	*Niphal* (be bound)
Perfect	Sg.	1 m/f.	קָשַׁרְתִּי	נִקְשַׁרְתִּי
		2 m.	קָשַׁרְתָּ	נִקְשַׁרְתָּ
		2 f.	קָשַׁרְתְּ	נִקְשַׁרְתְּ
		3 m.	קָשַׁר	נִקְשַׁר
		3 f.	קָשְׁרָה	נִקְשְׁרָה
	Pl.	1 m/f.	קָשַׁרְנוּ	נִקְשַׁרְנוּ
		2 m.	קְשַׁרְתֶּם	נִקְשַׁרְתֶּם
		2 f.	קְשַׁרְתֶּן	נִקְשַׁרְתֶּן
		3 m./f.	קָשְׁרוּ	נִקְשְׁרוּ
Imperfect	Sg.	1 m/f.	אֶקְשֹׁר	אֶקָּשֵׁר
		2 m.	תִּקְשֹׁר	תִּקָּשֵׁר
		2 f.	תִּקְשְׁרִי	תִּקָּשְׁרִי
		3 m.	יִקְשֹׁר	יִקָּשֵׁר
		3 f.	תִּקְשֹׁר	תִּקָּשֵׁר
	Pl.	1 m/f.	נִקְשֹׁר	נִקָּשֵׁר
		2 m.	תִּקְשְׁרוּ	תִּקָּשְׁרוּ
		2 f.	תִּקְשֹׁרְנָה	תִּקָּשַׁרְנָה
		3 m.	יִקְשְׁרוּ	יִקָּשְׁרוּ
		3 f.	תִּקְשֹׁרְנָה	תִּקָּשַׁרְנָה
Imperative			קְשֹׁר ...	הִקָּשֵׁר ...
Infinitive			קָשׁוֹר, (לִ)קְשֹׁר	(לְ)הִקָּשֵׁר
Participle			קֹשֵׁר, קָשׁוּר	נִקְשָׁר

Verbs (Regular)
פָּקַד, Oversee

Intensive (Heavy) Form			Causative Form, פָּקַד	
Piel (bind fast)	*Pual* (be bound fast)	*Hitpael* (bind oneself, conspire)	*Hiphil* (make overseer)	*Hophal* (be made overseer)
קִשַּׁרְתִּי	קֻשַּׁרְתִּי	הִתְקַשַּׁרְתִּי	הִפְקַדְתִּי	הָפְקַדְתִּי
קִשַּׁרְתָּ	קֻשַּׁרְתָּ	הִתְקַשַּׁרְתָּ	הִפְקַדְתָּ	הָפְקַדְתָּ
קִשַּׁרְתְּ	קֻשַּׁרְתְּ	הִתְקַשַּׁרְתְּ	הִפְקַדְתְּ	הָפְקַדְתְּ
קִשֵּׁר	קֻשַּׁר	הִתְקַשֵּׁר	הִפְקִיד	הָפְקַד
קִשְּׁרָה	קֻשְּׁרָה	הִתְקַשְּׁרָה	הִפְקִידָה	הָפְקְדָה
קִשַּׁרְנוּ	קֻשַּׁרְנוּ	הִתְקַשַּׁרְנוּ	הִפְקַדְנוּ	הָפְקַדְנוּ
קִשַּׁרְתֶּם	קֻשַּׁרְתֶּם	הִתְקַשַּׁרְתֶּם	הִפְקַדְתֶּם	הָפְקַדְתֶּם
קִשַּׁרְתֶּן	קֻשַּׁרְתֶּן	הִתְקַשַּׁרְתֶּן	הִפְקַדְתֶּן	הָפְקַדְתֶּן
קִשְּׁרוּ	קֻשְּׁרוּ	הִתְקַשְּׁרוּ	הִפְקִידוּ	הָפְקְדוּ
אֲקַשֵּׁר	אֲקֻשַּׁר	אֶתְקַשֵּׁר	אַפְקִיד	אָפְקַד
תְּקַשֵּׁר	תְּקֻשַּׁר	תִּתְקַשֵּׁר	תַּפְקִיד	תָּפְקַד
תְּקַשְּׁרִי	תְּקֻשְּׁרִי	תִּתְקַשְּׁרִי	תַּפְקִידִי	תָּפְקְדִי
יְקַשֵּׁר	יְקֻשַּׁר	יִתְקַשֵּׁר	יַפְקִיד	יָפְקַד
תְּקַשֵּׁר	תְּקֻשַּׁר	תִּתְקַשֵּׁר	תַּפְקִיד	תָּפְקַד
נְקַשֵּׁר	נְקֻשַּׁר	נִתְקַשֵּׁר	נַפְקִיד	נָפְקַד
תְּקַשְּׁרוּ	תְּקֻשְּׁרוּ	תִּתְקַשְּׁרוּ	תַּפְקִידוּ	תָּפְקְדוּ
תְּקַשֵּׁרְנָה	תְּקֻשַּׁרְנָה	תִּתְקַשֵּׁרְנָה	תַּפְקֵדְנָה	תָּפְקַדְנָה
יְקַשְּׁרוּ	יְקֻשְּׁרוּ	יִתְקַשְּׁרוּ	יַפְקִידוּ	יָפְקְדוּ
תְּקַשֵּׁרְנָה	תְּקֻשַּׁרְנָה	תִּתְקַשֵּׁרְנָה	תַּפְקֵדְנָה	תָּפְקַדְנָה
קַשֵּׁר ...		הִתְקַשֵּׁר	הַפְקֵד	
(לְ)קַשֵּׁר	קֻשַּׁר	(לְ)הִתְקַשֵּׁר	(לְ)הַפְקִיד	הָפְקֵד
מְקַשֵּׁר	מְקֻשָּׁר	מִתְקַשֵּׁר	מַפְקִיד	מָפְקָד

CHAPTER III

VOCABULARY

The lexicon of Old Testament Hebrew contains some 3,000 words which are derived from some 1,500 roots. Of these, 103 occur more than 500 times; 490 occur only once (*hapax legomena*); 150 are recognized as foreign words[1] usually referring to things imported from foreign countries.

For the student, the term "vocabulary" is usually associated with the idea of lengthy lists of words facing their respective "fixed" meanings. Vocabulary means "words" to be looked up in the dictionary, or to be learned by heart mechanically, in a rote manner. Besides the boredom this assignment implies, it does not do justice to the reality of Hebrew semantics.

In this section the student will learn the Hebrew vocabulary in two ways. First, he will understand the dynamic nature of the Hebrew word which is characterized by three phenomena: 1) the phenomenon of "ramification": the word moves outside and ramifies itself into a multiplicity of related words; 2) the phenomenon of permutation: the word moves within itself and has its letters permuted, thereby producing related words; 3) the phenomenon of polysemy: the word moves on the semantic level into several different meanings.

Secondly, he will learn the most important words, i.e., those words that occur the most in the Bible. A first list will provide him with the 40 words which occur more than 1000 times (to be learned from English to Hebrew and conversely); a second list will provide him with the 157 words which occur more than 200 times (to be learned only from Hebrew to

---

[1]Numerically the largest group of foreign words comes from Akkadian (50%) followed by Egyptian (22%), and by Persian (18%), and finally by Indian and Greek (10%). See Maximilian Ellenbogen, *Foreign Words in the Old Testament, Their Origin and Etymology* (London, 1962).

English). In order to facilitate the learning of these words, they have been classified according to their respective world of thought (God, man, space, time), and as far as possible, they have been enlightened by their etymology or a related word.

Thus, the student will learn "intelligently" not only through understanding the linguistic phenomena but also through a thinking process.

I. The Dynamic Nature of the Hebrew Word

A. Ramification

Virtually every Hebrew word goes back to a root. Thus we have for example:

> From the root: בָּנָה, to build, Gen 22:9
> | בְּ | in |
> | בֵּן | son, Gen 22:2 |
> | בַּת | daughter |
> | בַּיִת | house, family, Mic 4:2; Ps 23:6 |

> From the root: עָלָה, to go up
> | עַל | on, Gen 22:9 |
> | עֹלָה | burnt offering, that which goes up, Gen 22:2 |
> | עֶלְיוֹן | the Most High (God), Gen 14:18 |
> | מַעֲלָה | ascent, stair, Ps 120:1 |

This phenomenon implies two observations with regard to the Hebrew word.

a)   There is a basic idea which is carried over through the diverse ramifications.

b)   Subsequently the tracing of the correct root of the word (etymology) is of great importance for the essential meaning of this word.

1. The Nature of the Basic Idea

The basic idea which is contained in the Hebrew words is concrete and refers to an action and a totality.

a. It refers to an action.

The soul, the individual, נֶפֶשׁ (Ps 23:3), comes from a root meaning "to breathe."

Grace, חֶסֶד (Ps 23:6), comes from a root meaning "to assemble strongly."

Peace, שָׁלוֹם (Gen 43:23), comes from a root meaning "to be complete."

Glory, כָּבוֹד (Ps 24:7), comes from a root meaning "heavy."

Truth, אֶמֶת (Gen 24:49), comes from a root meaning "confirm."

Righteousness, צֶדֶק (Ps 23:3), comes from a root meaning "straightness (of a stick)."

Covenant, בְּרִית (Gen 21:27), comes from a root meaning "to cut."

Intelligence, בִּינָה (Deut 4:6), comes from a root meaning "to distinguish, to separate." (See the preposition, בֵּין = between.)

The idea of "sin" is conveyed by several words whose roots express action. To miss the goal, חָטָא (usually translated: sin). To deviate from the right direction, עָוֹן (usually translated: iniquity). To turn back, פָּשַׁע (usually translated: revolt).

By contrast, the idea of "law," תּוֹרָה (Mic 4:2), is derived from a root that means "to aim in the right direction, to show the way."

To be happy, אַשְׁרֵי (See Ps 1:1) is derived from a root that means "to walk forward," אָשַׁר (see the relative pronoun אֲשֶׁר, which, what).

Blessing, בְּרָכָה, is derived from a root that means to kneel down, בָּרַךְ (Gen 22:17).

To forgive is the action which covers and erases the sin, כִּפֶּר, or lifts up and withdraws it, נָשָׂא (Gen 22:4; Mic 4:3).

To comfort, נִחַם (Ps 23:4) is derived from a root that means to "breathe, to sigh."

b. It refers to a totality.

The word for sin, חַטָּאת, is not only the act of sin, but also the result of sin, the guilt of sin, the punishment for sin, the sacrifice for sin, etc.

The word for judging, שָׁפַט, not only refers to the sentence, but also to the act of collecting the evidence; it is both the act of charging and punishing the culprit, and the act of saving the innocent.

When the Israelite refers to the תּוֹרָה (law), he does not only think of law as a set of rules, but also as the book which contains this law, the way of life which is indicated by this law, and ultimately the Israelite religion.

The word for listening (שָׁמַע) does not just refer to the act of hearing with one's ears, it also means the actual result of listening, that is the act of obeying.

2. The Tracing of the Root

a. The Method

The process of discovering the root (usually of three letters) consists at this stage at least of two operations:

1) Eliminate the prefixes (and the inseparable words, if any): for the verbs, the preformatives, and for the nouns, the two letters, מ and ת (mnemotechnic word: האמנתיו, I believed him).

(הַ)דְּבָרִים	Gen 22:1
(אֲ)בָרֶכְךָ	Gen 22:17
(הַמַּ)אֲכֶלֶת	Gen 22:6
(נֶ)אֱחַז	Gen 22:13
(יִ)צְחָק	Gen 22:2

2) Eliminate the suffixes; endings of gender and number, and pronominal suffixes.

(הַ)דְּבָרִ(ים)	Gen 22:1
(אֲ)בָרֶכְ(ךָ)	Gen 22:17
(הַמַּ)אֲכֶלֶ(ת)	Gen 22:6

b. A Warning

The fact that two words are made of the same letters does not mean that these two words are derived from the same root. Five letters carry the evidence of at least two originally various sounds: צ, ז, שׁ, ח, ע.

Examples:

ע = *gh*, or ᶜ, or *ṣ*.
The ע of עֲמֹרָה (Gomorrah) comes from an original sound, *gh*[1] (preserved in our pronunciation from the Greek transliteration); this ע sound *gh* is different from the ע of עָמְרִי (Omri), sound ᶜ.
The ע of עָצַם, sound ᶜ (meaning "strong" in Mic 4:3) is different from the ע sound of עצם, sound *gh* (meaning "close" in Isa 33:15).
The ע of אַרְבַּע, sound ᶜ (meaning "four") is different from the ע of רבע, sound *ṣ* (meaning "lie down" in Ps 139:3; cf. רבץ in Ps 23:2).

ח = *ḥ* or *kh*
The ח of חוֹל, sound *ḥ* (meaning "sand" in Gen 22:17) is different from the ח of מְחֹלָל, sound *kh* (meaning "to pierce" in Isa 53:5)

שׁ = *š* or *th* (like thing)
The שׁ of שֶׁמֶן, sound *š* (meaning "oil" in Ps 23:5) is different from the שׁ of שְׁמֹנֶה, sound *th* (meaning "eight").

ז = *z* or hard *dh* (like "the")
The ז of זֶרַע, sound *z* (meaning "seed" in Gen 22:17) is different from the ז of זְרוֹעַ, sound *dh* (meaning "arm" in Exod 6:6).

---

[1]See Roland E. Loasby, "'Har-Magedon' According to the Hebrew in the Setting of the Seven Last Plagues of Revelation 16," *Andrews University Seminary Studies* 27 (Summer, 1989): 129-132.

צ = ṣ or ẓ or ḍ or ᶜ

The צ of עֵץ sound ḍ (meaning "wood" in Gen 22:9) is different from the צ of עֵצָה, sound ẓ (meaning "counsel" in Judg 20:7), and also from the צ of עָצֶה, sound ṣ (meaning "spine" in Lev 3:9).

*Table 3.8:
Letters Representing Two Sounds

ע	=	ᶜ or *gh*
ח	=	*ḥ* or *kh*
שׁ	=	*š* or *th*
ז	=	*z* or *dh*
צ	=	*ṣ* or *ẓ*

B. Permutation[1]

1. By Metathesis

The permutation of consonants may produce either synonyms or antonyms.

  a. Synonyms

אָהֵב	to love, to desire, Gen 22:2
אבה	wish, to desire, Gen 24:5
אַל	negation, Gen 22:12
לֹא	negation, Gen 22:12

[1]For a more complete list, see A. Weizer, מקרא ולשון, 183ff.

יָדַע	to know, conjugal relationship, Gen 22:12; cf. Gen 4:1
יָעַד	to betroth, Exod 21:9
מַיִם	water, Gen 1:6
יָם	sea, Gen 1:26
רָבָה	to increase, Gen 22:17
רָהַב	to increase, Ps 138:3.

b. Antonyms

לָקַח	to take, Gen 22:2
חָלַק	to share, to give, Josh 14:5
נָחָה	to guide, to drive, Ps 23:3
חָנָה	to camp, to settle, Exod 19:2
חָסֵר	what is missing, Ps 23:1
סָרַח	the superfluous, what remains, Exod 26:12
חָרַם	to kill without mercy, Deut 7:2
רָחַם	to have mercy, Exod 33:19

2. By Phonetical Connection

שָׁחָה	to bow, to prostrate, Gen 22:5
שָׁחַח	to bow, Job 38:40
כָּתַת	to break, Mic 4:3
חָתַת	to break, Isa 30:14
שָׁלַח	to send, Gen 22:10
שָׁלַךְ	to throw, Gen 37:22
שָׁחַט	to slay, Gen 22:10
שָׁחַת	to kill, Gen 9:15
שֵׁבֶט	rod, scepter, Ps 23:4
שָׁפַט	judge, Mic 4:3

שׁוֹט   whip, Prov 26:3

3. By Alphabetic Order

אַל   Negation, Gen 22:12
בַּל   Negation, Isa 14:21

יָצָא   to go out, Mic 4:2
יָצַב   to present oneself, Exod 8:16
יָצַג   to present, Gen 47:2

לָקַח   to take, Gen 22:2
לָקַט   to take, to pick, Song of Songs 6:2

C. Polysemy[1]

אָב   father, Gen 22:7
          master, 1 Sam 10:12
          prince, Gen 45:8

בַּיִת   house, Mic 4:1
          tent, 2 Kgs 23:7
          family, Gen 7:1
          place, Neh 2:3
          temple, 1 Kgs 6:27

בָּרַךְ   to bless, Gen 22:17
          to curse, 1 Kgs 21:10

דָּבָר   event, Gen 22:1
          thing, 1 Sam 20:2
          word, 1 Sam 17:29

---

[1]For more Hebrew words with several meanings, see James Strong's *Exhaustive Concordance of the Bible*. The dictionary at the end of the concordance provides all the different renderings of the word according to the Authorized English Version. By searching out these renderings in the main concordance and noting the corresponding number in the margin, the reader is able to find the passages where the Hebrew word occurs with its particular shade of meaning.

cause, motif, Josh 5:4
problem, Exod 18:16

דֶּשֶׁן   oil, fatness, Ps 63:6
ashes, Lev 4:12

חֶרֶב   sword, Mic 4:3
drought, Deut 28:22

יָד   hand, Gen 22:10
power, strength, Is 8:11
side, Ex 2:5
place, Jer 6:3
lot, share, Gen 47:24
monument, 1 Sam 15:12

פָּקַד   to pay attention to, to see, Exod 3:16
to visit, Gen 21:1
to punish, Jer 6:15
to number, 1 Sam 11:8
to appoint, Jer 15:3
to avenge, Hos 1:4
to remember, 1 Sam 15:2

II. Important Hebrew Words[1]

*A. 40 Words Over 1000 Times[2]

1. God

1)   אֱלֹהִים   **God** (Strength; plural of majesty; cf. Allah)[3]
2)   אָמַר   **say** (most frequent word)
3)   דָּבָר   **word, thing, event**; verb *Piel*: **to speak**

[1]In order to facilitate the learning process, the words have not been organized according to the alphabetic order but rather according to the principle of association of ideas.

[2]To be known from English to Hebrew and conversely.

[3]The comments in parenthesis give the original meaning of the root and as far as possible refer to related words which are familiar to the student.

4) עָשָׂה **do**
5) מֶלֶךְ **king** (to own exclusively; cf. Moloch)
6) יָשַׁב **to sit down**
7) אָב **father** (cf. אַבְרָהָם Abraham: father of multitude)
8) נָתַן **give** (cf. Nathan, Nathanael: God has given)
9) יְהֹוָה **Yahweh** [read *Adonay*], **the Lord** (to be, to speak)
10) הָיָה **be, happen**
11) אֲשֶׁר **who, which, that** (to go on, happy; cf. Asher)

2. *Man*

12) אִישׁ **man** (social, weak)
13) בֵּן **son** (to build)
14) עַם **people** (be united, related)
15) עִם **with** (side; cf. people; cf. Immanuel: God with us)
16) אֵת **with** (closer than עִם, mark of the accusative)
17) כֹּל **all** (complete, finish)
18) פָּנִים **face** (turn toward; cf. Peniel: face of God)
19) רָאָה **see**
20) שָׁמַע **hear, obey** (cf. Ishmael: God has heard)
21) יָד **hand** (strength; cf. letter Yod; cf. יְהוּדָה Judah)
22) דָּוִד **David** (the beloved)

3. *Space*

23) אֶרֶץ **earth, land, ground** (delimited space)
24) עִיר **city** (agitation?)
25) בַּיִת **house, family** (to build; cf. Bethel: house of God)
26) יָצָא **go out**
27) הָלַךְ **go, walk**
28) בּוֹא **enter, come**
29) שׁוּב **return, repent**
30) עַל **on, against**
31) מִן **from, part of, than** (portion; cf. the Manna)

32) אֶל **toward**

33) זֶה **this,** masculine; זֹאת **this,** feminine; אֵלֶּה these, masculine/feminine.

34) לֹא **no, not** (Perfect); אַל (Imperfect); אַיִן (participle)

4. Time

35) יוֹם **day**

36) לִפְנֵי **before** (preposition לְ [to] and the word פָּנִים: to the face of)

37) עַד **until** (pass on, advance)

38) הִנֵּה **behold, lo**

39) כִּי **for, when, that, indeed**

40) אִם **if**

*B. 157 Words Between 200 and 1000 Times[1]

1. God

1) אֵל **God** (power; cf. יִשְׂרָאֵל Israel: wrestling with God)

2) אָדוֹן; אֲדֹנִי **Lord, my lords** (firm, basis, cf. god Adonis)

3) אֶחָד **one, unique** (idea of monotheism and of unity)

4) מַלְאַךְ **angel, messenger** (to send; cf. Malachi: my angel)

5) רוּחַ **spirit, wind, air** (onomatopoeia, idea of widening)

6) חַי; חַיִּים **alive, life** (plural of intensity; see חַוָּה Eve)

7) חַיִל **strength, army**

8) חָזַק **be strong**

9) צָבָא **host, army** (cf. יְהֹוָה צְבָאוֹת the Lord of Host)

10) מְאֹד **very, exceedingly, might**

[1]To be learned from Hebrew to English.

11)	כָּבוֹד	**honor, glory** (to be heavy)
12)	גָּדוֹל	**great**
13)	יָרֵא	**fear God** (tension between fear and joy)
14)	אֹהֶל	**tent, tabernacle**
15)	אָרוֹן	**ark, chest**
16)	אַהֲרֹן	**Aaron**
17)	כֹּהֵן	**priest, cohen** (divine?)
18)	לֵוִי	**Levi** (to join)
19)	קֹדֶשׁ	**holy** (to separate)
20)	מִזְבֵּחַ	**altar** (to slaughter)
21)	אֵשׁ	**fire** (social, man?)
22)	צֹאן	**flock, sheep** (good, docile)
23)	עֹלָה	**burnt offering** (עָלָה to go up, to lift up)
24)	חַטָּאת	**offering** (to miss the goal)
25)	עָוֹן	**iniquity, transgression** (to err from the way)
26)	נָשָׂא	**lift up, bear** (with עָוֹן: forgive)
27)	מִנְחָה	**offering** (gift)
28)	חֶסֶד	**kindness, grace, love** (to assemble; cf. the Hassidim)
29)	אָהֵב	**love** (idea of emotion and total commitment)
30)	יָדַע	**to know, to love** (idea of conjugal relationship)
31)	שָׁלוֹם	**peace** (complete; שְׁלֹמֹה Solomon)
32)	יָשַׁע	**to save** (wide cf. יֵשׁוּעַ Jesus: The Lord saves)
33)	נָא	**please** (cf. Hosanna! "Save please")
34)	נָצַל	*Ni.*: **be delivered**; *Hi.*: *take away*
35)	בָּרַךְ	**bless** (knee, to kneel down)
36)	צַדִּיק	**righteous, just** (be straight)
37)	תּוֹרָה	**law, teaching** (to aim, to shoot)
38)	שָׁמַר	**keep, watch** (stay awake; cf. Samaria)
39)	מִשְׁפָּט	**judgment, time of judgment, sentence, custom**
40)	צָוָה	*Pi*: **command**; (מִצְוָה commandment)
41)	כָּרַת	**cut off, make a covenant**
42)	בְּרִית	**covenant** (to cut; cf. בָּרָא: create)
43)	פָּקַד	**visit, number, remember**
44)	עָזַב	**leave, forsake** (be remote, absent)

45)	נְאֻם	**declaration, revelation** (sigh)
46)	נָבִיא	**prophet** (to call, speak)
47)	כֹּה	**thus**
48)	נָגַד	*Hi*: **report, tell** (נֶגֶד against)
49)	כָּתַב	**write**
50)	בָּקַשׁ	*Pi.*: **seek**
51)	מִי	**who?** (מָה what?)
52)	מָצָא	**find**

2. Man

53)	אָדָם	**man** (red earth, or red blood)
54)	אִשָּׁה	**woman**
55)	אֵם	**mother** (be wide, womb or onomatopoeia)
56)	נֶפֶשׁ	**life, self, living being** (throat, breathe)
57)	בָּשָׂר	**flesh, living being**
58)	דָּם	**blood** (resemble?; idea of life and individuality)
59)	לֵב	**heart** (seat of thoughts, mind, will, feelings)
60)	רֹאשׁ	**head** (cf. רֵאשִׁית beginning, cf. *Rosh Hashana*)
61)	פֶּה	**mouth** (cf. the letter פ; לְפִי according to)
62)	קָרָא	**call, meet, read** (cf. the *qorᵓan*)
63)	עָנָה	**answer** (cf. עָנִי poor, humble)
64)	עַיִן	**eye, fountain** (cf. the form of the letter ע)
65)	אַף	**nose, anger** (snort?)
66)	רֶגֶל	**foot, leg**
67)	שָׁכַב	**lie down**
68)	זֶרַע	**seed, posterity**
69)	יָלַד	**to bring forth** (cf. יֶלֶד child; תּוֹלֵדוֹת genealogy)
70)	נַעַר	**lad, young man**
71)	בַּת	**daughter**
72)	אָח	**brother** (hearth, fire pot?)
73)	שֵׁם	**name, reputation** (cf. the name Shem)
74)	מִשְׁפָּחָה	**family, clan**

75)	גּוֹי	**people, nation** (often non Israelite)
76)	אוֹיֵב	**enemy** (cf. the name אִיּוֹב Job)
77)	פַּרְעֹה	**Pharaoh** (great house; or noble, eminent)
78)	מִצְרַיִם	**Egypt** (adversary; dual for Upper and Lower Egypt)
79)	פְּלִשְׁתִּי	**Philistine**
80)	רָשָׁע	**wicked** (be loose, ill regulated, abnormal)
81)	רָע	**evil** (cf. רֵעַ friend, not the same origin)
82)	מִלְחָמָה	war
83)	לֶחֶם	**bread, food**
84)	אָכַל	**eat, devour**
85)	שָׁתָה	**drink**
86)	בֶּגֶד	**garment, covering** (cf. בָּגַד to deceive?)
87)	נָכָה	Hi.: **smite**
88)	חֶרֶב	**sword**
89)	עָבַד	**serve, work** (cf. עֶבֶד servant)
90)	יַעֲקֹב	**Jacob** (the heel)
91)	מֹשֶׁה	**Moses** (to draw?)
92)	שָׁאוּל	**Saul** (to enquire, ref. to necromancy)

3. Space

93)	שָׁמַיִם	**heaven, sky** (be high, lofty)
94)	אֲדָמָה	**ground, earth** (red)
95)	מִדְבָּר	**wilderness** (to be behind)
96)	שָׂדֶה	**field**
97)	עֵץ	**tree**
98)	הַר	**mountain** (cf. Armageddon: mountain of Magedon)
99)	מַיִם	**water** (cf. form of letter מ suggesting waves)
100)	יָם	**sea, West**
101)	דֶּרֶךְ	**way, journey, custom**
102)	שָׁם	**there**
103)	שָׁלַח	**send, stretch out**
104)	קָרַב	**draw near**; Hi: **to sacrifice** (קָרְבָּן offering)

105)	מָקוֹם	place (to stand)
106)	מַחֲנֶה	camp, army (cf.local name Mahanaim: two camps)
107)	בָּנָה	build
108)	כּוּן	Ni.: be firm; Hi.: prepare (כֵּן base, yes, so)
109)	אֶבֶן	stone
110)	נָטָה	stretch out, bend
111)	גְּבוּל	boundary
112)	שַׁעַר	gate
113)	בֵּין	between (cf. בִּין to understand)
114)	סָבִיב	all around
115)	סוּר	turn aside, apostatize
116)	(בְּ)תוֹךְ	in the middle, within
117)	תַּחַת	under, instead of
118)	נָפַל	fall
119)	יָרַד	go down (cf. יַרְדֵּן the Jordan, flowing down)
120)	קוּם	rise, resurrect
121)	עָמַד	stand, be victorious
122)	שִׂים	put
123)	כְּלִי	vessel, utensil
124)	זָהָב	gold
125)	כֶּסֶף	silver
126)	אָסַף	gather (cf. אָסָף Asaph: recorder)
127)	יָסַף	add (cf. יוֹסֵף Joseph: he adds, increases)
128)	גַּם	also
129)	רָבָה	be numerous, great (cf. רַב many; רַבִּי Rabbi)
130)	מָלֵא	be full, fulfill
131)	אַמָּה	forearm (about eighteen inches)
132)	יָרַשׁ	possess, dispossess, inherit
133)	לָקַח	take
134)	נַחֲלָה	inheritance (to give)
135)	בָּבֶל	Babylon (door of God)
136)	יְרוּשָׁלַם[1]	Jerusalem (city of peace)

[1]Read *yerushalayim*; note the *hireq* under the ם as an indication for this reading (like *Adonay* in יְהוָה).

4. Time

137)	עֵת	**time**; עַתָּה now, this time
138)	עוֹד	**still, again** (turn about, repeat; עֵד: witness)
139)	מוֹעֵד	**appointed time or place** (יעד: appoint)
140)	כַּאֲשֶׁר	**as, when**
141)	לַיְלָה	**night**
142)	חֹדֶשׁ	**new moon, month** (cf. חָדָשׁ new)
143)	שָׁנָה	**year** (to repeat, cf. מִשְׁנָה Mishna: teaching)
144)	שְׁנַיִם	**two**, masc. (repeat; note the dual form)
145)	שָׁלֹשׁ	**three**, fem.; שְׁלֹשָׁה three, masc.; שְׁלֹשִׁים thirty
146)	אַרְבַּע	**four**, fem.; אַרְבָּעִים forty
147)	חָמֵשׁ	**five**, fem.
148)	שֵׁשׁ	**six**, fem. (cf. our "six"); שִׁשִּׁים sixty
149)	שֶׁבַע	**seven**, fem.; שָׁבוּעַ week; שְׁבוּעָה oath
150)	עֶשֶׂר	**ten**, fem.
151)	מֵאָה	**hundred**
152)	אֶלֶף	**thousand** (cf. the letter א)
153)	אַחַר	**behind, after**
154)	עוֹלָם	**forever, eternity** (what is concealed)
155)	כָּלָה	**cease, finish**
156)	עָבַר	**pass over** (cf. עִבְרִי Hebrew: of the other side)
157)	זָכַר	**remember** (cf. זָכָר male)

Conclusion

This dynamic picture of Hebrew vocabulary is quite disturbing. Words move and seem to escape a fixed definition. This phenomenon of mobility may be attributed to two facts: 1) Hebrew words are derived from verbs; thus they have preserved in their semantic the traces of the dynamics which created them. Words are generated from within the action. 2) Hebrew words are not distinct and closed within their own semantic "ghetto," they are open to each other through the intricate pulses of their phonetic or alphabetic content. This flexibility may be one of the explanations for the limited vocabulary. Few words to say much. Certainly this particularity of the Hebrew words will make the task of interpretation difficult. Here the correct etymological analysis of the word is necessary but not enough. Also the statistical argument of the classical "word study" will often be misleading. For as Meir Weiss puts it, "the word is a wild growth in the personal garden of the past."[1] The meaning of the word depends ultimately on its context (of literary structure, history and ideas).

III. Exercises (Vocabulary)

27. From the following words, derive new words (same root or not); give biblical references for each word (use *A Hebrew and English Lexicon of the Old Testament* by F. Brown, S. Driver, and C. Briggs).

1)	דְּבָרִים	Gen 22:1
2)	הָאֱלֹהִים	Gen 22:1
3)	מָקוֹם	Gen 22:3
4)	יָד	Gen 22:6
5)	אֵשׁ	Gen 22:6
6)	יַחְדָּו	Gen 22:6
7)	אָבִי	Gen 22:7
8)	שָׁם	Gen 22:9
9)	מַלְאַךְ	Gen 22:11
10)	מְאוּמָה	Gen 22:12

28. 1) Give two examples of words whose roots refer to an action.

2) Give two examples of words whose roots refer to a totality.

3) Give two examples of words which are made of the same letters but do not derive from the same root (explain).

4) Give two examples of synonyms which have their letters permuted or connected phonetically (explain).

5) Give two examples of words which have several meanings.

---

[1] Meir Weiss, *The Bible from Within* (Jerusalem, 1984), 75.

Hebrew For Theologians

29. *1) Circle the words you know, and give the basic meaning of the roots (words occurring more than 1000 times) in Gen 22:1-9.

2) Circle the words you know, and give the basic meaning of the roots (words occurring more than 200 times) in Gen 22:1-9.

CHAPTER IV

TEXTS

At this stage, we shall not make an exegesis of the biblical texts. The main purpose will be to familiarize the student with the words in their context. Thus, our treatment of the text will focus on two assignments.

1. Each word or expression will be analyzed and translated literally, with the concern of reminding and applying the previous data in grammar and vocabulary.

2. Along the way, when it is necessary, supplementary information will be provided; on the other hand, when the same form or word is repeated, translation only will be indicated.

Text I. Genesis 22:1-19

Gen 22:1

1. וַיְהִי, "And it was (It came to pass)"

Analysis:
1) The verb has a preformative and is prefixed by a *vav* with a *patah* → Imperfect with *vav* consecutive; apocope.[1]
2) The preformative is י → person: third masculine singular.
3) Form: *paal* (*qal*)
4) Root: היה, to be; verb group: ל"ה, which means that its last letter (ל of פעל) is ה.

---

[1]The grammatical term "*apocope*" (from the original Greek meaning "cutting off") is used to indicate the loss of the end of the word.

Note:
1) The final ה of היה has been dropped (apocope), thus producing the shorter form וַיְהִי instead of the regular form וַיִּהְיֶה (remember that the *sheva* becomes *hireq* in lengthened form, see for example: דְּבָרֶי → דְּבַר).
2) The preformative, *yod*, now has a *sheva* and therefore cannot be doubled by the *dagesh* (regular after consecutive *vav*).
3) The word וַיְהִי (also וְהָיָה, see Mic 4:1) expresses the impersonal subject and is often used to introduce independent narratives.

2. אַחַר, "after," preposition

Note:
1) As preposition and conjunction, the plural construct אַחֲרֵי is more frequent; generally used with the pronominal suffix (Gen 18:10).
2) Words with the same root:

    אַחֵר   adjective: other (Lev 27:20)
    אָחוֹר   behind, back part (1 Chr 19:10)
    אַחֲרוֹן last (2 Sam 19:12)
    אַחֲרִית far, future, end (Dan 10:14)

3. הַדְּבָרִם, "the things (the events, the words)"

    הַ   article
    דְּבָרִים plural of דָּבָר

Of the same root is perhaps דְּבוֹרָה, bee (see Isa 7:18 with the implied meaning of murmuring).

Other words with the same letters, but not necessarily of the same root (different sounds behind the ד):

    דְּבִיר   the holy of holies, shrine (1 Kgs 6:5)
    דֶּבֶר   pestilence (Lev 26:25)
    מִדְבָּר wilderness (Ps 65:13)

Gen 22:1

4. הָאֵלֶּה

הַ, article; note the lengthening of the *patah* under the article to compensate for the impossible *dagesh* in the guttural א.

אֵלֶּה, plural of the demonstrative pronoun זֶה (this)

Note:
אֵלֶּה has an article like הַדְּבָרִים (adjective used attributively).

5. וְהָאֱלֹהִים, "and the God"

וְ   Conjunction of coordination
הָ   Article with *qametz* before the guttural א
אֱלֹהִים   Root אלה (See *Allah* in Arabic.)

Despite its plural form it is used with a singular verb. This is a plural of intensity or of majesty. In Hebrew, the plural is not only used to indicate multiplicity, but also to express the idea of strength and intensity implied in life. Thus words like "heaven, water, face, blood" are always used in the plural in order to express the idea of fullness of life contained in these notions. Likewise the plural form of God expresses the idea of power, of fullness of life, which is attached to His nature (cf. also the plural usage in Gen 1:26).

6. נִסָּה, "tested"

Analysis:
1) No preformative → Perfect
2) Third person masculine singular
3) Form: *piel* (*dagesh* in the second letter of the root)
4) Root: נסה; verb group: ל"ה; verb whose last letter (ל) is ה.

7. אֶת־, note the dash ־ called *maqqef* (without *maqqef*: אֵת), particle of the accusative.

8.   אַבְרָהָם, Abraham

אַבְרָהָם longer form of אַבְרָם
אַבְרָם   is composed of the two elements: אָב, "father" "prince," and
         רָם, "exalted." The idea is "the exalted prince (the noble
         man)."

In אַבְרָהָם, the added element is הם from הָמוֹן "many nations" (1
Sam 4:14). See Gen 17:4-5.

9.   וַיֹּאמֶר, "and he said"

Analysis:
1) Imperfect and *vav* consecutive
2) Third masculine singular
3) *Paal*
4) Root: אמר

Note:
     The Imperfect with *vav* consecutive always refers to a past action.
וַיֹּאמֶר is the most frequent word and form in the Hebrew Bible.

10. אֵלָיו, "to him"

     אֶל preposition, construct form of the absolute form אֶל plus
pronominal suffix third person masculine singular.

Note:
     The י before the pronominal suffix because of the original root
אלי (like עַל, on; עַד, until).

to me	אֵלַי
to thee	אֵלֶיךָ
to him	אֵלָיו
to her	אֵלֶיהָ
to us	אֵלֵינוּ

Gen 22:1

to you	(וָ)אֲלֵיכֶם	→	Note the vocal change from אֲ to אֵ
to them	(וָ)אֲלֵיהֶם		when the accent shifted to the last syllable.

11. אַבְרָהָם, "Abraham"

12. וַיֹּאמֶר, "and he said"

13. הִנֵּנִי, "here I am"

הִנֵּה, here, behold

Dagesh in the נ denotes a double *nun* in the primitive root, with pronominal suffix first person singular. The general usage is הִנְנִי (Gen 6:17) without *dagesh* in the נ because of its *sheva*; but in pause, with *silluq* (here): הִנֵּנִי.

Gen 22:2

1. וַיֹּאמֶר, "and he said"

2. קַח, "take"

Analysis:
1) Imperative masculine singular
2) Root: לקח
3) Form: *paal*

Note:
1) The ל (first letter of the root) has dropped like in the verb group פ"נ (verbs that begin with נ); cf. תֵּן, "give!" (Hos 9:14) from נתן.
2) Of the same root:

לֶקַח	learning, teaching (Deut 32:2)
מַלְקוֹחַ	booty, prey, jaw (Num 31:11)
מֶלְקָחַיִם	tongs, snuffers (Exod 25:38)

3. נָא, "please" Interjection expressing supplication.

   Note: the נא in Hosan*na*! (Save, please!)

4. אֶת־בִּנְךָ, your son

   בֵּן with pronominal suffix second person masculine singular
   Several applications:
   בֶּן־בֵּן   son of son, grandson (Exod 10:2)
   בֶּן דּוֹד   uncle's son, cousin (Num 36:11)
   בֶּן אָדָם   son of Adam, human (Ps 49:3)

   Expresses quality:
   בֶּן־חַיִל   son of might, mighty man (1 Sam 14:52)
   בֶּן מָוֶת   son of death, mortal man (2 Sam 12:5)

   Indicates how old one is:
   בֶּן־חֲמֵשׁ מֵאוֹת שָׁנָה   (he was) five hundred years old (Gen 5:32)

5. אֶת־יְחִידְךָ, your unique

   יָחִיד   unique, only one, with the pronominal suffix second person
            masculine singular
   Note that the *qametz* has become *sheva* with the pronominal suffix
   like in the construct state (דְּבַר → דָּבָר).

   Words of the same root:
   Adverbs יַחַד or יַחְדָּו, together (Gen 22:6); אֶחָד, one (Gen 22:2)

6. אֲשֶׁר־, whom

   Relative pronoun, used to mean: who, whom, which, what, etc.

   Words of the same root:
   אֲשֵׁרָה   sacred tree (1 Kgs 16:33)
   אָשַׁר   to go forward (Prov 9:6)
   אַשְׁרֵי   blessed, happy (Ps 2:12)

Gen 22:2

7. אָהַבְתָּ, you (fully) love

Analysis:
1) Perfect
2) Second person masculine singular
3) *Paal (qal)*
4) Root: אהב

Note that the meaning of the Perfect here is not so much to express a past event or a finished action, but rather to indicate the perfection of his love; the idea is that Abraham loved, has always loved, still loves and perfectly loves his son Isaac.

8. אֶת־יִצְחָק, Isaac

Root: צחק = to laugh (Gen 21:6)
See the root שׂחק = to laugh (Prov 29:9)

9. וְלֶךְ־, and go

Analysis:
1) Imperative with the conjunction of coordination וְ (and)
2) Root: הלך
3) Form: *paal (qal)*

Note:
1) The ה first letter of the root has dropped (like in לקח).
2) The regular form is לֵךְ (with *tsere*); we have here לֶךְ (with *segol*), because it is used with *maqqef*.

10. לְךָ, yourself

The preposition לְ expresses the idea of connection (genitive, dative, etc.).

Used here with the pronominal suffix of the second person masculine singular.

This construction (verb with לְ and pronominal suffix) is used to give emphasis to the action, or simply to express a reflexive (get

Gen 22:2

yourself), or is a dative of interest implying the exclusion of anyone else from sharing this test.

11. אֶל־, to

Preposition (note the abbreviated form: ל) denotes motion to, opposition, or actual presence at a given place.

12. אֶרֶץ, (the) land, earth

This means also earth (note the similarity of the root in the English word, "earth"; cf. also the German *"Erde"*).

13. הַמֹּרִיָּה (of Moriah)

Note the construct form, אֶרֶץ הַמֹּרִיָּה, "the country of Moriah," where the article comes at the second word.

The etymology of Moriah is not clear. Perhaps related to the verb "to see" (ראה) in the local name Abraham gives in verse 14, or (and) the verb "to fear" (ירא) in verse 12, by means of alliteration. Jewish tradition relates the etymology of Moriah to the name of Jerusalem through the root, ירו implied in the first syllable מֹר. The prefix מ often indicates place; the suffix, יָה, is the contracted form of Yahweh.

Moriah reappears only in 2 Chr 3:1.

14. וְהַעֲלֵהוּ, and offer him up

Analysis:
1) Imperative
2) Second person masculine singular
3) *Hiphil* (Note the prefix ה, with the *patah*.)
4) Root: עלה (to go up); verb group: ל"ה
5) Pronominal suffix הוּ (Third person masculine singular)

Note:
1) *The pronominal suffix* has caused the dropping of the final ה of the root. The pronominal suffix of the verb is another way of

expressing the accusative of the personal pronoun. The pronominal suffix of the verb has more or less the same form as the pronominal suffix of the noun.

me	נִי	יַרְבִּיצֵנִי	He makes **me** to lie down. (Ps 23:2)
you (M)	דְ	אֲבָרֶכְךָ	I will bless **you**. (Gen 22:17)
you (F)	ךְ		
him	הוּ, וֹ	וַיַּעֲלֵהוּ	He offered **him** up. (Gen 22:13)
her	הָ		
us	נוּ	וְיוֹרֵנוּ	He will teach **us**. (Mic 4:2)
you (M, F)	כֶם , כֶן		
them (M)	הֶם , ם		
them (F)	הֶן, ן		

2) The ָ under the ע instead of ְ (under the guttural, the *sheva* becomes *hatef patah*).

15. שָׁם, there

Idea of distance, something far away

Word of the same root שָׁמָּה = there (Gen 14:10); also perhaps שָׁמֵם = to be desolated, deserted by men (Gen 47:19); שַׁמָּה = awful, dreadful event (Deut 28:37)

16. לְעֹלָה, for offering

    לְ preposition: for עֹלָה "offering" from the verb עלה, idea of "going up." The absence of an article indicates an indefinite sense for offering.

17. עַל, upon, on

    Note the relation between עַל and עֹלָה. The preposition עַל expresses the idea of "on," "upon," but also the idea of direction towards, against (Gen 34:25).

18. אֶחָד, one

    אֶחָד is the absolute form of the construct form, אַחַד.

19. הֶהָרִים, the mountains

    The vowel under the article is *segol* (הֶ), because it comes before the guttural ה with a *qametz* הָ. (See Table 4.9 below.)

*Table 4.9: Vocal Variations of the Article

regular		ה	Ex: הַדְּבָרִים	the things (Gen 22:1)
before	א ע ר	הָ	Ex: הָאֱלֹהִים	the God (Gen 22:1)
before	הָ חָ עָ	הֶ	Ex: הֶהָרִים	the mountains (Gen 22:2)
before	ה ח	הַ	Ex: הַחֲמוֹר	the donkey (Gen 22:5)

20. אֲשֶׁר, which

Gen 22:2

21. אֹמַר, I shall say

Analysis:
1) Imperfect
2) First person singular
3) Root: אמר
4) Form: *paal*; verb group: פ"א

Note:
1) The א of the root אמר disappears in the first person (to avoid two consecutive א) and is quiescent (not pronounced) in all the other persons.
2) The *holem* on the preformative in all persons: אֹמַר, תֹּאמַר, etc.

22. אֵלֶיךָ, to you

Gen 22:3

1. וַיַּשְׁכֵּם, And he got up early

Analysis:
1) Imperfect with *vav* consecutive (note the *patah* under the ו and the *dagesh* in the preformative); apocope
2) Third person masculine singular (preformative י)
3) *Hiphil* (Note the *patah* ַ under the preformative י)
4) Root: שכם

Note:
1) The basic idea of the root, שכם, is "to carry on the shoulder" (שְׁכֶם); the place name Shechem (שְׁכֶם) has probably been given because of the effect of shoulders by Mounts Ebal and Gerizim where Shechem was located. This word belongs to the nomadic vocabulary when people used to get up early and load the shoulders (of the donkey) in order to move. By extension the word came to mean "to get up early in the morning."
2) The infinitive absolute הַשְׁכֵּם is used as an adverb meaning "early" (Jer 7:13).

3) Instead of the regular form, יַשְׁכִּים, we have וַיַּשְׁכֵּם (with *tsere* instead of long *hireq*). This shortening of the Imperfect (apocope) comes after the *vav* consecutive. (This is not a *jussive*.)

2. אַבְרָהָם, Abraham

3. בַּבֹּקֶר, in the morning

בַּ is the contraction of the preposition בְּ "in," with the article הַ (בְּ + הַ = בַּ).

Note the *dagesh* in בֹּקֶר because of the article implied in the preposition.

Words of the same root: בִּקֵר (*piel*) "to enquire," seek (Lev 27:33).

See the related words: בִּקֵּשׁ (ר/שׁ) "to seek" (Deut 13:11) and בָּקָר "cattle" (Gen 12:16).

4. וַיַּחֲבֹשׁ, and he saddled

Analysis:
1) Imperfect with *vav* consecutive
2) Third person masculine singular
3) *Paal*
4) Root: חבשׁ

Note:
1) The *hatef patah* under the guttural ח instead of *sheva*.
2) The *patah* under the preformative (influence of the guttural ח).

5. אֶת־חֲמֹרוֹ, his donkey

Word with the same letters but not necessarily of the same root:

חֹמֶר   cement, mortar, clay (Jer 18:6)
          homer, dry measure, load of a donkey (Isa 5:10)
          heap (Exod 8:10). See the play on words with חֲמוֹר, donkey
          in Judg 15:16.

Gen 22:3

6. וַיִּקַּח, and he took

Analysis:
1) Imperfect with *vav* consecutive
2) Third person masculine singular
3) *Paal*
4) Root: לקח

7. אֶת־שְׁנֵי, two

שְׁנֵי is the construct form (two of) from the absolute form שְׁנַיִם, two (plural, dual).

Words of the same root:
שָׁנָה   to change (Mal 3:6)
שָׁנָה   year (Amos 2:10)
שָׁנָה   to repeat (1 Sam 26:8)

8. נְעָרָיו, of his young men

Singular absolute, נַעַר; plural, נְעָרִים with pronominal suffix: third person masculine singular.

9. אִתּוֹ, with him

Analysis:
1) Preposition אֵת (not to be confused with the particle of the accusative אֵת)
2) With the pronominal suffix third person singular (אִתִּי, with me; אִתְּךָ, with you; אִתּוֹ, with him; etc.)
3) The *dagesh* in the ת denotes a primitive root אנת (assimilation).

10. וְאֵת and . . . particle of the accusative, here without *maqqef.*

11. יִצְחָק, Isaac

12. בְּנוֹ, his son; בֵּן, son, with pronominal suffix third person masculine singular.

Gen 22:3

13. וַיְבַקַּע, and he split

   Analysis:
   1) Imperfect with *vav* consecutive
   2) Third person masculine singular
   3) *Piel* (*sheva* under the preformative, and *dagesh* in the second letter of the root)
   4) Root: בקע

   Note:
   1) No *dagesh* in the preformative *yod* with a *sheva*.
   2) Words of the same root:
       בֶּקַע   fraction, half shekel (Gen 24:22)
       בִּקְעָה   valley, plain (Gen 11:2)
       בָּקִיעַ   fissure, breach (Amos 6:11)

14. עֲצֵי, woods

15. עֹלָה, of offering

16. וַיָּקָם, and he arose

   Analysis:
   1) Imperfect with *vav* consecutive; apocope
   2) Third person masculine singular
   3) *Paal*
   4) Root: קוּם; verb group: ע"ו

   Note:
   1) ע"ו verbs mean that the second letter of the root is ו (see Paradigm B, pages 168-169). The name of the root is not taken, as usual, from the Perfect form (here: קָם) but from the infinitive קוּם, because this form brings out the characteristic letter of the root, i.e., ו.

       → The ו is preserved:
           a. With its long vocalization וּ in the Imperfect *paal* (אָקוּם, תָּקוּם, etc.: I, you, will stand up, etc. . . .) with the long

vowel *qametz* under the preformative. Note the second or third person feminine plural תְּקוּמֶינָה (you, they, will stand up) with the conjunctive *yod* before the suffix נָה.

b. With its short vocalization ו in the *niphal*. (Perfect נָקוֹם) he was stood up; Imperfect יִקּוֹם he will be stood up), and in the Intensive forms.[1]

→ The ו is not preserved:

a. In the Perfect *paal* (קַמְתִּי stood up קַמְתָּ you stand up, etc.) note the *patah* under the first syllable קַ of every person (closed syllable) except for the third persons (masculine, feminine, singular, plural) which have long *qametz* קָמוּ (open syllable).

b. In the *hiphil* because of its vocalization הֵקִים

2) Apocope of the last syllable קוֹם → קָם because of the consecutive *vav* (this is a short *qametz* ָ to be pronounced *o*). The accent has moved back from the syllable קָם (here long *qametz* because accented to be pronounced *ā*) to the preformative וַיָּקָם.

17. וַיֵּלֶךְ, and he went

Analysis:
1) Imperfect with consecutive *vav*; apocope
2) Third person masculine singular
3) *Paal*; verb group: פ"ה (like פ"י; belongs also to פ"ו)
4) Root: הלך (See Gen 22:2 note on word No. 9.)

Note:
1) The ה, first letter of the root has gone before the preformative.

---

[1] These forms are characterized by the doubling of the last letter, here the מ which gives the form *polel* instead of *piel* (Perfect, קוֹמֵם, he raised up; Imperfect, יְקוֹמֵם, he will raise up, etc.); the form *polal* instead of *pual* (Perfect, קוֹמַם, he was raised up; Imperfect, יְקוֹמַם, he will be raised up); the form *hitpolel* instead of *hitpael* (Perfect הִתְקוֹמֵם, he raised himself; Imperfect יִתְקוֹמֵם, he will raise himself).

Gen 22:3

2) Apocope of the last syllable because of the *vav* consecutive: וַיֵּלֶךְ
(with *segol* under ל, instead of יֵלֵךְ *tsere*)

18. אֶל־, to

19. הַמָּקוֹם, the place

Words of the same root:
    קוּם   to stand
    קוֹמָה   height (Exod 38:18)
    קָמָה   standing grain (mature) (Exod 22:5)

20. אֲשֶׁר־, which

21. אָמַר־, he said

Analysis:
1) Perfect
2) Third person masculine singular
3) *Paal*
4) Root: אמר

22. לוֹ, to him

23. הָאֱלֹהִים, the God

Gen 22:4

1. בַּיּוֹם, In the day

בַּ is the contraction of the preposition בְּ with the article הַ (note the *dagesh* in the *yod*).
    יוֹם day, as division of time (this text)
        day, in opposition to night (Gen 7:4)

Other usages:
1) With the article הַיּוֹם today (Gen 22:14); בַּיּוֹם הַהוּא this particular day (eschatological formula, Mic 4:6)

Gen 22:4

2) Adverbs: יוֹמָם, by day, Jer 15:9; especially the expression יוֹמָם וָלַיְלָה by day and night, continually (Exod 13:21)

2. הַשְּׁלִישִׁי, the third

שְׁלִישִׁי is the ordinal number "third," from the cardinal number שָׁלֹשׁ = three.

Table 4.10: Numbers

Feminine	Masculine	
אַחַת	אֶחָד	one
שְׁתַּיִם	שְׁנַיִם	two
שָׁלֹשׁ	שְׁלֹשָׁה	three
אַרְבַּע	אַרְבָּעָה	four
חָמֵשׁ	חֲמִשָּׁה	five
שֵׁשׁ	שִׁשָּׁה	six
שֶׁבַע	שִׁבְעָה	seven
שְׁמֹנֶה	שְׁמֹנָה	eight
תֵּשַׁע	תִּשְׁעָה	nine
עֶשֶׂר	עֲשָׂרָה	ten

The feminine form is the most simple one; the masculine is the same form ending with ה from 3 to 10.

The tens, 20 to 90, are expressed by the plural form.
Example: שָׁלֹשׁ → שְׁלֹשִׁים = 30

Gen 22:4

The ordinal numbers are generally formed from the corresponding cardinal numbers by adding ‍י. (*î*) in the last syllable and between the last syllable and the previous one.

Example: שָׁלֹשׁ → שְׁלִישִׁי = the third

3. וַיִּשָּׂא, and he lifted

Analysis:
1) Imperfect with *vav* consecutive
2) Third person masculine singular
3) From: *paal*
4) Root: נשׂא; verb group: פ"ן

Note:
1) Verb group: פ"ן, means that the first letter is נ. The נ drops before the preformative, hence the *dagesh* in the next letter (here שׂ).
2) The *qametz* of the last syllable results from the influence of the guttural א which lengthens the syllable (like ה).
3) Figurative usages: נָשָׂא רֹאשׁ, to lift up one's head, to be bold (Judg 8:28), or to restore, to honor (Gen 40:13); נָשָׂא עָוֹן, to take up sin, to forgive (Lev 10:17)
4) Words of the same root:
   נָשִׂיא   chief, prince (Num 1:16)
   מַשָּׂא   burden (Neh 13:19)
            oracle (Isa 14:28)

4. אַבְרָהָם, Abraham

5. אֶת־עֵינָיו, his eyes

עַיִן = eye → plural form is dual עֵינַיִם → construct עֵינֵי (here, with pronominal suffix third person masculine singular).

Note:
1) The parentage of עַיִן with regard to the corresponding word in European languages (English: *eye*; German: *Augen*; French: *œil*)
2) עַיִן also means spring of water (Gen 16:7).

Gen 22:4

6. וַיַּרְא, and he saw

Analysis:
1) Imperfect with consecutive *vav*; apocope
2) Third person masculine singular
3) Root: ראה; verb group: ל"ה
4) Form: *paal*

Note:
1) The preformative receives a *patah* under the influence of the following ר which like the gutturals is attracted by the sound *a*.
2) Apocope: the ה of ראה has been deleted giving the form, וירא, instead of יראה (see Gen 22:8), identical with the *hiphil* apocopated וַיַּרְא, he showed (2 Kgs 11:4).

7. אֶת־הַמָּקוֹם, the place

8. מֵרָחֹק, from afar off

מֵ from the preposition מִן (from)

Note:
   The *tsere* under מ instead of *hireq* compensates for the impossible *dagesh* which should come in the following letter (assimilation of the נ), but is impossible in the guttural ר.

Gen 22:5

1. וַיֹּאמֶר, and he said

2. אַבְרָהָם, Abraham

3. אֶל־, to

4. נְעָרָיו, his young men

5. שְׁבוּ, stay, sit

    Analysis:
    1) Imperative
    2) Second person plural
    3) Form: *paal*
    4) Root: יָשׁב; verb group: פ"י

    Note:
    The פ"י verbs are verbs whose first letter of the root is י (see Paradigm C, pages 170-171).
    1) This י is preserved in the *paal* Perfect יָשַׁבְתִּי; יָשַׁבְתָּ; etc. (I sat, you sat, etc.).
    2) This י disappears when the preformative of the Imperfect *paal* is added, אֵשֵׁב, תֵּשֵׁב, etc. (I will sit, you will sit, etc.). Note the *tsere* under the preformative (*e - e* pattern); to compensate for the loss of the *yod* the regular *hireq* has been lengthened to *tsere*.
    3) This י becomes ו in the *niphal*, the *hiphil* and the *hophal*.

6. לָכֶם, to yourselves

    Nuance of reflexive, or emphasis (Abraham does not want to be followed).

7. פֹּה, here

    Also used with the interrogative adverb אֵי (what? who? where?) giving the form, אֵיפֹה, where (Gen 37:16).

8. עִם־, with

    אֵת (with) expresses closer association than עִם: compare the compound preposition מֵעִם, from the surrounding (1 Sam 10:9), and מֵאֵת from close proximity (Gen 27:30).

9. הַחֲמוֹר, donkey

    Note the article הַ before חֲ (see Table 4.9).

Gen 22:5

10. וַאֲנִי, while I myself

   1) Before a *hatef*, the conjunction of coordination *vav* (and) takes the vowel of the *hatef*, here the *patah*.
   2) The function of *vav* introduces an antithetical clause (here rendered "while").

11. וְהַנַּעַר, and the young man

12. נֵלְכָה, we shall go (we are determined to go)

   Analysis:
   1) Imperfect, cohortative (Note the ה at the end of the form.)
   2) First person masculine plural
   3) Form: *paal*
   4) Root: הלך to go; verb group: פ"ה

13. עַד־, until (as far as)

   Note the related words (idea of time)

עוֹד	again, still (Gen 9:11, 15)
לָעַד	for ever (Ps 21:7)
עֵת	time (Exod 18:22)
מוֹעֵד	appointed time (Exod 9:5)

14. כֹּה, there

   כֹּה also means "thus" (adverb of manner)

   Related words:
   כָּכָה (composed with כ and כה) = thus (Exod 12:11)
   אֵיכָה or אֵיךְ (composed with אי and כה) = how? (Gen 26:9)

15. וְנִשְׁתַּחֲוֶה, and we shall worship (we are determined to worship)

   Analysis:
   1) Imperfect with conjunction of coordination *vav*

Gen 22:5

2) First person plural
3) Form: *hitpael*

Note on etymology:

1) Traditional explanation, root: שחו
    a. Phenomenon of metathesis: when the root of the verb begins with a sibilant, that is a hissing sound (ס, צ, שׁ or שׂ) the ת and the sibilant change places, thus, instead of התשׁחו, we have the better sounding השׁתחו.
    b. The final ה may be explained as denoting the cohortative.
    c. Note the semantic relation between the root שחו (to bow, prostrate) and the root שׁחה (to bow down, to be cast down, Ps 42:7) and שׂוח (to meditate, Gen 24:63). See also the word שָׁחִי (to lie down, perhaps from the root שׁחה, Isa 51:23). These examples attest the existence of a root שׁחה, שׁחו, שׁחח, or שׁוח with the basic meaning of prostrating, meditating.
2) More recent explanation, root: חוה
    a. This root is prefixed with *št* as in Ugaritic or in Akkadian; this is a *hištaf ᶜal*, kind of reflexive (characterized by *t*) of the causative form *šaf ᶜel* (characterized by *š*).
    b. The meaning of חוה is to prostrate, to wind (like a serpent). See the Arabic *taḥawwa* (fifth form) and especially the Ugaritic *yšthwy*.

16. וְנָשׁוּבָה, and we shall return (we want, we wish to return)

Analysis:

1) Imperfect with conjunctive *vav*; cohortative
2) First person plural
3) Form: *paal*
4) Root: שׁוב; verb group: ע"ו

Note:

1) The root שׁוב means: to come back (here)
                               to turn away (Num 14:43)
                               to repent (Hos 3:5)
                               to be restored (Ps 23:3)

Gen 22:5

2) Words of the same root:
מְשׁוּבָה apostasy, Jer 2:19
תְּשׁוּבָה answer, Job 34:36

17. אֲלֵיכֶם, to you

Gen 22:6

1. וַיִּקַּח, and he took

2. אַבְרָהָם, Abraham

3. אֶת־עֲצֵי, (the) woods

4. הָעֹלָה, of the offering

5. וַיָּשֶׂם, and he put

Analysis:
1) Imperfect with *vav* consecutive; apocope
2) Third person masculine singular
3) *Paal*
4) Root: שִׂים; verb group: ע"י (also found שׂוּם, Exod 4:11)

Note:
1) ע"י verbs behave like ע"ו verbs (see קוּם); the only difference is in the Imperfect יָשִׂים versus יָקוּם.
2) Apocope because of the consecutive *vav*, the last syllable שִׂים has been shortened into שֶׂם.
3) The expression שִׂים לֵב, literally put one's heart, i.e., to pay attention (Deut 32:46; Hag 1:5).

6. עַל־, on

7. יִצְחָק, Isaac

8. בְּנוֹ, his son

9. וַיִּקַּח, and he took

10. בְּיָדוֹ, in his hand

    Analysis:
    בְּ   preposition in, or by the means of
    יָד   hand with pronominal suffix third person masculine singular

    Words of the same root:
    יָדָה   *paal*: to throw (Jer 50:14)
    הוֹדָה   *hiphil*: to thank, to confess (1 Kgs 8:33)
    תּוֹדָה   thanksgiving, offering (Lev 7:12)
    יְהוּדָה   name Judah

11. אֶת־הָאֵשׁ, the fire

    Note the *qametz* under the article ה before the guttural א.

    Words of the same root:
    אֱנוֹשׁ   man, social dimension, Deut 32:26
    אִישׁ   man, Gen 2:23

12. וְאֶת־הַמַּאֲכֶלֶת, and the knife

    Note the *hiphil* participle form of the word מַאֲכֶלֶת.

    Words of the same root:
    אָכַל = to eat, Exod 34:28
    מַאֲכָל = food, Gen 2:9

13. וַיֵּלְכוּ, and they went

    Analysis:
    1) Imperfect with *vav* consecutive
    2) Third person masculine plural
    3) *Paal*
    4) Root: הלך; verb group: פ"ה

Gen 22:6

14. שְׁנֵיהֶם, the two of them

    Analysis: שְׁנַיִם (construct שְׁנֵי) with pronominal suffix, third person masculine plural.

15. יַחְדָּו, together

    Original form, יַחְדָּיו (Jer 46:12); idea of becoming one (see the related word אֶחָד, one).

Gen 22:7

1. וַיֹּאמֶר, and he said

2. יִצְחָק, Isaac

3. אֶל־, to

4. אַבְרָהָם, Abraham

5. אָבִיו, his father אָב (father) with pronominal suffix, third person masculine singular

    Note:
    The *yod* before the pronominal suffix denotes a primitive root אבה (י and ה are often interchangeable, see verbs ל"ה).

6. וַיֹּאמֶר, and he said

7. אָבִי, my father אָב with pronominal suffix, first person

    Note:
    Irregular plural in אוֹת (feminine form) אָבוֹת: fathers, ancestors (Exod 6:14) like שֵׁם (name) → שֵׁמוֹת names (Exod 1:1)

8. וַיֹּאמֶר, and he said

9.   הִנֵּֽנִי, here I am

Note:
    From הִנֵּה (behold, here), with pronominal suffix first person; compare with v. 1, No. 13; the *segol* (instead of the normal *sheva*, or of *tsere* in pause) under the נ is exceptional. (See also Gen 27:18.)

10.   בְנִי, my son

Note: The ב has no *dagesh*.

Rule:
    The *begedkefet* does not take *dagesh* when it follows an open syllable (here, the נִי of הִנֵּֽנִי).

11.   וַיֹּאמֶר, and he said

12.   הִנֵּה, here (is)

13.   הָאֵשׁ, the fire

14.   וְהָעֵצִים, and the woods

15.   וְאַיֵּה, but where (is)

Note:
1) The verb "to be" is implied, it is never used in the present tense or to introduce a predicate.
2) Function of the *vav*: introduces an antithetical clause (here rendered "but").

16.   הַשֶּׂה, the lamb

17.   לְעֹלָה, for offering

Gen 22:8

1.   וַיֹּאמֶר, and he said

Gen 22:8

2. אַבְרָהָם, Abraham

3. אֱלֹהִים, God

4. ־יִרְאֶה, he will see

Analysis:
1) Imperfect
2) Third person masculine singular
3) *Paal*
4) Root: ראה; verb group: ל"ה

Note:
    Verb group: ל"ה. In the Imperfect, final ה remains in every person except when the person requires a specific termination; then ה drops before vocal termination or changes into י before consonantal termination. (See Paradigm D, pages 172-173.)

Table 4.11: ל"ה Imperfect

I shall see	אֶרְאֶה
you shall see (M)	תִּרְאֶה
you shall see (F)	תִּרְאִי
he shall see	יִרְאֶה
she shall see	תִּרְאֶה
we shall see	נִרְאֶה
you shall see (M)	תִּרְאוּ
you shall see (F)	תִּרְאֶינָה
they shall see (M)	יִרְאוּ
they shall see (F)	תִּרְאֶינָה

Gen 22:8

5. לֹו, for Himself, nuance of reflexive, or emphasis (God will certainly see, provide)

Note:
      Dagesh in lamed; this *dagesh* is a conjunctive *dagesh*; so called because it comes from the close connection between two words. Two main conditions for this *dagesh*:

1) The last vowel of the preceding word is *segol* or *qametz*.
       יִרְאֶה־לֹּו
2) Comes on an accented syllable.
       יִרְאֶה־לֹּו

Table 4.12: *Dagesh*

Two Kinds of *Dagesh*
Weak *Dagesh* (*qal*) in *Begedkefet*
Exception: No *dagesh* in *begedkefet* preceded by a word ending with an open syllable.
Strong *Dagesh* (*hazaq*)
After article and *vav* consecutive Assimilation Verbal forms (*piel, pual, hitpael*) Conjunctive *dagesh* Trace of *nun* or double letter in original root Exception: No *dagesh* in yod יְ or mem מְ with a *sheva*

6. הַשֶּׂה, the lamb

7. לְעֹלָה, for offering

8. בְּנִי, my son

Gen 22:8

9. וַיֵּלְכוּ, and they went

10. שְׁנֵיהֶם, the two of them

11. יַחְדָּו, together

Gen 22:9

1. וַיָּבֹאוּ, and they came

   Analysis:
   1) Imperfect with *vav* consecutive
   2) Third person masculine plural
   3) *Paal*
   4) Root: בוא; verb group: ע"ו

2. אֶל־, to

3. הַמָּקוֹם, the place

4. אֲשֶׁר, which

5. אָמַר־, he said

6. לוֹ, to him

7. הָאֱלֹהִים, the God

8. וַיִּבֶן, and he built

   Analysis:
   1) Imperfect with *vav* consecutive; apocope
   2) Third person masculine singular
   3) *Paal*
   4) Root: בנה; verb group: ל"ה

9. שָׁם, there

10. אַבְרָהָם, Abraham

11. אֶת־הַמִּזְבֵּחַ, the altar

   Words of the same root:
   זָבַח   to slaughter, to sacrifice (Exod 20:24)
   זֶבַח   sacrifice (Gen 31:54)
   Note the related word טַבָּח cook (1 Sam 9:24), or the bodyguard
   (2 Kgs 25:8).

12. וַיַּעֲרֹךְ, and he arranged

   Analysis:
   1) Imperfect with *vav* consecutive
   2) Third person masculine singular
   3) *Paal*
   4) Root: ערך

   Note:
   1) *Hatef patah* under the guttural ע instead of *sheva*; affects the
      preformative which receives the basic vowel, i.e., *patah* (instead
      of *hireq*).
   2) Various meanings:
      - arrange in order (Num 23:4)
      - arrange in battle (Judg 20:22)
      - compare, evaluate (Isa 40:11)
   3) Words of the same root:
      עֵרֶךְ   order, row (Exod 40:23)
               evaluation (Lev 5:15)
      מַעֲרָכָה battle line (1 Sam 4:2)

13. אֶת־הָעֵצִים, the wood

14. וַיַּעֲקֹד, and he bound

   Analysis:
   1) Imperfect with *vav* consecutive
   2) Third person masculine singular

Gen 22:9

3) *Paal*

4) Root: עָקַד

Note:

1) *Hatef patah* under the guttural עֲ instead of *sheva*; affects the preformative which receives *patah*.

2) The expression עֲקֵדַת יִצְחָק, the binding of Isaac characterizes this event in Jewish tradition.

3) Word of the same root, עָקֹד, striped (of Jacob's sheep, Gen 30:40)

15. אֶת־יִצְחָק, Isaac

16. בְּנוֹ, his son

17. וַיָּשֶׂם, and he put

18. אֹתוֹ, him

אֵת particle of the accusative with the pronominal suffix of the third person; אֵת becomes אֹת (with *holem*) when it receives a pronominal suffix, except for the heavy suffix of the second person plural.

me	אֹתִי
you (m)	אֹתְךָ
you (f)	אֹתָךְ
him	אֹתוֹ
her	אֹתָהּ
us	אֹתָנוּ
you (m)	אֶתְכֶם
you (f)	אֶתְכֶן
them (m)	אֹתָם
them (f)	אֹתָן

19. עַל־, on

20. הַמִּזְבֵּחַ, the altar

Gen 22:9

21. מִמַּעַל, upon

מִמַּעַל is composed of the word מַעַל (upon) and the inseparable preposition מִן, hence the *dagesh* in the מ of מַעַל (assimilation of the נ). The force of the meaning "from" in מִן has been lost.

22. לָעֵצִים, to the woods

The preposition לְ after מִמַּעַל indicates the connection; it has *qametz*, לָ, because of the implied article הָ before the guttural ע.

Gen 22:10

1. וַיִּשְׁלַח, and he sent

Analysis:
1) Imperfect with *vav* consecutive
2) Third person masculine singular
3) *Paal*
4) Root: שׁלח

Note:
1) *Patah* under ל in וַיִּשְׁלַח because of the influence of the guttural ח.
2) Word of the same root:
    שֶׁלַח, weapon (Joel 2:8)
3) שֻׁלְחָן, table (Ps 23:5). It has the same letters, but comes probably from a different root (שׁ is originally different).

2. אַבְרָהָם, Abraham

3. אֶת־יָדוֹ, his hand

Note the idiomatic expression, שָׁלַח אֶת־יָדוֹ, "he sent his hand" to mean "he stretched out his hand."

4. וַיִּקַּח, and he took

5. אֶת־הַמַּאֲכֶלֶת, the knife

Gen 22:10

6. לִשְׁחֹט, to slay

Analysis:
1) infinitive construct; preposition לְ
2) *Paal*
3) Root: שׁחט

Note:
1) The preposition לְ becomes לִ before the *sheva* (collision of shevas).
2) The related root שׁחת, to destroy (Gen 6:17).

7. אֶת־בְּנוֹ, his son

Gen 22:11

1. וַיִּקְרָא, and he called

Analysis:
1) Imperfect with *vav* consecutive
2) Third person masculine singular
3) *Paal*
4) Root: קרא

Note:
1) The verb קרא means to call, to cry (Judg 9:7), to name (Gen 4:26), to read aloud (Jer 36:6).
2) Word of the same root: מִקְרָא convocation, sacred assembly (Exod 12:16), reading (Neh 8:8). Later the word מִקְרָא came to mean the Holy Scriptures (the expression מִקְרָאוֹת גְּדוֹלוֹת designates the Rabbinic Bible).
3) The Arabic word, *Koran*, (of the same Semitic root) refers also to the sacred reading of the Muslims.

2. אֵלָיו, to him

3. מַלְאַךְ, (the) angel of

    Also means:
    - a messenger (Gen 32:4)
    - a prophet (Isa 42:19)
    - a priest (Mal 2:7)
    - a heavenly being (1 Chr 21:15)

    Note:
    The word מַלְאַךְ is here in construct with יְהוָה. The absolute form is מַלְאָךְ (with *qametz* under א).

4. יְהוָה, *YHWH* (my Lord)

    1) The vowels of יְהוָה are taken from the word אֲדֹנָי, my Lord, to indicate that "Adonai" should be read (*qerê*). The *hatef patah* under the guttural א becomes *sheva* under *yod*, and the *patah* under the closed syllable נָ becomes *qametz* under the open syllable וָה. Thus the addition of the vowels by the Masoretes has followed the rules of Hebrew phonetics.
        The combination of the two--the Tetragrammaton (the four letters, *YHWH*) and the vowels of Adonai--makes the artificial name Jehovah (probably 16th century origin).
    2) The meaning of יְהוָה.
        a. The root הוה means "to be," or (see Ugaritic) "to speak." In Hebrew the idea of existence and of word are related (cf. the word דָּבָר, meaning thing, event and word).
        b. The form, יהוה, is probably to be analyzed as a *hiphil*. Imperfect, third person, meaning "he will cause to be." The approximate original pronunciation is Yahweh.

5. מִן־, from

    Preposition expressing the idea of origin (from, out of). This preposition indicates also the comparison (than).
    Example: הַכֹּהֵן הַגָּדוֹל מֵאֶחָיו, the priest that is greater than his brethren (Lev 21:10).

Gen 22:11

This Hebrew expression of the *comparative* accounts for the Hebrew idea of totality. "To compare" means in Hebrew to refer to an object in relation to a totality of which this object is a part. Thus, "the priest is greater than his brethren" will be translated in Hebrew "the priest is greater out of his brethren."

6. הַשָּׁמַיִם, the heavens

Probably related to the word שָׁם expressing the idea of far distance (Arabic *shama*: be high, lofty).

7. וַיֹּאמֶר, and he said

8. אַבְרָהָם, Abraham

9. אַבְרָהָם, Abraham

10. וַיֹּאמֶר, and he said

11. הִנֵּנִי, here I am

Gen 22:12

1. וַיֹּאמֶר, and he said

2. אַל־, not, do not (negation for Imperfect)

3. תִּשְׁלַח, you shall send

   Analysis:
   1) Imperfect
   2) Second person masculine singular
   3) *Paal*
   4) Root: שלח

4. יָדְךָ, your hand; יָד, hand, with pronominal suffix of second person masculine singular

5.　אֶל־, to, on; the preposition אֶל may also connote agressivity (see Gen 4:8).

6.　הַנַּעַר, the young man

7.　וְאַל־תַּעַשׂ, and don't do

   Analysis:
   1) Imperfect; apocope; *jussive*
   2) Second person masculine singular
   3) *Paal*
   4) Root: עשׂה; verb group: ל"ה

   Note:
   　　The *jussive* is found in the second and the third person singular and plural. With the negation אַל, it expresses a strong prohibition.

8.　לוֹ, to him

9.　מְאוּמָה, anything

   　　From מָה וּמָה: what and what, or from מָאוּם, מוּם: spot, point (Lev 21:17)

10.　כִּי, because (since)

   　　Like for other conjunctions, the meaning of כִּי is very flexible and has a wide range of applications:
   　　- that, Gen 22:12 (below)
   　　- when, Gen 6:1

11.　עַתָּה, now

   1) From עֵת time (Hos 10:12)
   2) Original root ענה, hence the *dagesh* in the ת of עַתָּה (assimilation)

Gen 22:12

3) The termination הָ indicates probably the trace of a primitive accusative case ending[1] (like the old Arabic *a*), meaning *this* time, i.e., "now."

12. יָדַעְתִּי, I have known.

Analysis:
1) Perfect
2) First person masculine singular
3) *Paal*
4) Root: ידע; verb group: פ"י

Note:
1) The meaning of the Perfect implying complete knowledge
2) The word ידע "to know" implies intellectual, as well as physical knowledge. This word is used to express the intimacy and the experience of the conjugal relationship (Gen 4:1).

13. כִּי־, that

Another usage of this conjunction (see 10) is to introduce a clause depending on a verb.

14. יָרֵא, fearing

Analysis:
1) Participle
2) Masculine singular

---

[1]Case endings have disappeared in biblical Hebrew. Only some rare words have preserved remains of the primitive forms. For instance the ending ה, *ā*, (accusative) to express direction (example: בָּבֶלָה "to Babel," 2 Kgs 24:15); or the ending וֹ, *o*, (probably from the accusative; example: חַיְתוֹ אֶרֶץ "the beast of the earth," Gen 1:24, cf. vs. 25); or the ending וּ, *u*, in the proper names (nominative; example: פְּנוּאֵל Gen 32:32); or the ending מִי = *y*, in the proper names (genitive; example: מַלְכִּיצֶדֶק "the king of righteousness," Gen 14:18). The ancient Semitic declension had indeed three cases: nominative (*û*), genitive (*î*), and accusative (*a*).

Gen 22:12

3) Construct form (absolute יָרֵא → יְרֵא)
4) Root: ירא; verb group: פ"י

Note:
1) Usually in relation to God
2) Word of the same root:
   נוֹרָע (*niphal*) something frightful, terrible, in relation to God (Judg 13:6)
3) The form *pael* characterizes generally the stative verbs--i.e., the verbs which express a state or a quality (intransitive meaning). Example: כָּבֵד heavy, Gen 41:31

15. אֱלֹהִים, God

16. אַתָּה, you

17. וְלֹא, for not

Note the function of the conjunctive *vav*: it introduces a clause of cause (here rendered "for").

18. חָשַׂכְתָּ, you have (not) withheld

Analysis:
1) Perfect
2) Second person masculine singular
3) *Paal*
4) Root: חשׂך

19. אֶת־בִּנְךָ, your son

20. אֶת־יְחִידְךָ, your unique

21. מִמֶּנִּי, from me

The preposition מִן with the pronominal suffix of the first person. With heavy suffixes the simple form remains (for example: מִכֶּם from you, plural); with light suffixes, the מ is doubled מִמֶּנִּי.

Gen 22:12

Gen 22:13

1. וַיִּשָּׂא, and he lifted

2. אַבְרָהָם, Abraham

3. אֶת־עֵינָיו, his eyes

4. וַיַּרְא, and he saw

5. וְהִנֵּה־, and here

6. אַיִל, ram

   Words of the same root:
אַיָּל	deer, 1 Kgs 5:3
אַיִל	leader, Exod 15:15
	terebinth, Isa 1:29 perhaps
also אֱלֹהִים	God, Gen 22:1

7. אַחַר,[1] after

8. נֶאֱחַז, it was caught

   Analysis:
   1) Perfect[2]
   2) Third person masculine singular
   3) *Niphal*
   4) Root: אחז; verb group: פ"א

[1]Several manuscripts and versions have the word אֶחָד (one); ר and ד are often confused in Hebrew writing.

[2]Participle if we have a *qametz* נֶאֱחָז as indicated in some manuscripts and versions; the Perfect fits better the reading אחר (after), whereas the participle fits better the reading אֶחָד (one).

Note:
1) The *hatef segol* under the guttural א instead of *hireq* (*niphal*); this is a compromise between the sound "a" to which is attached the guttural and the required *hireq*.
2) The נ influenced by the guttural has taken the basic vowel *segol*.

9.   בַּסְּבַךְ, in the thicket

1) Preposition בַּ with the article הַ, hence the *dagesh* in ס.
2) Word of the same root: סְבַךְ, verb, to interweave (Nah 1:10).

10. בְּקַרְנָיו, by its horns

Analysis:
1) בְּ preposition meaning "in" or "by means of" (instrumental).
2) The form *segolate*, קֶרֶן, horn (feminine singular), has a dual plural קַרְנַיִם (absolute form) which becomes קַרְנֵי in construct state; the latter form is the one used here with the pronominal suffix (third person masculine singular) קַרְנָיו.
3) The accent on קרניו has lengthened the regular *patah* to a *qametz* under the נ.
4) קֶרֶן has several meanings:
   - wind instrument (שׁוֹפָר), Josh 6:5
   - symbol of strength, Deut 33:17
   - rays, Exod 34:29[1]

11. וַיֵּלֶךְ, and he went

12. אַבְרָהָם, Abraham

13. וַיִּקַּח, and he took

14. אֶת־הָאַיִל, the ram

[1]St. Jerome who understood קרן in its primitive sense of "horn" translated the verse "Horns formed in his face" in the Vulgate. Later, drawing upon the Vulgate mistranslation, Michelangelo created his sculpture of Moses with two horns extended from his forehead.

Gen 22:13

15. וַיַּעֲלֵהוּ, and he offered it up

Analysis:
1) Imperfect with consecutive *vav*
2) Third person masculine singular with pronominal suffix (third person masculine singular)
3) *Hiphil*
4) Root: עלה; verb group: ל"ה

Note:
1) The *hatef patah* comes under the guttural ע instead of *sheva* (laryngals are attracted by the sound "a").
2) The ה of the root עלה has been dropped before the pronominal suffix.

16. לְעֹלָה, for offering

17. תַּחַת, instead

1) Preposition, means "under, beneath," Gen 7:19
2) In idiomatic expression:
    - the place in which one stands: שְׁבוּ אִישׁ תַּחְתָּיו stay everyone in his place, Exod 16:29
    - in place of, instead of, עַיִן תַּחַת עַיִן eye for eye, Exod 21:24

18. בְּנוֹ, his son.

Gen 22:14

1. וַיִּקְרָא, and he called

2. אַבְרָהָם, Abraham

3. שֵׁם־, name

1) In construct state with the following word
2) שֵׁם has several meanings
    a. Name, Gen 26:33

    b.   Reputation; note the play on words between שֵׁם (name) and
שֶׁמֶן (oil, perfume) in Eccl 7:1: טוֹב שֵׁם מִשֶּׁמֶן טוֹב: A good
name is better than a good oil.

    c.   Monument, Isa 55:13, note the idiomatic expression יָד וָשֵׁם
(literally "hand and name") which means "memorial" (Isa
56:5).

4.   הַמָּקוֹם, (of) the place

5.   הַהוּא, this very one

    1) Literally "the it" (here referring to place) or "the he." הוּא, third
person masculine singular is used as a demonstrative, "this very
place." For example: בַּיוֹם הַהוּא, in that very day, Mic 4:6.

    2) Other usages:

        a.   Personal pronoun (subject), emphatic: "he" or "it" (Gen
3:15)

        b.   Used as emphatic predicate of God: אֲנִי הוּא, אֲנִי, I, I am He.
Deut 32:39 (cf. Isa 41:4)[1]

        c.   In a neuter sense, "that," "it"; also with an emphatic note:
הוּא אֲשֶׁר דִּבַּרְתִּי, that (is) what I said (Exod 16:23)

6.   יְהֹוָה, the Lord

7.   יִרְאֶה, will see

8.   אֲשֶׁר, so that

    1) This is another meaning of אֲשֶׁר close to כִּי.

    2) May also have a causal force: אֲשֶׁר טִמֵּא, because he defiled (Gen
34:13).

---

[1]The Septuagint usually translates this expression by *ego eimi*, I am, as in
Exod 3:14 (cf. John 8:58).

Gen 22:14

9. יֵאָמֵר, it will be said

Analysis:
1) Imperfect
2) Third person masculine singular
3) *Niphal*
4) Root: אמר; verb group: פ"א

Note:
    Tsere is used under the preformative *yod* instead of *hireq* as a compensation for the impossible *dagesh* (assimilation of the נ of *niphal*) in the guttural א.

10. הַיּוֹם, today

    Literally "the day" with a demonstrative force, namely, "this day"

11. בְּהַר, in (the) mountain

    בְּ preposition, without the article הַ, in construct state with the following word

12. יְהֹוָה, of the Lord

13. יֵרָאֶה, it will be seen.

Analysis:
1) Imperfect
2) Third person masculine singular
3) *Niphal*
4) Root: ראה; verb group: ל"ה

Note:
    Tsere is used under the preformative *yod* instead of *hireq* as a compensation for the impossible *dagesh* (assimilation of the נ of *niphal*) in the guttural ר.

Gen 22:14

Gen 22:15

1. וַיִּקְרָא, and he called

2. מַלְאַךְ, (the) angel

3. יְהֹנָה, (of) the Lord

4. אֶל־, to

5. אַבְרָהָם, Abraham

6. שֵׁנִית, a second time

    1) Feminine ordinal number; the masculine form is שֵׁנִי
    2) Here used as an adverb with the feminine ending ת. because the
       feminine word פַּעַם (time) is implied. See בַּפַּעַם הַשְּׁבִיעִית, the
       seventh time (Josh 6:16).

7. מִן־, from

8. הַשָּׁמַיִם, the heavens (For the plural form, see our comment on v. 1,
    No. 5.)

Gen 22:16

1. וַיֹּאמֶר, and he said

2. בִּי, by (in) Myself

    Preposition בְּ, with pronominal suffix first person

3. נִשְׁבַּעְתִּי, I have sworn

    Analysis:
    1) Perfect
    2) First person singular
    3) *Niphal*

Gen 22:15, 16

4) Root: שׁבע

Note:
1) Here the Perfect tense expresses the completeness of God's swearing; it is definitive.
2) Words of the same root:
   שֶׁבַע   seven (Gen 21:28)
   שְׁבוּעָה oath (Gen 26:3) שָׁבוּעַ week, period of seven days (Dan 9:27)

4. נְאֻם־, declaration (oracle)

This word is always used in construct state and before divine names by the prophet citing the divine word (Isa 14:22; Amos 2:11).

5. יְהוָה, (of) the Lord

6. כִּי, since

1) This is another usage for the conjunction כִּי.
2) Note the construction (v. 17) כִּי...כִּי; the first כִּי introduces the clause of reason or cause; the second כִּי (v. 17), introduces the clause of result (cf. 1 Kgs 1:30).

7. יַעַן אֲשֶׁר, because that

Note:
1) This locution is rarely used; with כִּי it denotes a strong causal nuance.
2) Words of the same root:
   ענה   to be occupied, worried (Eccl 1:13)
   עִנְיָן concern, occupation (Eccl 1:13)
   לְמַעַן for the motif of, on account of (Ps 23:3)
3) Other words with the same letters, but not necessarily of the same root.
   ענה   to answer (Mic 6:5)
   ענה   to be afflicted, humiliated (Ps 119:107)
   עָנִי   poor (Ps 10:2)

Gen 22:16

8. עָשִׂיתָ, you have done

Analysis:
1) Perfect
2) Second person masculine singular
3) *Paal*
4) Root: עשׂה; verb group: ל"ה

Note: ל"ה verbs in Perfect
1) The final ה *remains* only in the third person masculine singular עָשָׂה, he made (feminine עָשְׂתָה, she made).
2) The final ה *drops out* before a vocal ending (only עָשׂוּ, they made) and changes into י before a consonantal ending, עָשִׂיתִי, I made. (See Paradigm D, pages 172-173.)

Table 4.13: ל"ה Perfect

I made	עָשִׂיתִי
you made (singular masculine)	עָשִׂיתָ
you made (singular feminine)	עָשִׂיתְ
he made	עָשָׂה
she made	עָשְׂתָה
we made	עָשִׂינוּ
you made (plural masculine)	עֲשִׂיתֶם
you made (plural feminine)	עֲשִׂיתֶן
they made	עָשׂוּ

9. אֶת־הַדָּבָר, the thing

10. הַזֶּה, (the) this (this thing)

Note on the demonstrative pronoun זֶה, this.

Gen 22:16

1) Is used like the adjective (follows the substantive and can also receive the article ה).
2) Used as an adverb when attached to certain words, אֵי זֶה, which, where (Job 28:20).
3) Feminine word זֹאת;
    a. When related to feminine word (Gen 2:23)
    b. With a neuter sense עָשִׂיתָ זֹּאת, you did this (Gen 3:14)
    c. The locution בְּכֹל זֹאת, in spite of this (Ps 78:32)

11. וְלֹא, and not

12. חָשַׂכְתָּ, you (did not) withdraw

13. אֶת־בִּנְךָ, your son

14. אֶת־יְחִידְךָ, your unique

Note the *segol* under the ד; the regular *sheva* has been lengthened under the influence of the accent (pause).

Gen 22:17

1. כִּי, then; conjunction introducing the result clause (see above, v. 16, No. 6).

2. בָרֵךְ, (to) bless

Analysis:
1) infinitive absolute
2) *Piel*
3) Root: ברך

Note:
1) The *qametz* under ב (instead of *patah*) to compensate for the impossible *dagesh* (*piel*) in the guttural ר.
2) The infinitive absolute expresses the idea of the verb (idea of blessing).

3.   אֲבָרֶכְךָ, I shall bless you

Analysis:
1) Imperfect with pronominal suffix (second person masculine singular)
2) First person masculine singular
3) *Piel*
4) Root: ברך

Note:
1) The form, בָּרֵךְ אֲבָרֶכְךָ (infinitive absolute), followed by the Imperfect meaning literally "bless I will bless"; this pleonastic language is used to emphasize the certainty of the statement, thus meaning: "I shall certainly bless you."
2) The *tsere* under ר has been shortened into *segol* because of the addition of the pronominal suffix.

4.   וְהַרְבָּה, and (to) cause increase

Analysis:
1) infinitive absolute with conjunction of coordination *vav*.
2) *Hiphil*
3) Root: רבה; verb group: ל"ה

Note:
1) The form, הַרְבָּה, instead of the common form הַרְבֵּה, which is used as an adverb in the sense of "much" (Gen 41:49).
2) Words of the same root:

רַב	Adjective, great (Gen 24:25)
רַב	Noun, chief (Dan 1:3)
רבב	Verb, to be numerous (Gen 6:1)
רְבָבָה	Noun, myriad (Gen 24:60)
אַרְבֶּה	Noun, locust (Joel 1:4)

5.   אַרְבֶּה, I shall cause to increase

Analysis:
1) Imperfect

Gen 22:17

2) First person masculine singular Gen 22:17
3) *Hiphil*
4) Root: רבה; verb group: ל"ה

Note:

Like the preceding form, the infinitive absolute is followed by the Imperfect to emphasize the certainty of the promise "I shall certainly cause to increase."

6. אֶת־זַרְעֶךָ, your seed (from the absolute form זֶרַע seed, with pronominal suffix [second person masculine singular])

Note:
1) *Segolate* form like מֶלֶךְ which becomes מַלְךְּ in the declined form.
2) *Hatef patah sheva* under the guttural ע instead of *sheva*
3) Words of the same root:
   זָרַע   to sow (Gen 47:23)
   זֵרֹעַ   vegetable (Dan 1:12)
4) Words with the same letters but not of the same root (ז has a different sound): זְרוֹעַ arm, strength (Exod 6:6)

7. כְּכוֹכְבֵי, like the stars of

כְּ, like

כּוֹכָב, star (absolute form); כּוֹכָבִים stars → כּוֹכְבֵי construct state plural (stars of)

Note:
1) Used metaphorically, when the word is plural it refers to the posterity, and when the word is singular to a supernatural being (Num 24:17; Isa 14:13).
2) The name Bar Kochba בַּר כּוֹכְבָא, son of the star (Aramaic); Jewish leader of the second Revolt against Rome (A.D. 132-135).

8. הַשָּׁמַיִם, the heavens

Gen 22:17

9.   וְכַחוֹל, and like the sand

     Note:
     The article is implied under כ with *patah* before the guttural ח.

     Words of the same root:
     חוּל   Verb, to whirl, dance (Judg 21:21)
     מָחוֹל   Noun, dance (Ps 30:12)

10. אֲשֶׁר, which, that

11. עַל־, on

12. שְׂפַת, (the) shore; construct state from the absolute form, שָׂפָה

     Note:
     1) The final ה becomes ת in feminine nouns in the construct state.
     2) Other meanings: lip (Isa 29:13), language (Gen 11:1)
     3) Word of the same root, perhaps שָׂפָם, moustache (Mic 3:7)

13. הַיָּם, (of) the sea

     Means also "West" (Gen 13:14), i.e., position of the Mediter-
     ranean Sea from the point of view of Palestine.

14. וְיִרַשׁ, and he will take possession (inherit)

     Analysis:
     1) Imperfect with conjunction of coordination
     2) Third person masculine singular
     3) *Paal*
     4) Root: ירשׁ; verb group: פ"י

     Note:
     1) יָרַשׁ is a stative verb (like יָרֵא).

Gen 22:17

2) Imperfect of stative verbs usually follow the pattern יִפְעַל; if they are פ"י, they generally keep the *yod* of the root.[1]

Examples: יִכְבַּד   he will be heavy (Exod 9:7)
                   יִירָא   he will fear (Amos 3:8)
                   יִירַשׁ   he will inherit (Gen 22:17)

3) The *yod* of the root is mute, however, (no vowel) and tends, therefore, to disappear. Thus our וַיִּרַשׁ; also וַיִּרָא, he will fear (Jer 26:21).

4) The form of the infinitive construct of the פ"י is worth noting; they generally loose the *yod* in the beginning, and as a compensation receive a ת in the end.

Examples: שֶׁבֶת   from יָשַׁב, to sit (1 Sam 7:2)
                 רֶשֶׁת   from יָרַשׁ, to inherit (Deut 2:31)

15.   זַרְעֶךָ, your seed

16.   אֶת שַׁעַר, the door

Word in construct state with the following word (same form in absolute state).

Note:
1) Word of the same root, שׁוֹעֵר, porter (2 Chr 31:14)
2) Word with the same letters, but not necessarily of the same root (different original sounds in שׁ):

    שָׁעַר   Verb, to measure, evaluate (Gen 26:12)
    שֹׁעָר   Adjective, disgusting (Jer 29:17)

17.   אֹיְבָיו, (of) his enemies

1)   אֹיְבֵי enemies of (construct form in plural), with pronominal suffix third person (from אֹיֵב, אֹיְבִים, absolute form)

---

[1]Compare with the form of the Imperfect in active verbs פ"י: יֵשֵׁב, he will sit (Gen 22:19).

2) Words of the same root:

    אֵיבָה   enmity (Gen 3:15)

    אִיּוֹב   the name Job (object of enmity) (Job 1:1)

Gen 22:18

1. וְהִתְבָּרֲכוּ, and they will bless themselves

Analysis:
1) Perfect with *vav* consecutive (prophetic Perfect)
2) Third person masculine plural
3) *Hitpael*
4) Root: ברך

Note:
1) *Hitpael* conveys the idea of reflection, denoting a nuance of participation in the blessing.
2) *Qametz* under ב (instead of *patah*) to compensate for the *dagesh* that is required in the *hitpael*, but is impossible in the guttural ר.
3) *Hatef patah* under the guttural ר instead of the regular *sheva*. (Gutturals are attracted by the sound *a*.)

2. בְזַרְעֲךָ, (in) your seed

Note:
No *dagesh* in the *begedkefet* ב because it follows a word ending with the open syllable כוּ-.

3. כֹּל, all

More usual form, כָּל- (short *qametz* pronounced *o*), with *maqqef* (Ps 23:6).

Words of same root:

    כָּלִיל   Adjective, entire, whole (Exod 28:31)

    כָּלָה   Verb, to finish, be complete (Gen 2:2)

    מִכְלָה   Noun, completeness, perfection (2 Chr 4:21)

4. גּוֹיֵי, peoples (of)

Construct form from גּוֹיִם (plural absolute of גּוֹי)

Words of the same root:
    גְּוִיָה   body (Gen 47:18)
    גַּו   back (1 Kgs 14:9)
Note the related word גּוּפָה, body (1 Chr 10:12).

5. הָאָרֶץ, the earth

6. עֵקֶב, following (as a result of, since)

Words of the same root:
    עָקֵב   heel, footprint (Gen 3:15)
    עָקַב   to follow; adverb, the heel (Hos 12:4)
    עָקֹב   insidious, deceitful (Jer 17:9)
    יַעֲקֹב   Jacob (Gen 25:26)

7. אֲשֶׁר, that, which

8. שָׁמַעְתָּ, you have heard

Analysis:
1) Perfect
2) Second person masculine singular
3) *Paal*
4) Root: שׁמע; stative verb

Note:
1) The use of the Perfect suggests that Abraham heard, obeyed completely.
2) When followed by בְּ, לְ, or אֶל, it means "to obey" (1 Sam 8:7, Gen 3:17).
3) Words of the same root:
    שְׁמוּעָה   Report, tidings (2 Sam 4:4)
    שִׁמְעוֹן   Simon (Gen 29:33)
    יִשְׁמָעֵאל   Ishmael (Gen 16:11)

Gen 22:18

9. בְּקֹלִי, (in) my voice

    בְּ   preposition "in"

    קֹלִי   construct form of קוֹל (absolute form); with pronominal suffix (first person masculine singular)

Note:
1) Also means "sound" (Exod 9:23).
2) Words of the same root, perhaps:

        קָלַל   Verb, to be light, easy (Amos 2:15)

        קְלָלָה   Noun, curse (Gen 27:12)

Gen 22:19

1. וַיָּשָׁב, and he returned

Analysis:
1) Imperfect; consecutive *vav*; apocope
2) Third person masculine singular
3) *Paal*
4) Root: שׁוּב; verb group: ע"ו

Note:
The apocopated form of שׁוּב is שָׁב (short *qametz* pronounced *o*).

2. אַבְרָהָם, Abraham

3. אֶל־, to

4. נְעָרָיו, his young men

5. וַיָּקֻמוּ, and they rose

Analysis:
1) Imperfect; *vav* consecutive
2) Third person masculine plural
3) *Paal*
4) Root: קוּם; verb group: פ"ו

Gen 22:19

Note:

Compare with v. 3, No. 16, where the form is וַיָּקָם (short *qametz* under the ק); here we have a *qibbutz* instead of short *qametz* although it is the same form (Imperfect consecutive); cf. וַיָּקָם in 1 Kgs 3:21.

The third person masculine plural (our form) and the first person singular are the only persons of the Imperfect consecutive to keep the regular non-apocopated form (with קָם or קוּם).

6. וַיֵּלְכוּ, and they went

7. יַחְדָּו, together

8. אֶל־, to

9. בְּאֵר שָׁבַע, Beersheba

    בְּאֵר   well
    שָׁבַע   seven, oath

10. וַיֵּשֶׁב, and he stayed

Analysis:
1) Imperfect; *vav* consecutive; apocope
2) Third person masculine singular
3) *Paal*
4. Root: ישׁב; verb group: פ"י

11. אַבְרָהָם, Abraham

12. בִּבְאֵר שָׁבַע, in Beersheba

Note:

The preposition בְּ has received *hireq* instead of the regular *sheva* (collision of two *shevas*).

Gen 22:19

Text II. Psalm 23:1-6

Ps 23:1

1. מִזְמוֹר, Song (melody)

   Note:
   1) Technical term in some titles in the Psalms
   2) Words from the same root:

      זָמַר   Verb, to sing (to God), Ps 27:6 to play musical instruments (to God), Ps 149:3

      זִמְרָה   melody, song in praise of God, Ps 81:3

      זָמִיר   song (to God and secular), Isa 25:5

   3) Words with the same letters but not necessarily of the same root (ז is different):

      זָמַר   verb, to trim, prune, Lev 25:3, 4

2. לְדָוִד, of David

   לְ preposition expressing the idea of connection; may also mean "concerning David," or "belonging to David" (collection of Psalms).

   לְ this preposition is very flexible.
   - denotes direction (to, towards), Ps 99:5
   - expresses locality (at, near), Gen 49:13
   - expresses time (towards), Gen 3:8
   - transition into new state (into), Gen 2:22
   - belonging to, Deut 22:14
   - concerning, about, Gen 20:13
   - purpose (in order to), Gen 1:17

   דָוִד, David
       Note the passive form of the noun, פָּעִיל, meaning "beloved" (Cant 1:13).

Compare with the forms of:

מָשִׁיחַ   Messiah, Dan 9:25

נָבִיא   prophet, Gen 20:7

נָשִׂיא   prince, Ezek 7:27

3. יְהֹנָה, the Lord

4. רֹעִי, (is) my Shepherd

Note:
1) The participle form; masculine singular with pronominal suffix (first person masculine singular); from the verb רעה (to pasture, to tend), *paal*, verb group ל"ה
2) Meaning:

    Transitive sense: to tend, to give pasture, Gen 30;31

                           to rule, to teach, 2 Sam 5:2

                           to guide, Prov 10:21

    Intransitive sense: to graze, to feed, Gen 41:2
3) Words of the same root: מִרְעֶה, pasturage, Gen 47:4
4) Words with the same letters, but not necessarily from the same root (different ע):

    רֵעַ   friend, Deut 5:20

    רְעוּת   fellow (see the name of Ruth), Exod 11:2

    רְעוּת   longing, desiring (see רצה; to desire), Eccl 1:14

    רַע   bad, evil (see perhaps רצע;רעע, רצע, to break), Gen 6:5
5) The verb "to be" is not needed to introduce the predicate, especially when present time is implied.

5. לֹא, no

6. אֶחְסָר, I shall (not) be in need

Analysis:
1) Imperfect
2) First person masculine singular
3) *Paal*
4) Root: חסר (to be in need; stative verb)

Ps 23:1

Note:
1) The vowel *a* under the last syllable (form, יִפָּעֵל) is characteristic of the stative verbs (*qametz* instead of *patah* because of pause).
2) Words from the same root:

הֶסֶר   poverty, Prov 28:22

חָסֵר   needy (Passive form), Eccl 6:2

Ps 23:2

1. בִּנְאוֹת, in (the) pastures

Note:
1) The *hireq* under the preposition בְּ, "in," collision of two *shevas*)
2) נְאוֹת comes from the absolute form, נָוֶה, pasture, meadow; plural construct נְוֹת (Zeph 2:6), usually נְאוֹת (here).
3) See the related word נוּחַ, to rest, Exod 23:12.

2. דֶּשֶׁא, (of) fresh grass

Note:
1) The related word דּוּשׁ, verb, to tread, to thresh, Jer 50:11
2) The related word שָׂדֶא (metathesis and שׂ/שׁ): field, Gen 2:5

3. יַרְבִּיצֵנִי, he will make me lie down

Analysis:
1) Imperfect, with pronominal suffix (first person masculine singular)
2) Third person masculine singular
3) *Hiphil*
4) Root רבץ to lie down

Words from the same root:

רָבַע   verb, to lie down (ע/צ), Lev 20:16

רֵבֶץ   dwelling place, Isa 35:7

4. עַל־, by

This preposition is very flexible:
- upon, Gen 1:11
- expresses excess, preeminence (see מִן), Gen 48:22
- expresses addition, Ps 69:28
- denotes proximity (by), Gen 14:6
- expresses motion, direction, Gen 2:5

Note the expression אֶל עַל upwards, Hos 11:7.

5. מֵי, (the waters)

Construct form from the absolute מַיִם (always plural)

Note the related word (metathesis) יָם, sea, Gen 1:10.

6. מְנֻחוֹת, (of) quietness

Plural of מְנוּחָה • resting place, Mic 2:10
• quietness, rest, 1 Chr 22:9

Note:
1) The construct form used to express qualification. The phrase "the waters of quietness" means "the quiet waters."
2) A number of plurals (especially in poetry) are used to intensify the idea of the root (plural of amplification).
   אֱלֹהִים Godhead (idea of power), Job 1:16
   גְּבוּרוֹת exceptional strength, Job 41:4
   חֲמוּדוֹת greatly beloved, Dan 9:23
   רַחֲמִים great compassion, Gen 43:14
   נְקָמוֹת complete vengeance, Judg 11:36
3) Words from the same root:
   נוּחַ to rest, Exod 20:11
   נֹחַ the name of Noah, Gen 5:29 (cf. the related word נָחַם, to comfort, Gen 5:29)

Ps 23:2

7. יְנַהֲלֵנִי, he will lead me

    Analysis:
    1) Imperfect with pronominal suffix (first person masculine/feminine singular)
    2) Third person masculine singular
    3) *Piel*
    4) Root: נהל, to lead

    Note:
    1) *Hatef patah* under the guttural ה instead of *sheva*. (Gutturals are attracted by the sound *a*.)
    2) The *dagesh* is impossible in the guttural ה; yet the preceding vowel is not lengthened by compensation (before ה or ח, the vowel remains short).
    3) Meanings:
       • to lead to a watering place, Isa 49:10
       • to refresh, Gen 47:17
       • to lead to a goal, Exod 15:13
    4) Words of the same root:
       נַהֲלֹל   pasture, watering place, Isa 7:19

    Related words:
       נַחַל (ה/ח)   torrent, Isa 7:19
       נהר (ל/ר)   stream river, Gen 2:10.

Ps 23:3

1. נַפְשִׁי, my breath (life, being, soul)

    Construct form from the absolute *segolate* נֶפֶשׁ

    Several meanings:
       • that which breathes, Jer 15:9
       • life, Exod 21:23
       • the man himself, the person, Gen 17:14
       • "my soul" means "me," Judg 16:30
       • seat of appetites, Ps 107:9

• seat of emotions, Deut 12:20
• seat of mental acts, Ps 139:14

Note the related words:

נָפַח	to breathe, to blow, Jer 15:9
נְשָׁמָה	breath, Gen 2:7
נָשַׁב	to blow, Isa 40:7 (metathesis and פ/ב)
נָשַׁף	to blow, Exod 15:10 (metathesis)
נָשַׁק	to kiss, to smell, Cant 1:2 (metathesis and פ/ק)
נָשַׁךְ	to bite, Amos 5:19 (metathesis and פ/ב)

2. יְשׁוֹבֵב, he will restore

Analysis:
1) Imperfect
2) Third person masculine singular
3) *Piel* (*polel*)
4) Root: שׁוב; verb group: ע"ו

Note:
1) ע"ו verbs (see note on Gen 22:3, word No. 16) have the form *polel* instead of *piel*; the ע of the root is doubled (as in שׁובב), hence the name of the form *polel*. Otherwise, the conjugation remains the same.
2) The *polel* (*piel* of ע"ו) has a causative force here: to bring back (Ps 60:3).
3) It has the same meaning as in the *hiphil*; remember that in the *hiphil*, the ו drops and is replaced by י:
    e.g.: Perfect הֵשִׁיב he brought back (Gen 14:16)
           Imperfect יָשִׁיב he will bring back (Gen 50:15)

3. יַנְחֵנִי, he will guide me

Analysis:
1) Imperfect with pronominal suffix (first person masculine singular)
2) Third person masculine singular
3) *Hiphil*
4) Root: נחה, to guide; verb group: ל"ה

Note:
1) The final ה of the root has dropped out before the pronominal suffix (the regular *hiphil* of נחה would be יַנְחֶה).
2) The connective vowel *tsere* has taken the place of *segol* under ה (in Perfect, the connective vowel is *patah*. Example: נָחַנִי, he guided me, Gen 24:27).

4. בְּמַעְגְּלֵי־, in (the) tracks

Analysis:
1) בְּ (preposition "in"); no *dagesh* because it is preceded by the open syllable נִי
2) מַעְגְּלֵי, plural construct of מַעֲגָּל

Words of the same root:
    עֶגְלָה   heifer, Gen 15:9
    עֲגָלָה   cart, 1 Sam 6:7
    עָגוֹל   adjective, round, 1 Kgs 7:23

5. צֶדֶק, (of) righteousness

Meanings:
1) What is right, normal, straight, Deut 25:15 (our text)
2) Righteousness in government, Lev 19:15
3) Righteousness in salvation, Isa 62:1

Note the construct form to express qualification; the phrase "paths of righteousness" means "right paths."

6. לְמַעַן, for the sake of (on account of)

7. שְׁמוֹ, his name

שֵׁם with pronominal suffix (third person masculine singular)

Ps 23:4

1. גַּם, even (also)

Ps 23:4

2. כִּי־, though (when)

    The association נַם כִּי is often used to express a concession (Isa 1:15).

3. אֵלֵךְ, I shall go

    Analysis:
    1) Imperfect
    2) First person masculine singular
    3) *Paal*
    4) Root: הלך; verb group: פ"ה

4. בְּנֵיא, in (the) valley

    בְּ   preposition "in"
    גֵּיא   construct form from גַּיְא (absolute form), Num 21:20

    Note:
    1) The expression גֵּי . . . הַנֹּם, Josh 15:8, valley of Hinnom (from which our "Gehenna").
    2) Word of the same root גָּאָה, verb, to rise up (of waters), Ezek 47:5.

5. צַלְמָוֶת, (of) the shadow of death

    Composite noun, צֵל shadow, and מָוֶת death

    Note:
    1) The expression shadow of death expresses the dark character of death.
    2) Words related to צֵל:
       צָלַל   to grow dark, Neh 13:19
       צֶלֶם   image, likeness, Gen 1:26
       Words with same letters but not of the same root:
       צָלַל   verb, to tingle, 1 Sam 3:11
       צְלְצְלִים   cymbals, Ps 150:5

Ps 23:4

3) Words related to מָוֶת:

מוּת   verb, to die, Gen 2:17

מֵת   man (mortal), Isa 3:25

6. לֹא־, No

7. אִירָא, I shall (not) fear

Analysis:
1) Imperfect
2) First person masculine singular
3) *Paal*
4) Root: ירא; verb group: פ"י; stative verb

Note:

The *yod* of the root remains after the preformative (*atynty*), and affects the preceding vowel under the א of the *atynty*: the *segol* becomes *hireq*.

8. רַע, evil

Meaning:
injury, harm, Gen 31:29
ethical evil, Deut 30:15

Words of the same root:
רָעָה   evil, misery, distress, Prov 1:33
רעע   verb, to be evil, displeasing, Num 11:10
Perhaps רעע, verb (cf. רצץ) to break Jer 11:16

9. כִּי־, for

10. אַתָּה, you (thou)

Note:
1) Second person masculine singular
2) *Dagesh* in ת from an original form *anta* (assimilated noun)

Ps 23:4

11. עִמָּדִי, with me

Note:
1) The word עִמָּדִי is probably the contraction of the two words: עִם, with, and יָדִי, my hand; it conveys the idea of close active association.
2) The verb, to be, is not needed to introduce the predicate.

12. שִׁבְטְךָ, your rod

שֵׁבֶט   Absolute form (*segolate*) with pronominal suffix (second person masculine singular)

Note:
1) Means: rod, Exod 21:20; scepter, Isa 14:5; tribe, Gen 49:16
2) The related word, שַׁרְבִיט (with ר), Esth 5:2

13. וּמִשְׁעַנְתֶּךָ, and your staff

1) The conjunction of coordination וְ has become וּ before מ (בומ״ף).
2) From מִשְׁעֶנֶת (absolute form), with pronominal suffix (second person masculine singular)

Word of the same root: שָׁעַן, verb, to lean, support, Num 21:15

14. הֵמָּה, they

Words of the same root:
הָמָה   roar (of peoples, waves), Ps 46:7
הָמוֹן   roar, crowd, great number, 2 Chr 11:23
הָמַם   verb, he makes a noise, Isa 28:28

15. יְנַחֲמֻנִי, (they) will comfort me

Analysis:
1) Imperfect with pronominal suffix (first person masculine singular)
2) Third person masculine plural
3) *Piel*

Ps 23:4

4)   Root: נחם to comfort

Note:
1) *Hatef patah* under the guttural ח instead of *sheva*
2) *Dagesh* is inadmissible in the guttural ח, but no lengthening of the preceding vowel is required before ח. (See v. 2, No. 7.)
3) The *shurek* has been shortened into *qibbutz* because of the addition of the pronominal suffix נִי which has lengthened the word.

Ps 23:5

1. תַּעֲרֹךְ, you will prepare

 Analysis:
 1) Imperfect
 2) Second person masculine singular
 3) *Paal*
 4) Root: עֶרךְ, to prepare

2. לְפָנַי, before me

 לְ   preposition, to
 פָנַי Construct form from the absolute form plural
 פָּנִים face (Gen 43:31), with the pronominal suffix (first person masculine singular); means literally "to my face"

Note:
1) The usage of פָּנִים in some expressions:
  פָּנִים אֶל פָּנִים face to face, Gen 32:31
  מִפָּנִים וּמֵאָחוֹר before and behind (2 Sam 10:9)
  לְפָנִים   formerly (Deut 2:12)
  לִפְנֵי   at the face of, in the presence of, Gen 18:22
2) Words of the same root:
  פָּנָה verb, to turn, Gen 24:49
  פְּנִימָה within, Lev 10:18
  פִּנָּה corner, 2 Kgs 14:13

3. שֻׁלְחָן, table

4. נֶגֶד, in the front of
   - what is conspicuous, Exod 34:10
   - against, Job 10:17

Note:
1) Expression כְּנֶגֶד, corresponding to, Gen 2:18.
2) Words of the same root:
   נגד   verb (*hiphil*), to declare, to tell, Gen 9:22
   נָגִיד   leader, Dan 9:25

5. צֹרְרָי, my enemies

   Noun from the participle form masculine plural of the root צרר (*paal*): to show hostility, to vex, Is 11:13; with pronominal suffix (first person masculine singular)

   Words of the same root:
   צָר   enemy, Esth 7:6
   צוּר   rock, Exod 17:6

   Words with the same letters but not of the same root (צ is different):
   צרר   to bind, Exod 12:34
   צַר   narrow, Num 22:26

6. דִּשַּׁנְתָּ, you have anointed

Analysis:
1) Perfect
2) Second person masculine singular
3) *Piel*
4) Root: דשׁן, to be fat; stative verb

Note:
1) The *piel* has here a causative form, meaning "to make fat," Prov 15:30.

2) Words of the same root:

    דֶּשֶׁן   fatness, ashes, Lev 1:16

7. בַּשֶּׁמֶן, with the oil

    בַּ, preposition with the article; without *dagesh* in the *begedkefet* בּ because of the preceding open vowel תָּ

Words of the same root:

    שָׁמֵן   fat, robust, Gen 49:20

Word with the same letters but not of the same root (not the same שׁ):

    שְׁמֹנָה   eight, Judg 3:8

8. רֹאשִׁי, my head

    רֹאשׁ with pronominal suffix (first person masculine singular)

Words of the same root:

    רִאשׁוֹן   first, Isa 41:4
    רֵאשִׁית   beginning, Gen 1:1

With the same letters but not of the same root:

    רֹאשׁ   (or רוֹשׁ) poison, Jer 9:14; Deut 32:32

9. כּוֹסִי, my cup

    כּוֹס with pronominal suffix (first person masculine singular)

Related words:

    כִּיס   bag, purse, Deut 25:13
    כָּסָה   to cover, to clothe, Judg 4:19

10. רְוָיָה, saturation, over flow

Words of the same root:

    רוה   verb, to be saturated (See Ps 36:9, also associated with דשׁן.)

Ps 23:5

Note the related word, יוֹרֶה (by metathesis) early rain, Deut 11:14.

Ps 23:6

1. אַךְ, only (surely)

   Interjection meaning "surely," "no doubt," Gen 26:9; only, Gen 23:13.

2. טוֹב, happiness (good thing)

   Words from same root:
   טוֹב   verb, to be delightful, Num 24:5
   טוֹב   adjective, pleasant, good, Ps 133:1

3. וָחֶסֶד, and grace

   The conjunction וְ has become וָ before an accented syllable חֶ (also the case before monosyllabic words).
   Example: וָמֵת, he died, Exod 21:12).

חֶסֶד, meaning:
1) Kindness, grace (men to men), Ps 141:5
2) Love to God, piety (Jer 2:2)
3) Lovely appearance, Isa 40:6

Words from the same root:
חָסִיד   kind, pious, Ps 4:4
חֲסִידָה   stork, Lev 11:19

Words with the same letters but not same root (ס is different):
חֶסֶד   shame, reproach, Lev 20:17

4. יִרְדְּפוּנִי, they will pursue me

   Analysis:
   1) Imperfect with pronominal suffix (first person masculine singular)
   2) Third person masculine plural

3) *Paal*
4) Root: רדף, to pursue

Note the aggressive connotation:
1) To pursue (with hostile purpose), Gen 31:23
2) To pursue (knowledge of God), Hos 6:3

5. כָּל-, all

6. יְמֵי, days

     Construct form from the plural absolute יָמִים

7. חַיָּי, (of) my life

     Construct form from the absolute חַיִּים, life, with pronominal suffix (first person masculine singular)

Note:
1) Plural of intensity
2) *Dagesh* in *yod*, probably denoting assimilation of *vav* from primitive root (see the connection between the name חַוָּה, Eve, and the word חַיִּים, living, in Gen 3:20).

3) Words of same root:
         חָיָה   verb, to live, 2 Kgs 1:2
         חַי   adjective, alive, living, Job 19:25
         חַיָּה   animal, Gen 8:17

8. וְשַׁבְתִּי, and my staying

     וְ   conjunction of coordination: and.

שַׁבְתִּי
1) Construct form with pronominal suffix (first person masculine singular) derived from the infinitive שֶׁבֶת, of יָשַׁב (to stay, to sit) by analogy to *segolates* (for example: מַלְכִּי, my king, from the *segolate* מֶלֶךְ; cf., however, שִׁבְתִּי, in Ps 27:4).

Ps 23:6

2) Or should be corrected into וְיָשַׁבְתִּי (Perfect first person singular).
3) Do not confuse with the same form, שַׁבְתִּי, I shall return (Perfect first person singular of שׁוּב); the context does not allow this interpretation because of the preposition בְּ.

9. בְּבֵית־, in (the) house

10. יְהֹנָה, (of) the Lord

11. לְאֹרֶךְ, for length

Preposition לְ, to, for

Words from the same root:
אָרַךְ   verb (especially in *hiphil*), to prolong, Deut 4:26
אֶרֶךְ   (construct form of אָרֵךְ) adjective, long, in expression like אֶרֶךְ אַפַּיִם, long of nose (= patient), Prov 14:29
אֲרוּכָה   healing (of a wound), Jer 30:17

12. יָמִים, of days

Note:
    The whole expression אֹרֶךְ יָמִים, length of days, is often used to express the idea of continuity (Ps 91:16; Deut 30:20, etc.).

Text III.　Micah 4:1-4

Mic 4:1

1.　וְהָיָה, and it will be (it shall come to pass)

Analysis:
1) Perfect; consecutive *vav*; prophetic Perfect
2) Third person masculine singular
3) *Paal*
4) Root: היה, to be; verb group: ל"ה

2.　בְּאַחֲרִית, in the end (latter part)

בְּ　preposition in

Note אַחֲרִית:
1) The word is always in construct state.
2) Meaning, extremity, end:
　　applies to space (far islands), Ps 139:9
　　to time (far future), Isa 41:22
　　to man (posterity), Ps 37:37
3) Words of the same root: see אחר in Gen 22:1

3.　הַיָּמִים, of the days

　　The בְּאַחֲרִית הַיָּמִים is a technical expression to designate the end of the days (for this eschatological terminology, see Dan 12:8, Gen 49:1).

4.　יִהְיֶה, it will be

Analysis:
1) Imperfect
2) Third person masculine singular
3) *Paal*
4) Root: היה; verb group: ל"ה

Mic 4:1

Note:
    The expression, אֶהְיֶה אֲשֶׁר אֶהְיֶה, I will be what I will be, Exod 3:14.

5.   הַר, mountain (of)

Word in construct (same form, הַר, in absolute)

6.   בֵּית־, house (of)

Construct form from the absolute בַּיִת

7.   יְהֹנָה, the Lord

    Note the construct form, הַר בֵּית יְהֹנָה, mountain of the house of *YHWH*, where the two words הַר and בַּיִת are in construct state with the word יְהֹנָה.

8.   נָכוֹן, established

Analysis:
1) Participle
2) Masculine singular
3) *Niphal*
4) Root: כּוּן, to be firm; verb group: ע"ו

Note:
1) The participle with היה (to be) to express the durative aspect of the verb: it will be (it will stay) established.
2) Do not confuse with:
   a. The Perfect *niphal* third person masculine singular נָכוֹן (he has been established) same form; . . . נְכוֹנֹתָ ,נְכוֹנֹתִי (I, you have been established)
   b. The Imperfect *niphal* first person plural נִכּוֹן (we shall be established) with *hireq* under the *nun* (*atynty*); . . . אֶכּוֹן,תִּכּוֹן (I, you shall establish). See Gen 22:3, note on word No. 16.

Mic 4:1

9. בְּרֹאשׁ, in top

   בְּ   preposition, in

   Note on רֹאשׁ:
   - head, Gen 40:16
   - beginning, Judg 7:19
   - best, Exod 30:23

10. הֶהָרִים, of the mountains

11. וְנִשָּׂא, and will be exalted

   Analysis:
   1) Perfect; consecutive conversive *vav*; prophetic Perfect
   2) Third person masculine singular
   3) *Niphal*
   4) Root: נשׂא, to lift, to carry; verb group: פּ"ן and ל"א

   Note:
   1) *Dagesh* in שׂ to compensate for the assimilated נ of the root פּ"ן, before the *nun* of the *niphal*.
   2) Verbs: ל"א
      The final א has lost its consonantal value; then the last syllable is always an open *ā*, except before the ending נָה in Imperfect second and third person feminine plural, where it becomes *ē*, תִּשֶּׂאנָה.

   Note:
   The conjugation of the ל"א verbs is often influenced by that of ל"ה.

12. הוּא, it

   Often the pronoun, הוּא, it (or he), emphatically resumes the subject.

Mic 4:1

13. מִגְּבָעוֹת, above the hills

Preposition מִן; the נ has been assimilated, hence the *dagesh* in the ג.

Note:
1) The comparative usage of מִן meaning "higher than the hills," literally "high (exalted) away from the hills"
2) Note on גְּבָעוֹת:
    - plural of גִּבְעָה, hill, 2 Sam 2:25
    - words of the same root:
        גָּבִיעַ, cup, bowl, Gen 44:12
        מִגְבָּעוֹת, turban (of priest: conical form), Lev 8:13
    - note the related word:
        גָּבֹהַּ high, Gen 7:19

14. וְנָהֲרוּ, and they shall flow

Analysis:
1) Perfect; conversive *vav*; prophetic Perfect
2) Third person masculine plural
3) *Paal*
4) Root: נהר, to follow

Note:
1) *Hatef patah* under the guttural ה instead of *sheva*.
2) Words of same root:
        נָהָר, stream, river, Gen 2:10
        נָהַר, is to shine, Isa 60:5

15. עָלָיו, to him

The preposition, עַל, generally means "on, upon," and may also express the idea of direction with a special connotation of pressure—meaning here that the peoples will press to this city (cf. Isa 2:2 where the preposition, אֶל, to, is used).

16. עַמִּים, peoples

Mic 4:1

Mic 4:2

1. וְהָלְכוּ, and they will come

   Analysis:
   1) Perfect; conversive *vav*; prophetic Perfect
   2) Third masculine plural
   3) *Paal*
   4) Root: הלך, to go; verb group: פ"ה

2. גּוֹיִם, nations

3. רַבִּים, numerous

   Masculine plural adjective; agrees with the word nations

4. וְאָמְרוּ, and they will say

   Analysis:
   1) Perfect; conversive *vav*; prophetic Perfect
   2) Third plural
   3) *Paal*
   4) Root: אמר, to say; verb group: פ"א

5. לְכוּ, go

   Analysis:
   1) Imperative
   2) Masculine plural
   3) *Paal*
   4) Root: הלך, to go up; verb group: פ"ה

6. וְנַעֲלֶה, and let us go up

   Analysis:
   1) Imperfect; cohortative (context)
   2) First person masculine plural

3) *Paal*
4) Root: עלה, to go up; verb group: ל"ה

Note:

1) *Hatef patah* under the guttural ע instead of *sheva*; affects the preceding vowel hence the *patah* under the preformative like in *hiphil*.

2) The context only determines if the verb is cohortative; the root being ל"ה one cannot add another ה. See the Imperative of the preceding verb לְכוּ and the clear cohortative form in the next verse, נֵלְכָה.

7. אֶל־, to

8. הַר־, mountain

   Construct state, same form as the absolute הַר.

9. יְהֹנָה, of the Lord

10. וְאֶל־, and to

11. בֵּית, the house

    Construct state from the absolute בַּיִת.

12. אֱלֹהֵי, of the God

    Construct state from the absolute אֱלֹהִים.

13. יַעֲקֹב, of Jacob

    Note the construct state of the two words בֵּית אֱלֹהֵי יַעֲקֹב.

14. וְיוֹרֵנוּ, and he will teach us

Mic 4:2

Analysis:
1) Imperfect; conjunction of coordination; pronominal suffix (first person masculine plural)
2) Third person masculine singular
3) *Hiphil*
4) Root: ירה, to shoot; verb group: פ"י

Note:
1) The י of the root ירה has become ו after the preformative (cf. Gen 22:5, note on word No. 5).
2) The final ה has dropped out before the pronominal suffix נו.
3) Meaning of the root ירה:
    Paal: to throw, Exod 19:13
4) Words of the same root:
    יוֹרֶה, early rain (October-November), Deut 11:14
    מוֹרֶה, teacher, Prov 5:13
    תּוֹרָה, law, Exod 12:49

15. מִדְּרָכָיו, from his ways

Note:
1) The preposition מִ from מִן; the נ has been assimilated, hence the *dagesh* in the ד.
2) דְּרָכָיו from the absolute דְּרָכִים (singular *segolate* דֶּרֶךְ with pronominal suffix [third person masculine singular])
3) דְּרָכָיו read the ending יו, *av* (transliteration: *āw*).
4) On the meaning of דֶּרֶךְ:
    toward, 1 Kgs 8:44
    usage, Gen 31:35
    intentions, 1 Kgs 13:33
5) Words of the same root:
    דָּרַךְ verb, to tread, Num 24:17

16. וְנֵלְכָה, that we may go

Mic 4:2

Analysis:
1) Imperfect; conjunction of coordination; cohortative
2) First person masculine plural
3) *Paal*
4) Root: הלך, to go; verb group: פ"ה

Note:

This cohortative with "*vav* conjunction of coordination" is used to express an intention, an intended consequence.

Example: וְאֹכֵלָה, Gen 27:4, (bring it to me) that I may eat.

17. בְּאֹרְחֹתָיו, in his paths

בְּ in

אֹרְחֹתָיו construct form from the absolute אֹרְחוֹת (singular אֹרַח) with pronominal suffix (third person masculine singular)

Words of the same root:
אֲרֻחָה meal, Prov 15:17

18. כִּי, for

19. מִצִּיּוֹן, from Zion

מִ preposition from מִן

צִיּוֹן stronghold captured by David, 2 Sam 5:7.

Words of the same root:
צָיוֹן   dryness, Isa 25:5
צִיָּה   drought, Ezek 19:13

Words with same letters but from another root:
צִיּוּן   signpost, monument, Ezek 39:15
מִצְוָה   commandment, Deut 8:1

Mic 4:2

20. תֵּצֵא, will go out

    Analysis:
    1) Imperfect
    2) Third person feminine singular
    3) *Paal*
    4) Root: יצא; verb group: פ"י and ל"א

21. תּוֹרָה, law

    Other meanings:
    1) Human instruction, Prov 13:14
    2) Divine instruction, Dan 9:10
    3) Codes of law, Exod 24:12
    4) Way of life, 2 Sam 7:19

22. וּדְבַר־, and word

    Conjunction וּ (instead of וְ) before *sheva*; דְּבַר construct form from the absolute דָּבָר

23. יְהֹוָה, of the Lord

24. מִירוּשָׁלָם, from Jerusalem

    1) The preposition מִ from מִן, נ has been assimilated; but no *dagesh* (by compensation) in the י with *sheva* because י with *sheva* cannot be doubled, hence the form מִי with long *hireq*.
    2) The name יְרוּשָׁלָם:
        a. Composed with יְרוּ; root: ירה, to cast (Job 38:6, with the sense of laying foundation), and שָׁלֵם, peace, meaning "foundation of peace."
        b. Popular midrashic etymology relates יְרוּ to Moriah (allusion to Abraham's sacrifice) and שָׁלֵם to Melchizedek (Genesis Rabbah 56:10; cf. Midrash Tehillim 76:3).

Mic 4:2

3) Written יְרוּשָׁלֵם *yerushalem* (*ktiv*), but read *yerushalayim*. The reading (*qerê*) is indicated by the vowels under the last two letters לַ֫יִ (*ā, î*)--a dual form which may have preserved the oldest pronunciation of Jerusalem (*ayîm*).

Mic 4:3

1. וְשָׁפַט, and he will judge

Analysis:
1) Perfect; conversive *vav*; prophetic Perfect
2) Third person masculine singular
3) *Paal*
4) Root: שׁפט, to judge

Note on meaning:
    to govern, 1 Kgs 3:9
    to deliver, Ps 10:18
    to punish, Ezek 7:3

Word from the same root:
    מִשְׁפָּט, judgment (Exod 21:31)

2. בֵּין, between

1) The act of judging שָׁפַט often goes with this preposition (Exod 18:16) because judging implies discerning "between" two parties.
2) Usage of בֵּין, between
    בֵּין . . . וּבֵין, Gen 13:3
    בֵּין . . . לְ, Gen 1:6
3) Words from same root:
    בִּין, verb, to discern, Dan 9:23
    בִּינָה, intelligence, Prov 3:5

3. עַמִּים, peoples

4. רַבִּים, numerous

5. וְהוֹכִיחַ, and will convict

Analysis:
1) Perfect; conversive *vav*; prophetic Perfect
2) Third person masculine singular
3) *Hiphil* (*pual* not attested in the Bible)
4) Root: יכח; verb group: פ"י

Note:
1) The י of the root יכח has become ו after the ה of the *hiphil* (cf. Mic 4:3, note on word No. 14 and Gen 22:5, note on word No. 5).
2) Meanings:
    to decide, Gen 31:42
    to decide, convict (with preposition ל), Isa 2:4, Job 32:12
    to chide, Job 22:4
    to correct, Job 13:10

Word from the same root:
    תּוֹכַחַת, argument, Ps 38:15

6. לְגוֹיִם, (to) nations

7. עֲצֻמִים, mighty

    Plural of the adjective עָצוּם, mighty, agrees in gender with the noun nations.

Words with the same root:
    עָצְמָה   might, Isa 40:29
    עֶצֶם   bone, Mic 3:2

Word with the same letters but not from the same root (צ is different):
    עצם   verb, to shut (the eyes), Isa 29:10

8. עַד־רָחוֹק, until far

9. וְכִתְּתוּ, they will crush (beat into pieces)

Analysis:
1) Perfect; conversive *vav*; prophetic Perfect
2) Third person masculine plural
3) *Piel*
4) Root: כתת, to crush; verb group: ע"ע

Note:
1) ע"ע verbs are verbs whose second letter is repeated (see Paradigm E, pages 174-175). The same two letters tend to fuse into one; hence we note two possibilities: either the two letters remain (rare) (for example: כָּתוּת, beaten, Isa 30:14), or we have only one doubled letter, i.e., with a *dagesh* (more frequent)—if there is a vowel after it (for example: כַּתּוֹתִי, I have beaten, Ps 89:24).
2) Words from the same root:
   כָּתִית, crushed, in the expression שֶׁמֶן כָּתִית, oil crushed (Exod 29:40) refers to the oil made by crushing the olives in a mortar.
   מְכִתָּה, crushed fragments, Isa 30:14
3) Note the related word:
   מַכְתֵּשׁ (ת/שׁ), mortar, Prov 27:22

10. חַרְבֹתֵיהֶם, their swords

Construct form from the absolute חַרָבוֹת (singular חֶרֶב *segolate*) with pronominal suffix (third person masculine plural); cf. Isa 2:4, where we have חַרְבוֹתָם, probably the oldest form.

Note:
1) Word from the same root:
   חָרַב, to attack, Jer 50:21
2) Related words:
   חָרַם verb (מ/ב by phonetics), to exterminate, Josh 8:26
   חֵרֶם (מ/ב by phonetics), devoted thing, ban, Josh 6:17
   חָרַג (ב/ג by alphabetic order), to quake, Ps 18:46
   חָרַד (ב/ג/ד by alphabetic order), to tremble, Isa 19:16

Mic 4:3

3) Words with the same letters but not from the same root (ח is different, note the semantic parentage however):
חֹרֶב, desolation, Isa 61:4
חָרַם, to mutilate, Lev 21:18

11. לְאִתִּים, into plowshares

לְ preposition to; denotes the movement of change
אֵת plowshare; note *dagesh* in ת, denoting perhaps an original נ

Words with the same letters but not from the same root:
אֵת, with
אֶת, before accusative

12. וַחֲנִיתֹתֵיהֶם, and their spears

Construct form from the absolute חֲנִיתוֹת (חֲנִית singular) with pronominal suffix (third person masculine plural)

Words from the same root:
חָנָה verb, to encamp, Gen 26:17
מַחֲנֶה, camp, Gen 32:3

13. לְמַזְמֵרוֹת, into pruning knives

לְ preposition, to; denotes the movement of change.

מַזְמֵרָה pruning knife; note the form of the Participle *hiphil*.

Words from the same root:
זָמַר verb, to trim, to prune, Lev 25:3
זְמוֹרָה, branch, Ezek 8:17

Words with the same letters but not from the same root (different ז):
מִזְמוֹר, melody, psalm, Ps 23:1

14. לֹא־, no

Mic 4:3

15. יִשְׂאוּ, they will (not) lift

16. גּוֹי, people

Note the plural of the verb in accordance to the meaning of גּוֹי (people) which has a collective sense.

17. אֶל־, to (against)

18. גּוֹי, people

19. חֶרֶב, sword

20. וְלֹא־, and no

21. יִלְמְדוּן, they will (not) study

Analysis:
1) Imperfect
2) Third person masculine plural
3) *Paal*
4) Root: למד, to study

Note:
Compare with Isa 2:4 where we have the form יִלְמְדוּ (without נ); the נ has been added in Mic 4 to avoid having two vowels following each other (hiatus), here before *ō* (cf. יָדְעוּן, before *ā*, in Deut 8:3, 16).

22. עוֹד, again

The adverb עוֹד is used to express the idea of repetition and continuance (still, yet, again, besides).
- besides, still, Gen 19:12
- with the negation means, "no longer," (our passage)

Words from the same root; see Gen 22:5 (cf. word No. 13):

עֵד, witness, Gen 31:44

עוֹדֵד verb, to restore, Ps 146:9

23. מִלְחָמָה, war

Words from the same root:

לחם verb, to fight, come to close quarters, Judg 9:17

לָחוּם, intestines (idea of pressed together), Job 20:23, Zeph 1:17

לֶחֶם, bread, compact food, Exod 29:23

Mic 4:4

1. וְיָשְׁבוּ, and they will sit

Analysis:
1) Perfect; conversive *vav*; prophetic Perfect
2) Third person masculine plural
3) *Paal*
4) Root: ישׁב, to sit; verb group: פ"י

2. אִישׁ, man (everyone)

Note:
1) The word אִישׁ, man, is often used to express the idea of "each," "everyone" with reference to persons (here) or even animals (Gen 15:10).
2) The verb is in plural because אִישׁ is understood as a collective.
3) The use אִישׁ־אִישׁ, one another, Exod 36:4
4) Words from the same root:
   אִישׁוֹן,[1] pupil of eye, Deut 32:10
   אָשַׁשׁ verb, to found (idea of firmness), Isa 46:8
   יֵשׁ, there is (being), 2 Sam 9:1
5) Words with the same letters but not necessarily from the same root.

[1]The suffix וֹן is a diminutive ending, meaning here "the little man" (reflection in the eye).

Mic 4:4

אִשָּׁה, woman, Gen 2:23
אָנַשׁ, to be weak, 2 Sam 12:15
אֱנוֹשׁ, mankind (idea of sociability), Jer 20:10

6) The plural form, אֲנָשִׁים, men (Gen 12:20), should be related to אנשׁ rather than to אִישׁ; the original plural of אִישׁ is אִישִׁים, men (Isa 53:3). The etymological distinction between the two groups is not settled however (see especially the connection between אִישׁ and אִשָּׁה in Gen 2:23).

3. תַּחַת, under

4. גַּפְנוֹ, his vine

Construct form from the absolute גֶּפֶן with pronominal suffix (third person masculine singular)

5. וְתַחַת, and under

6. תְּאֵנָתוֹ, his fig tree

Construct form from the absolute תְּאֵנָה with pronominal suffix (third person masculine singular)

Words from the same root:
אנה verb, to be opportune, Prov 12:21
תַּאֲנָה, opportunity, time of copulation, Jer 2:24

7. וְאֵין, and no

וְ conjunction of coordination, and אֵין construct form from the absolute אַיִן, nothing, Isa 40:17

Note:

אֵין particle of negation used before the noun or the participle (here), meaning "there is not," corresponding to the affirmative יֵשׁ, "there is."

8. מַחֲרִיד, causing to tremble (frightening)

Mic 4:4

Analysis:
1) Participle
2) Masculine singular
3) *Hiphil*
4) Root: חרד, to tremble

Note:
1) *Hatef patah* under the guttural ח, instead of *sheva.*
2) Word from the same root:
      חֲרָדָה trembling, anxiety, Gen 27:33

9.   כִּי־, for

10.   פִּי, (the) mouth

   פִּי is the construct form of פֶּה mouth

Note:
1) No *dagesh* in the *begedkefet* פ because it follows the open syllable
      כִּי.
2) Other meanings:
          - edge of sword, Prov 5:4
          - opening, Gen 29:2
          - extremity, 2 Kgs 10:21
3) Used with the preposition לְ, לְפִי means "according to," Lev
      25:16.

11.   יְהֹוָה, (of) the Lord

12.   צְבָאוֹת, of armies

1) Plural form of the word צָבָא
2) Several meanings:
          · army, Gen 21:22
          · angels, Dan 8:10
          · stars, Deut 4:19
          · units, Num 4:3, 23

Mic 4:4

Word from the same root:

צבא verb, to wage war, Num 31:7, or to serve in the sanctuary, Num 4:23

13. דִּבֶּר, has spoken

Analysis:
1) Perfect
2) Third person masculine singular
3) *Piel*
4) Root: דבר, to speak

Mic 4:4

IV. Exercises (Texts)

Gen 22:1-19

*30. Analyze each word (etymology, parsing of verbs) and translate (Gen 22:1-19).

31. Find words with pronominal suffixes, and indicate the person, in Gen 22:1-10 (31 cases).

32. Translate the following sentences:

1) And he said to him, Gen 22:1.
2) I will say to you (singular masculine), Gen 22:2.
3) And he said to me, Gen 24:40.
4) And the men said to us, Gen 42:33.
5) From her to you a son, Gen 17:16.
6) And he said to them (masculine plural), Gen 24:6.

33. Explain the 23 *dagesh* in Gen 22:1-5.

34. Translate the following sentences:

1) The Lord took (לקח) you (masculine plural), Deut 4:20.
2) Israel took my land, Judg 11:13.
3) And he took them (masculine plural) from their hand, Exod 29:25.
4) I have taken you (masculine plural) from there, Gen 27:45.
5) The Lord sent (שלח) me, 1 Sam 15:1.
6) The Lord has not sent you (masculine singular), Jer 28:15.
7) We came to a country where you sent us, Num 13:27.
8) I have not sent them, Jer 23:32.
9) And Moses sent them (masculine plural), Num 31:6.

35. Translate the following sentences:

1) For from her you have been taken (לקח), Gen 3:19.
2) Do not hide (סתר *hiphil*) your face from me, Ps 27:9.
3) And kings from you will go out, Gen 17:6.
4) Send from you, one, Gen 42:16.

5) You shall not eat from it, Gen 2:17.

36. Verbs: ע"ו (קוּם rise, arise, stand), translate the following sentences:

1) A prophet has not arisen in Israel like Moses, Deut 34:10.
2) You will stand (prophetic Perfect) and you will speak to them, Jer 1:17.
3) I will rise against (on) the house of Jeroboam, Amos 7:9.
4) Every man in Israel stood up from his place, Judg 20:33.
5) You have stood up instead of your fathers, Num 32:14.
6) We stood up, Ps 20:9.
7) Stand up (masculine plural) and let us stand up upon her for war, Obad 1.
8) A prophet shall stand up, Deut 13:2.
9) I will make my covenant stand up with you, Gen 9:11.
10) To stand up to me, 1 Sam 22:13.
11) I will cause a prophet to stand up for them, Deut 18:18.
12) Moses caused the tabernacle to stand up (מִשְׁכָּן), Exod 40:18.
13) And they stood up to make it stand up from the earth, 2 Sam 12:17.
14) Deborah stood up and went, Judg 4:9.
15) And he stood up and went to the place, Gen 22:3.

37. Verbs: ל"ה (רָאָה, see), translate the following sentences:

1) Samuel saw Saul, 1 Sam 9:17.
2) What have you (masculine singular) seen that you have done, Gen 20:10.
3) I have seen you righteous (צַדִּיק), Gen 7:1.
4) Our eyes have not seen, Deut 21:7.
5) You (masculine plural) have seen what I have done, Exod 19:4.
6) We have seen that the Lord (is) with you, Gen 26:28.
7) All the earth that you (masculine singular) are seeing, Gen 13:15.
8) All the people were seeing the voices, Exod 20:18.
9) See (masculine singular) with your eyes, Ezek 40:4.
10) See (masculine plural) what you are doing, 2 Chr 19:6.

11) I said: I shall not see, Isa 38:11.
12) Now, you will see what I will do to Pharaoh, Exod 6:1.
13) The Lord will see to him a lamb for offering, Gen 22:8.
14) And the women saw, Gen 3:6.

38. Consonantal Text

1) Write down the consonantal text of Gen 22:1-2; add vowels by yourself and check afterwards.
2) Learn to read the text of Gen 22:1-5 without vowels.

Ps 23

*39. Analyze each word (etymology, parsing of verbs) and translate Ps 23.

40. Translate the following sentences:

1) To restore (*hiphil*) the king to his house, 2 Sam 19:11.
2) He has not brought back his hand, Josh 8:26.
3) I will not bring back the people, Deut 17:16.
4) To bring back (*polel*) Jacob to him, Isa 49:5.
5) You will come back to the Lord your God, Deut 30:10.

41. 1) Learn by heart Ps 23 in Hebrew.
    2) Write down the transliteration of Ps 23.
    3) Write down the consonantal text of Ps 23.
    4) Add the vowels to the consonantal text of Ps 23.

Mic 4:1-4

*42. Analyze each word (etymology, parsing of verbs) and translate Mic 4:1-4.

43. Verbs: ע"ו (כּוּן, establish), translate the following sentences:

1) Man will not be established, Prov 12:3.
2) The word is established from God, Gen 41:32.
3) I have established, 2 Sam 7:13.
4) My hand shall be established, Ps 89:22.

5) And you (masculine singular) have established (*polel*) for you, 2 Sam 7:24.

44. Verbs: ל"א (נשׂא, left up), translate the following sentences:

1) I have lifted up your face (masculine singular), Gen 19:21.
2) You (masculine singular) have lifted up, 2 Kgs 19:4.
3) I will lift up my hand to them, Ezek 20:5.
4) The Lord will lift up his face to you, Num 6:26.
5) We shall lift up, Lam 3:41.
6) He has been lifted up, Exod 25:28.
7) He has lifted up (with intensity), 2 Sam 5:12.

45. Verbs: ע"ע (סבב, turn about), translate the following sentences:

1) I have turned about, Eccl 7:25.
2) He turned about, 1 Sam 7:16.
3) Turning about in the city, Cant 3:3.
4) The Jordan will turn about, Ps 114:5.
5) David turned about (Imperfect consecutive) to bless his house, 1 Chr 16:43.

46. 1) Write the consonantal text of Mic 4:1-2 and its transliteration.
    2) Learn to read the consonantal text of Mic 4:1-2.

Paradigm B: Verb
קוּם,

		Simple Form	
	Person	*Paal* (arise)	*Niphal* (be arisen)
Perfect	Sg. 1 m/f.	קַמְתִּי	נְקוּמוֹתִי
	2 m.	קַמְתָּ	נְקוּמוֹתָ
	2 f.	קַמְתְּ	נְקוּמוֹת
	3 m.	קָם	נָקוֹם
	3 f.	קָמָה	נָקוֹמָה
	Pl. 1 m/f.	קַמְנוּ	נְקוּמוֹנוּ
	2 m.	קַמְתֶּם	נְקוּמוֹתֶם
	2 f.	קַמְתֶּן	נְקוּמוֹתֶן
	3 m/f.	קָמוּ	נָקוֹמוּ
Imperfect	Sg. 1 m/f.	אָקוּם	אֶקּוֹם
	2 m.	תָּקוּם	תִּקּוֹם
	2 f.	תָּקוּמִי	תִּקּוֹמִי
	3 m.	יָקוּם	יִקּוֹם
	3 f.	תָּקוּם	תִּקּוֹם
	Pl. 1 m/f.	נָקוּם	נִקּוֹם
	2 m.	תָּקוּמוּ	תִּקּוֹמוּ
	2 f.	תְּקוּמֶינָה	תִּקּוֹמְנָה
	3 m.	יָקוּמוּ	יִקּוֹמוּ
	3 f.	תְּקוּמֶינָה	תִּקּוֹמְנָה
Imperative		קוּם ...	הִקּוֹם ...
Infinitive		קוּם ,(לְ)קוּם	נָקוֹם ,(לְ)הִקּוֹם
Participle		קָם	נָקוֹם

ʿayin vav (ע"ו)

Arise

Intensive (Heavy) Form			Causative Form	
Piel (*Polel*) (rise up)	*Pual* (*Polal*) (be raised up)	*Hitpael* (*Hitpolel*) (raise oneself)	*Hiphil* (cause to arise)	*Hophal* (be caused to arise)
קוֹמַמְתִּי	קוֹמַמְתִּי	הִתְקוֹמַמְתִּי	הֲקִימוֹתִי	הוּקַמְתִּי
קוֹמַמְתָּ	קוֹמַמְתָּ	הִתְקוֹמַמְתָּ	הֲקִימוֹת	הוּקַמְתָּ
קוֹמַמְתְּ	קוֹמַמְתְּ	הִתְקוֹמַמְתְּ	הֲקִימוֹת	הוּקַמְתְּ
קוֹמֵם	קוֹמַם	הִתְקוֹמֵם	הֵקִים	הוּקַם
קוֹמְמָה	קוֹמְמָה	הִתְקוֹמְמָה	הֵקִימָה	הוּקְמָה
קוֹמַמְנוּ	קוֹמַמְנוּ	הִתְקוֹמַמְנוּ	הֲקִימוֹנוּ	הוּקַמְנוּ
קוֹמַמְתֶּם	קוֹמַמְתֶּם	הִתְקוֹמַמְתֶּם	הֲקִימוֹתֶם	הוּקַמְתֶּם
קוֹמַמְתֶּן	קוֹמַמְתֶּן	הִתְקוֹמַמְתֶּן	הֲקִימוֹתֶן	הוּקַמְתֶּן
קוֹמְמוּ	קוֹמְמוּ	הִתְקוֹמְמוּ	הֵקִימוּ	הוּקְמוּ
אֲקוֹמֵם	אֲקוֹמַם	אֶתְקוֹמֵם	אָקִים	אוּקַם
תְּקוֹמֵם	תְּקוֹמַם	תִּתְקוֹמֵם	תָּקִים	תּוּקַם
תְּקוֹמְמִי	תְּקוֹמְמִי	תִּתְקוֹמְמִי	תָּקִימִי	תּוּקְמִי
יְקוֹמֵם	יְקוֹמַם	יִתְקוֹמֵם	יָקִים	יוּקַם
תְּקוֹמֵם	תְּקוֹמַם	תִּתְקוֹמֵם	תָּקִים	תּוּקַם
נְקוֹמֵם	נְקוֹמַם	נִתְקוֹמֵם	נָקִים	נוּקַם
תְּקוֹמְמוּ	תְּקוֹמְמוּ	תִּתְקוֹמְמוּ	תָּקִימוּ	תּוּקְמוּ
תְּקוֹמֵמְנָה	תְּקוֹמַמְנָה	תִּתְקוֹמֵמְנָה	תְּקִימֶינָה	תּוּקַמְנָה
יְקוֹמְמוּ	יְקוֹמְמוּ	יִתְקוֹמְמוּ	יָקִימוּ	יוּקְמוּ
תְּקוֹמֵמְנָה	תְּקוֹמַמְנָה	תִּתְקוֹמֵמְנָה	תְּקִימֶינָה	תּוּקַמְנָה
קוֹמֵם		הִתְקוֹמֵם	הָקֵם ...	
(לְ)קוֹמֵם	(לְ)קוֹמַם	(לְ)הִתְקוֹמֵם	(לְ)הָקִים	(לְ)הוּקַם
מְקוֹמֵם	מְקוֹמַם	מִתְקוֹמֵם	מֵקִים	מוּקַם

Paradigm C: Verb
יָשַׁב,

	Person	Simple
		Paal (sit, dwell)
Perfect	Sg. 1 m/f.	יָשַׁבְתִּי
	2 m.	יָשַׁבְתָּ
	2 f.	יָשַׁבְתְּ
	3 m.	יָשַׁב
	3 f.	יָשְׁבָה
	Pl. 1 m/f.	יָשַׁבְנוּ
	2 m.	יְשַׁבְתֶּם
	2 f.	יְשַׁבְתֶּן
	3 m/f.	יָשְׁבוּ
Imperfect	Sg. 1 m/f.	אֵשֵׁב
	2 m.	תֵּשֵׁב
	2 f.	תֵּשְׁבִי
	3 m.	יֵשֵׁב
	3 f.	תֵּשֵׁב
	Pl. 1 m./f.	נֵשֵׁב
	2 m.	תֵּשְׁבוּ
	2 f.	תֵּשַׁבְנָה
	3 m.	יֵשְׁבוּ
	3 f.	תֵּשַׁבְנָה
Imperative		שֵׁב ...
Infinitive		יָשׁוֹב , (לְ)שֶׁבֶת
Participle		יוֹשֵׁב , יָשׁוּב

Pey Yod (פ"י)
Sit

Form	Causative Form	
Niphal (be inhabited)	*Hiphil* (cause to dwell)	*Hophal* (be made to dwell)
נוֹשַׁבְתִּי	הוֹשַׁבְתִּי	הוּשַׁבְתִּי
נוֹשַׁבְתָּ	הוֹשַׁבְתָּ	הוּשַׁבְתָּ
נוֹשַׁבְתְּ	הוֹשַׁבְתְּ	הוּשַׁבְתְּ
נוֹשַׁב	הוֹשִׁיב	הוּשַׁב
נוֹשְׁבָה	הוֹשִׁיבָה	הוּשְׁבָה
נוֹשַׁבְנוּ	הוֹשַׁבְנוּ	הוּשַׁבְנוּ
נוֹשַׁבְתֶּם	הוֹשַׁבְתֶּם	הוּשַׁבְתֶּם
נוֹשַׁבְתֶּן	הוֹשַׁבְתֶּן	הוּשַׁבְתֶּן
נוֹשְׁבוּ	הוֹשִׁיבוּ	הוּשְׁבוּ
אִנָּשֵׁב	אוֹשִׁיב	אוּשַׁב
תִּנָּשֵׁב	תּוֹשִׁיב	תּוּשַׁב
תִּנָּשְׁבִי	תּוֹשִׁיבִי	תּוּשְׁבִי
יִנָּשֵׁב	יוֹשִׁיב	יוּשַׁב
תִּנָּשֵׁב	תּוֹשִׁיב	תּוּשַׁב
נִנָּשֵׁב	נוֹשִׁיב	נוּשַׁב
תִּנָּשְׁבוּ	תּוֹשִׁיבוּ	תּוּשְׁבוּ
תִּנָּשַׁבְנָה	תּוֹשֵׁבְנָה	תּוּשַׁבְנָה
יִנָּשְׁבוּ	יוֹשִׁיבוּ	יוּשְׁבוּ
תִּנָּשַׁבְנָה	תּוֹשֵׁבְנָה	תּוּשַׁבְנָה
... הִנָּשֵׁב	... הוֹשֵׁב	
(לְ)הִנָּשֵׁב	הוֹשֵׁב , (לְ)הוֹשִׁיב	הוּשַׁב
נוֹשָׁב	מוֹשִׁיב	מוּשָׁב

Paradigm D: Verb
נָלָה,

		Simple Form	
	Person	*Paal* (uncover)	*Niphal* (be uncovered)
Perfect	Sg. 1 m/f.	נָּלִיתִי	נִנְלֵיתִי
	2 m.	נָּלִיתָ	נִנְלֵיתָ
	2 f.	נָּלִית	נִנְלֵית
	3 m.	נָּלָה	נִנְלָה
	3 f.	נָּלְתָה	נִנְלְתָה
	Pl. 1 m/f.	נָּלִינוּ	נִנְלֵינוּ
	2 m.	גְּלִיתֶם	נִנְלֵיתֶם
	2 f.	גְּלִיתֶן	נִנְלֵיתֶן
	3 m/f.	נָּלוּ	נִנְלוּ
Imperfect	Sg. 1 m/f.	אֶגְלֶה	אֶנָּלֶה
	2 m.	תִּגְלֶה	תִּנָּלֶה
	2 f.	תִּגְלִי	תִּנָּלִי
	3 m.	יִגְלֶה	יִנָּלֶה
	3 f.	תִּגְלֶה	תִּנָּלֶה
	Pl. 1 m/f.	נִגְלֶה	נִנָּלֶה
	2 m.	תִּגְלוּ	תִּנָּלוּ
	2 f.	תִּגְלֶינָה	תִּנָּלֶינָה
	3 m.	יִגְלוּ	יִנָּלוּ
	3 f.	תִּגְלֶינָה	תִּנָּלֶינָה
Imperative		... נָּלֵה	... הִנָּלֵה
Infinitive		נָּלֹה, (לְ)נְלוֹת	הִנָּלֹה, לְהִנָּלוֹת
Participle		גֹּלֶה (נָּלוּי)	נִגְלֶה

Lamed Hey (ל"ה)
Uncover

Intensive (Heavy) Form			Causative Form	
Piel (reveal)	*Pual* (be revealed)	*Hitpael* (reveal itself)	*Hiphil* (carry into exile)	*Hophal* (be carried into exile)
גִּלִּיתִי	גֻּלֵּית	הִתְגַּלֵּיתִי	הִגְלֵיתִי	הָגְלֵיתִי
גִּלִּיתָ	גֻּלֵּיתָ	הִתְגַּלֵּיתָ	הִגְלֵיתָ	הָגְלֵיתָ
גִּלִּית	גֻּלֵּית	הִתְגַּלֵּית	הִגְלֵית	הָגְלֵית
גִּלָּה	גֻּלָּה	הִתְגַּלָּה	הִגְלָה	הָגְלָה
גִּלְּתָה	גֻּלְּתָה	הִתְגַּלְּתָה	הִגְלְתָה	הָגְלְתָה
גִּלִּינוּ	גֻּלֵּינוּ	הִתְגַּלֵּינוּ	הִגְלִינוּ	הָגְלֵינוּ
גִּלִּיתֶם	גֻּלֵּיתֶם	הִתְגַּלֵּיתֶם	הִגְלִיתֶם	הָגְלֵיתֶם
גִּלִּיתֶן	גֻּלֵּיתֶן	הִתְגַּלֵּיתֶן	הִגְלִיתֶן	הָגְלֵיתֶן
גִּלּוּ	גֻּלּוּ	הִתְגַּלּוּ	הִגְלוּ	הָגְלוּ
אֲגַלֶּה	אֲגֻלֶּה	אֶתְגַּלֶּה	אַגְלֶה	אָגְלֶה
תְּגַלֶּה	תְּגֻלֶּה	תִּתְגַּלֶּה	תַּגְלֶה	תָּגְלֶה
תְּגַלִּי	תְּגֻלִּי	תִּתְגַּלִּי	תַּגְלִי	תָּגְלִי
יְגַלֶּה	יְגֻלֶּה	יִתְגַּלֶּה	יַגְלֶה	יָגְלֶה
תְּגַלֶּה	תְּגֻלֶּה	תִּתְגַּלֶּה	תַּגְלֶה	תָּגְלֶה
נְגַלֶּה	נְגֻלֶּה	נִתְגַּלֶּה	נַגְלֶה	נָגְלֶה
תְּגַלֶּה	תְּגֻלֶּה	תִּתְגַּלּוּ	תַּגְלוּ	תָּגְלוּ
תְּגַלֶּינָה	תְּגֻלֶּינָה	תִּתְגַּלֶּינָה	תַּגְלֶינָה	תָּגְלֶינָה
יְגַלּוּ	יְגֻלּוּ	יִתְגַּלּוּ	יַגְלוּ	יָגְלוּ
תְּגַלֶּינָה	תְּגֻלֶּינָה	תִּתְגַּלֶּינָה	תַּגְלֶינָה	תָּגְלֶינָה
... גַּלֵּה		... הִתְגַּלֵּה	... הַגְלֵה	
(לְ)גַּלּוֹת	(לְ)גֻלּוֹת	(לְ)הִתְגַּלּוֹת	(לְ)הַגְלוֹת	הָגְלֹה
מְגַלֶּה	מְגֻלֶּה	מִתְגַּלֶּה	מַגְלֶה	מָגְלֶה

Paradigm E: Verb
סָבַב,

	Person	Simple
		Paal (turn about)
Perfect	Sg. 1 m/f.	סַבּוֹתִי
	2 m.	סַבּוֹתָ
	2 f.	סַבּוֹת
	3 m.	סָבַב(סַב)
	3 f.	סָבְבָה(סַבָּה)
	Pl. 1 m/f.	סַבּוֹנוּ
	2 m.	סַבּוֹתֶם
	2 f.	סַבּוֹתֶן
	3 m/f.	סָבְבוּ(סַבּוּ)
Imperfect	Sg. 1 m/f.	אָסֹב(אֶסֹּב)
	2 m.	תָּסֹב(תִּסֹּב)
	2 f.	תָּסֹבִּי(תִּסְּבִי)
	3 m.	יָסֹב(יִסֹּב)
	3 f.	תָּסֹב(תִּסֹּב)
	Pl. 1 m/f.	נָסֹב(נִסֹּב)
	2 m.	תָּסֹבּוּ(תִּסְּבוּ)
	2 f.	תְּסֻבֶּינָה(תִּסֹּבְנָה)
	3 m.	יָסֹבּוּ(יִסְּבוּ)
	3 f.	תְּסֻבֶּינָה(תִּסֹּבְנָה)
Imperative		סֹב ...
Infinitive		סָבוֹב, סֹב(לְ)
Participle		סוֹבֵב, (סָבוּב)

ᶜ*ayin Doubled* (ע"ע)
Turn About

Form	Causative Form	
Niphal (be turned about)	*Hiphil* (cause to turn about)	*Hophal* (be caused to turn about)
נְסַבּוֹתִי	הֲסִבּוֹתִי	הוּסַבּוֹתִי
נְסַבּוֹתָ	הֲסִבּוֹתָ	הוּסַבּוֹתָ
נְסַבּוֹת	הֲסִבּוֹת	הוּסַבּוֹת
נָסַב	הֵסֵב	הוּסַב
נָסַבָּה	הֵסֵבָּה	הוּסַבָּה
נְסַבּוֹנוּ	הֲסִבּוֹנוּ	הוּסַבּוֹנוּ
נְסַבּוֹתֶם	הֲסִבּוֹתֶם	הוּסַבּוֹתֶם
נְסַבּוֹתֶן	הֲסִבּוֹתֶן	הוּסַבּוֹתֶן
נָסַבּוּ	הֵסֵבּוּ	הוּסַבּוּ
אֶסַּב	אָסֵב	אוּסַב
תִּסַּב	תָּסֵב	תּוּסַב
תִּסַּבִּי	תָּסֵבִּי	תּוּסַבִּי
יִסַּב	יָסֵב	יוּסַב
תִּסַּב	תָּסֵב	תּוּסַב
נִסַּב	נָסֵב	נוּסַב
תִּסַּבּוּ	תָּסֵבּוּ	תּוּסַבּוּ
תִּסַּבֶּינָה	תְּסִבֶּינָה	תּוּסַבֶּינָה
יִסַּבּוּ	יָסֵבּוּ	יוּסַבּוּ
תִּסַּבֶּינָה	תְּסִבֶּינָה	תּוּסַבֶּינָה
הִסַּב ...	הָסֵב	
הִסּוֹב ,(לְ)הִסַּב	(לְ)הָסֵב	(לְ)הוּסַב
נָסָב	מֵסֵב	מוּסָב

CHAPTER V

SYNTAX

Syntax will be understood in its stricter sense as the Greek etymology of the term suggests, namely as the "together (*syn*) arrangement" (*tassein*) of the words. This definition means that we shall essentially pay attention to the life of the Hebrew discourse as a whole:[1] the way it is organized (word order), the way it is articulated (the *vav*), and the way it flows (the accents).

I. The Organization of the Discourse: Word Order

The Hebrew sentence is generally made up of the subject and the predicate. The predicate may be a noun (nominal clause) or a verb (verbal clause). In a nominal clause, the rule is simple; unless emphasis is intended, the natural order of the words is: subject, predicate.

Examples: יְהוָה רוֹעִי   the Lord (is) my Shepherd, Ps 23:1

אַתָּה עִמָּדִי   you (are) with me, Ps 23:4

Emphasis on predicate: יְרֵא אֱלֹהִים אַתָּה, fearing God you, Gen 22:12

In verbal clauses, the situation is more complex depending on whether the verb is in the Perfect or Imperfect, and also whether it is used with an object or not.

---

[1]The so-called syntax of the parts of the Hebrew discourse (nouns, verbs, etc.) has been indicated especially in the course of "the texts." For more on syntax, see especially Bruce K. Waltke and M. O'Connor, *An Introduction to Biblical Hebrew Syntax* (Winona Lake, IN, 1990).

177

a) If the verb is in the Perfect, unless emphasis is intended, the verb tends to come after the subject.

Examples:

אֱלֹהִים נִסָּה			God tested, Gen 22:1

פִּי יְהֹוָה . . . דִּבֵּר		the mouth of Lord . . . spoke, Mic 4:4

Emphasis on verb: אָמַר יְהֹוָה, said the Lord, Jer 45:25

b) If the verb is in the Imperfect, unless emphasis is intended, the verb tends to come before the subject.

Examples:

יִהְיֶה הַר			it will be the mountain, Mic 4:1

לֹא יִשְׂאוּ גוֹי			they will not lift up people, Mic 4:3

Emphasis on subject:

אֲנִי וְהַנַּעַר נֵלְכָה		I and the young man we shall go, Gen 22:5

אֱלֹהִים יִרְאֶה־לּוֹ		God himself will see, Gen 22:8

c) The object usually takes the third position regardless of the place of the verb.

Examples:

וְהָאֱלֹהִים נִסָּה אֶת־אַבְרָהָם		And God tested Abraham (S.V.C.)

וַיִּקַּח אַבְרָהָם אֶת־עֲצֵי הָעֹלָה	And took Abraham the wood of the offering, Gen 22:6

Two exceptions, however: the object comes at the beginning of the sentence if emphasis is intended or if it is a temporal object.

Emphasis on object:

מִצִּיּוֹן תֵּצֵא תוֹרָה		from Zion shall go out Torah, Mic 4:2

הַמָּקוֹם אֲשֶׁר־אָמַר־לוֹ הָאֱלֹהִים	the place that said to him God, Gen 22:3

Temporal object:

בַּיּוֹם הַשְּׁלִישִׁי וַיִּשָּׂא		the third day he raised, Gen 22:4

בְּאַחֲרִית הַיָּמִים יִהְיֶה		In the latter days it will be, Mic 4:1

II. The Articulation of the Discourse: The *Vav*

To articulate his discourse, the Hebrew uses several kinds of particles: conjunctions such as כִּי (because, if, that, if, cf. Gen 22:12, Ps 23:4), אֲשֶׁר (because, that, who, which, what, cf. Gen 22:2,3,14), prepositions such as לְ (to, in order to; cf. Gen 22:10), יַעַן (because, cf. Gen 22:16), verbs such as וַיְהִי (and it came to pass, cf. Gen 22:1, Mic 4:1), וַיֹּאמֶר to articulate dialogues (and he said, cf. Gen 22:1-19), adverbs such as הִנֵּה (behold, lo; cf. Gen 22:13 etc...). All these particles can be learned through a list of vocabulary or through consulting the dictionary.

The most important, and indeed the most frequently used articulating word in Hebrew discourse is the *vav*, which is so rich and so dynamic that it cannot be apprehended simply by consulting the dictionary; the *vav*, therefore, deserves a special treatment.

The primary function of the *vav*, whether it comes before a verb (Perfect, Imperfect) or before a noun, is to indicate a *correlation*. However the great semantic flexibility (see Polysemy) of the *vav* allows for a wide range of meanings.

Depending on the context this *correlation* can be understood "positively" in the sense of an addition, or "negatively" in the sense of an opposition. "Positively" the *vav* may introduce a close connection, a supplement of information, a continuation, an emphasis, an explanation, a consequence. "Negatively" the *vav* may introduce a distinction or a separation, a comparison, and eventually a contrast.

A. The *Vav* of Addition

1. Close connection (viewed as a unity)

אֲנִי וְהַנַּעַר   I *and* the young man (Gen 22:5)
טוֹב וָחֶסֶד   Goodness *and* mercy (Ps 23:6)

2. Supplement of information

וַיִּקַּח אֶת־שְׁנֵי נְעָרָיו אִתּוֹ וְאֵת יִצְחָק בְּנוֹ, He took two of his young men with him *and* (also) his son Isaac (Gen 22:3)

3.   Continuation (sequential)

וְהַעֲלֵהוּ . . . וְלֶךְ־לְךָ, go yourself . . . *and* (then) offer him (Gen 22:2)

וַיִּשָּׂא אַבְרָהָם אֶת־עֵינָיו וַיַּרְא, Abraham lifted his eyes *and* (then) he saw (Gen 22:4)

4.   Explanation (epexegetical)

עָשִׂיתָ אֶת־הַדָּבָר הַזֶּה וְלֹא חָשַׂכְתָּ אֶת־בִּנְךָ You have done this thing, *that is* you have not spared your son (Gen 22:16)

5.   Emphasis

יָדַעְתִּי כִּי־יְרֵא אֱלֹהִים אַתָּה וְלֹא חָשַׂכְתָּ אֶת־בִּנְךָ, I know that you fear God, (even) you have not spared your son (Gen 22:12)

6.   Consequence

וַיִּקְרָא אַבְרָהָם שֵׁם־הַמָּקוֹם, *Therefore* Abraham called the place (Gen 22:14)

בַּיּוֹם הַשְּׁלִישִׁי וַיִּשָּׂא אַבְרָהָם אֶת־עֵינָיו, On the third day (then) Abraham lifted his eyes (Gen 22:4)

B.   The *Vav* of Opposition

1.   A distinction (mark of new beginning)[1]

וְאַבְרָהָם זָקֵן . . . , *And* Abraham was old (Gen 24:1)
וַיִּקְרָא אֵלָיו מַלְאַךְ יְהוָה, *Then* (turning point) the angel of the Lord called (Gen 22:11)

---

[1]In the synagogue scroll, the *vav* marks normally the beginning of a new column (cf. Israel Yeivin, *Introduction to the Tiberian Masorah*, ed. and trans. E. J. Revell, Masoretic Studies 5 [Missoula, MT, 1980], 43).

2. Contemporary situation

שְׁבוּ־לָכֶם פֹּה . . . וַאֲנִי וְהַנַּעַר נֵלְכָה עַד־כֹּה, Sit yourselves here . .
. *while* I and the young man we shall go until there (Gen 22:5)

3. Contrast

הִנֵּה הָאֵשׁ . . . וְאַיֵּה הַשֶּׂה, Here is the fire . . . *but* where is the
lamb (Gen 22:7)

Note: The "*vav* of addition" always comes before a verb when it
is used to introduce subordinate clauses (3, 6); the "*vav* of opposition"
always comes before a non-verb when it is used to introduce a
non-sequential relation (2, 3).

The same word *vav* expresses the many facets of the idea of
correlation. The various shades seem to blend into each other as
colors on a palette. We have given some illustrations of that phenomenon. They are far from being exhaustive however, but they indicate
at least a principle, a direction of thought. There is no way of
determining a fixed and definitive pattern. Every meaning depends on
the life of the context.

This use of the *vav* keyword in the articulation of the Hebrew
discourse, is also indicative of a certain frame of mind. The Hebrew
thinks his discourse as a whole, is a totality. And the rich variety of
potential meanings behind the *vav* shows the dynamic interrelationship
of the context and an aptitude for flexibility. The Hebrew thinks in
synthesis rather than in analysis. Certainly this consideration bears
important implications on the level of interpretation. The exegete must
respect and follows the moving fluctuations of the *vav* if he wants to
understand and expose correctly the Hebrew text.

III. The Flowing of the Discourse: The Accents

The accents are different in prosaic text (the 21 books) and in the first
three books of the Hagiographa (איוב, Job; משלי, Proverbs; תהלים,
Psalms: mnemotechnic word אמ"ת, "truth," formed with the first letter of

each book).[1] The words of the verses are separated by the disjunctive accents or connected by the conjunctive accents according to the rules of syntax and the logic of the discourse.

A. Disjunctive Accents

1. Role and Value

The verse is unequally divided from the most important division marking the end of the verse or its middle, to the least important one usually affecting small words. The division is operated according to the principle of dichotomy by means of disjunctive accents graded along a straight hierarchical organization (hence the comparison of the disjunctive accents to the Lords of the Medieval Society). The first category of disjunctives (Grade I, also called Emperors) divide the verse into two sections. The second category of disjunctives (Grade II, also called Kings) divide each of these two sections which are in their turn subdivided by a third category of disjunctives (Grade III, also called Dukes) into subsections which are also subdivided by a fourth category of disjunctives (Grade IV, also called Counts). This means that a unit ending with Grade I is divided by Grade II; a unit ending with II is divided by III; a unit ending with III is divided by IV.

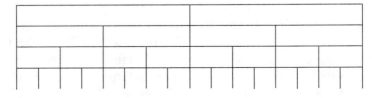

I iv iii iv II iv iii iv I iv iii iv II iv iii iv I

This dichotomic role of the disjunctive accents reveals that the values of these accents are not absolute. Their values depend

---

[1]For more on the accents, see especially William Wickes, *Two Treatises on the Accentuation of the Old Testament*, ed. Harry M. Orlinsky (New York, 1970); C. D. Ginsburg, *Introduction to the Massoretico-Critical Edition of the Hebrew Bible*, ed. Harry M. Orlinsky (New York, 1966); Israel Yeivin, *Introduction to the Tiberian Masorah*.

essentially on their relative place. In fact, the farther a disjunctive is from its superior, the greater value it has; thus, in a shorter verse, a king (Grade II) has less value than a count (Grade IV) in a long verse; also, if the same accent is used several times, the first usage has greater value than the next ones.

2. Table of Disjunctive Accents

a) In Prosaic Texts (21 books)

Grade I (Emperor)

(1)   :(ˌ) *Silluq*, "end," before *sof pasuq*, the verse divider (:)

(2)   (˰) *Athnah*, "the causing to rest," dividing the verse in two parts.

Grade II (Kings)

(3)   ( ) *Segolta*, form of *segol*, "grapes," points to the form of the sign.

(4)   ( ) *Shalshelet*, "chain," points to the melody, kind of double-trill.

(5)   ( ) *Zaqef*, "upright," points the upright finger to mark it in the cantillation (same disjunctive value as small *Zaqef* but with stronger tone).

(6)   ( ) Small *Zaqef*, "upright"

(7)   ( ) *Rebia*, "resting" from Aramaic רבע = Hebrew רבץ

(8)   (ˌ) *Tifha*, "handbreadth," points to the manual sign to mark a slow melody.

Grade III (Dukes)

(9) (ˋ) *Zarqa*, "to sprinkle," points to the character of melody "a turn."

(10) (ˋ) *Pashta*, "extending," points to an extension of the voice in the melody.

(11) (ˏ) *Yetib*, "to dwell," Hebrew יָשַׁב, points to an extension of the voice; same disjunctive value as *Pashta* but different melody.

(12) (ˌ) *Tebir*, "to break," Hebrew שָׁבַר, points to the broken note.

Grade IV (Counts)

(13) (´) *Geresh*, "expulsion," points to the high note produced by the expulsion of the voice.

(14) (˝) *Gershayim*, "double *Geresh*," same disjunctive value as *Geresh* but different melody

(15) (⊢) *Pazer*, "to scatter," points to the melody, kind of trill.

(16) ( ) Great *Pazer*, or *Qarne para*, "cow-horns," same disjunctive value as Pazer but different melody

(17) ( ) *Telisha*, "to pluck out," points to the very high note obtained by drawing out the voice.

(18) (ˌ) *Legarmeh*, "for itself," points to the disjunctive quality of the accent in contrast to the usually conjunctive *munah* (ˌ), see below.

b) **In Poetic Texts (Psalm, Job, Proverbs, אמ"ת)**

Grade I (Emperors)

(1) :(ˌ) Silluq

(2) ($\overset{\angle}{\jmath}$) *Oleh weyored*, "ascending and descending," points to the back and forth modulation; divides the verse in two parts in long verses.

(3) ($_\wedge$) *Athnah*, divides the verse in two parts in short verses; in longer verses follows *Oleh weyored*.

Grade II (Kings)

(4) ($\overset{\bullet}{}$) Great, *Rebia*

(5) ($\overset{\bullet\prime}{}$) *Rebia mugrash*, "*Rebia* with *geresh*"

(6) I($\overset{\ddagger}{}$) Great *Shalshelet*

Grade III (Dukes)

(7) ($\overset{\text{\textbackslash}}{}$) *Sinnor*, "canal," points to the meandering modulation.

(8) ($\overset{\bullet}{}$) Small *Rebia*

(9) ($_\mathsf{L}$) *Dehi*, "thrust back," points to the backward inclination of the sign.

Grade IV (Counts)

(10) ($^\mathsf{F}$) *Pazer*

(11) I($_\mathsf{L}$) *Mehuppakh legarmeh*, "*mehuppakh* by itself," points to the disjunctive quality of the accent, in contrast to the usually conjunctive *mehuppakh* ($_\mathsf{L}$), see below.

(12) I($\grave{}$) *Azla legarmeh*, "*azla by itself*," points to the disjunctive quality of the accent, in contrast to the usually conjunctive *azla* ($\grave{}$), see below.

3. Disjunctives and Syntax

The division of the sentence by the disjunctive accents depends not only on the logic of the discourse but also on the intention of emphasis which determines which part of that sentence should appear first. Thus, if the subject or the object precedes the verb, it indicates emphasis and is therefore generally marked off with a disjunctive. This order goes against the general tendency of Hebrew discourse, to have the verb in the first position, except if an emphasis is intended. The verb will not be marked off with a disjunctive but with a conjunctive (see below) because the dynamic of the verb pushes forward.

Examples:
When subject precedes: אַ֫יִל I אַחַ֫ר I וְאֶחַז בַּסְּבַךְ, Gen 22:13
When object precedes: בָּשָׂ֫ר I בְּנַפְשׁוֹ דָמוֹ לֹא תֹאכֵלוּ׃, Gen 9:4
But, when verb precedes: וְשַׁבְתִּי בְּבֵית־יְהֹוָ֫ה I לְאֹרֶךְ יָמִים, Ps 23:6

B. Conjunctive Accents

1. Role and Value

The conjunctive precedes and is related to the disjunctive just as the servant precedes and is related to his lord (hence the comparison of the conjunctive accents to the servants of the Medieval Society). There is no hierarchy which regulates the use of conjunctives, but every conjunctive is the servant of only one lord (except for two, *munah* and *merka*, which serve several lords). On the other hand, one lord may have several different conjunctives, alternatively or simultaneously.

2. Table of Conjunctive Accents

   a) **In Prosaic Texts (21 books)**

   (1) ( ) *Munah*, "rest," points to the sustained note, or the position of the sign in the form of a *shofar* under the word; this is the most frequent conjunctive.

(2) (˒) *Mahpak*, "inverted," from the root הָפַךְ, points to the descending and ascending modulation, or to the inverted position of the sign in the form of a *shofar*.

(3) (ˎ) *Merka*, "long," from the root אָרַךְ, points to the prolonging modulation.

(4) (ˌ) Double *Merka*

(5) (˻) *Darga*, "scale," points to the descending scale through the octave.

(6) (ˋ) *Azla*, "going on," indicates that we should not pause in the melody, in contrast to the disjunctive *Pashta*, with the same sign.

(7) (ˋ) Little *telisha*

(8) (ˬ) *Galgal*, "wheel" or *yerah*, "moon," points to the form of the sign.

(9) (˳) *Mayyela*, "inclined," points to the form of the sign.

b) **In Poetic Texts (Psalms, Job, Proverbs, אמ"ת**

(1) (ˌ) *Munah*

(2) (ˌ) *Merka*

(3) ( ) *Illuy*, "suspended," from the root עָלָה, points to the position of the accent in the form of a *shofar*.

(4) (˳) *Tarha*, "slow, heavy," points to the slow modulation.

(5) (ˬ) *Galgal* or *yerah*

(6) (˱) *Mahpak*

(7) (ˋ) *Azla*

(8) ( ) Small *shalshelet*

(9)   (˒) *Sinnorit*, feminine of *sinnor*, to distinguish
        from the disjunctive *sinnor* with the same sign.

3. Conjunctives and Syntax

The conjunctive accents relate the words which are connected by
the grammar and the meaning, such as the verb or the predicate to the
subject, the verb to the object, words in construct, pair of words, etc.

Examples:

Verb and subject	וַיִּשְׁלַח אַבְרָהָם	Gen 22:10
Predicate and subject	כּוֹסִי רְוָיָה	Ps 23:5
Verb and object	וַיִּקַּח אֶת־הָאַיִל	Gen 22:13
Words in construct	עֲצֵי הָעֹלָה	Gen 22:6
Pair of words	שִׁבְטְךָ וּמִשְׁעַנְתֶּךָ	Ps 23:4

*Table 5.14: Main Accents

Disjunctives:
׃(ֽ) *Silluq* = end of verse
(֑) *Athnah* = middle of verse
Conjunctives:
(ֻ) *Munah*
(ֹ) *Merka*

C. Application

Genesis 22:1:

וַיְהִי וו אַחַר ׀ הַדְּבָרִים הָאֵלֶּה וו וְהָאֱלֹהִים וו נִסָּה וו אֶת־אַבְרָהָם ווו
וַיֹּאמֶר אֵלָיו וו אַבְרָהָם וו וַיֹּאמֶר הִנֵּנִי׃

It-shall-come-to-pass, after these things, God tested Abraham;
and-he-said to-him Abraham, and-he-said here-I-am.

Psalm 23:1:

מִזְמוֹר לְדָוִד III יְהוָה רֹעִי II לֹא אֶחְסָר׃

Psalm of-David; *YHWH* (is) my-Shepherd, I-shall-not want.

Micah 4:1:

וְהָיָה I בְּאַחֲרִית הַיָּמִים II יִהְיֶה הַר בֵּית־יְהוָה נָכוֹן I בְּרֹאשׁ הֶהָרִים II
וְנִשָּׂא הוּא מִגְּבָעוֹת III וְנָהֲרוּ עָלָיו II עַמִּים׃

It-shall-come-to pass in-the-after of-days, shall the mountain
of-the-house-of-*YHWH* established, on-the-top of-mountains, and-shall-
be-exalted it, above the hills; and-shall-flow to-it, peoples.

Conclusion

Hebrew syntax does not display a stable picture. The regular order of
the words is often disturbed by the need for emphasis, showing greater
sensitivity to movements of life than to grammatical requirements. Also the
vav which articulates the Hebrew discourse indicates the importance of the
interrelated totality, and betrays thereby a point of view of synthesis rather
than of analysis; the *vav* relates the different parts of the discourse in many
ways to be determined according to the life of the context. The observation
of Hebrew syntax shows that the idea of totality and the idea of living
relationship between the different parts constitute the nerve which animates
the Hebrew discourse. Another symptom of this dynamic can be perceived
in the fact that the discourse tends to begin with the verb in the Imperfect,
again confirming previous observations on Hebrew thinking: the action
comes first and generates the rest.

The function of the accents is both grammatical, to indicate the
interrelationship of the words, and liturgical, to regulate the public reading
of the text. This twofold role of the accents shows again the connection
between language and the religious truth. The meaning is preserved by the
sacred reading. It is also noteworthy that the value of the accent, as a mark
of punctuation is always relative, depending both on the word to which it

is attached and the context.[1]   Thus the living meaning governs the interpretation of the grammatical signs; the two are related, the how following the fluctuations of the what.

IV. Exercises (Syntax)

*47.   Indicate the order of the phrases (place of s.v.o.) in Gen 22:1-10.

*48.   Indicate the disjunctive accents and their respective grade, and conjunctive accents, in Gen 22:1-5.

49.   Indicate the disjunctive accents, their respective grade, and the conjunctive accents, in Ps 23:1-3.

50.   Find in Gen 22:1-19 two *vavs* of addition and two *vavs* of opposition (identify their specific function).

[1]The great disjunctive *Athnah*, for instance, may sometimes indicate a very important break (as in Gen 1:4) and sometimes a very little one (as Gen 1:1). It may even function like a conjunctive, especially in enumerations and in numbers (see Lev 12:5; Num 1:46; see also perhaps Dan 9:25).

CHAPTER VI

HEBREW THOUGHT

Introduction

Biblical theologians,[1] philosophers,[2] and linguists[3] have united their efforts to trace and describe Hebrew thought as it is reflected in the Hebrew language within the context of biblical civilization.

The concept of "Hebrew Thought" implies 1) the assumption that the Hebrew Bible has been written by human persons who belonged to a specific culture and tradition, lived a specific experience, spoke a specific language and therefore had a specific way of thinking, 2) the observation

---

[1]See for instance classics like Gerhard von Rad, *Old Testament Theology*, trans. J. A. Baker (Philadelphia, 1961); Otto Procksch, *Theologie des Alten Testaments* (Gütersloh, 1949); Edmond Jacob, *Theology of the Old Testament*, trans. Arthur W. Heathcote and Philip J. Allcock (New York, 1958); André Neher, *The Prophetic Existence* (South Brunswick, NJ, 1969); André Lacocque, *But As For Me* (Atlanta, 1979), 13-93.

[2]See Claude Tresmontant, *A Study of Hebrew Thought*, trans. Michael F. Gibson (New York, 1960); Thorleif Boman, *Hebrew Thought Compared with Greek*, trans. Jules L. Moreau (Philadelphia, 1960); Johannes Pedersen, *Israel: Its Life and Culture*, trans. Mrs. Aslaug Moller (London, 1926); Abraham J. Heschel, *God in Search of Man: A Philosophy of Judaism* (New York, 1976); idem, *I Asked for Wonder: A Spiritual Anthology* (New York, 1983); idem, *Man is not alone; A Philosophy of Religion* (New York, 1972); idem, *The Prophets* (New York, 1969); idem, *The Sabbath; Its Meaning for Modern Man* (New York, 1951).

[3]See, for instance, J. Weingreen, *Classical Hebrew Composition* (Oxford, 1957); Edward Horowitz, *How the Hebrew Grew* (Hoboken, NJ, 1960); Theodore H. Robinson, *The Genius of Hebrew Grammar: A Presidential Address Delivered to the Society for Old Testament Study, December 1927* (London, 1928).

that there is a common thread of thought throughout the Old Testament and therefore the recognition of a certain philosophical unity in the Hebrew Bible. The former presupposition allows for "a philosophical" approach focusing on the mentality, the ideas, and the thoughts of the Hebrew people; the latter presupposition allows for "a synthetic" approach taking the Hebrew Bible as a whole. This "synchronic-philosophical" approach does not exclude, however, the diachronic approach. Indeed, the diachronic or the systematic analysis of the biblical concepts which pertain to the discipline of "Old Testament Theology" is necessary and complements the exposition of Hebrew thought as much as it needs it for its own purposes in order to develop a correct Old Testament Theology. For Hebrew thought takes us to the very heart of Old Testament Theology; it is the essence of Old Testament Theology.

Our presentation of Hebrew thought will proceed by steps. First, as a preliminary, we shall define the nature of Hebrew thought; then we will describe this thought through four basic concepts and around which, like around axes, revolve most biblical ideas, namely, the Hebrew concepts of the world, time, man, and God.

This picture of Hebrew thought does not purport, however, to be exhaustive as we are only concerned with drawing a synthesis of the main trends, a mere essay indicating directions of thought. Also, our presentation will be based on, or will refer to, what we have already observed and described in the grammar, the vocabulary, the syntax. Before, we proceeded from the language to the thought; now, we shall proceed conversely from the thought to the categories of language.

I. The Nature of Hebrew Thought

A. Action Precedes Thought

We shall start with a paradox: Hebrew thought as expressed in the Bible is not a thought. The Bible does not provide any treatise on the concept of the world, or of time, etc. Hebrew thought does not construct the truth as a philosophical system; rather it is essentially the response to an event. Thus, in Hebrew, it is the thought that follows the event and not the reverse.

This phenomenon has already been noticed on the level of the language. We find it in the nature of the Hebrew word etymologically derived from the verb, thereby attesting that the action had preceded the thinking process of designation. We find it in Hebrew syntax which legislates the order of the phrase and puts the verb expressing the action before the consciousness of the thinking subject.

The same truth is taught throughout the Hebrew Scriptures. The fact that the Hebrew Bible starts with the event of Creation points to that movement. Salvation history begins with an event in which the human genius is totally absent. The human involvement is described only as a passive reception, or an enjoyed reaction that comes after the event, in the "spiritual" life of the Sabbath (Gen 2:1-3, cf. Exod 20:8-11). Likewise the Israelite theology of salvation is drawn out of the event of Exodus, which will remain in biblical tradition the basic event of reference for any spiritual elaboration (Exod 20:2; Deut 5:6; Isa 40:3). The same principle shines through the Israelite response to God's giving of the law: נַעֲשֶׂה וְנִשְׁמָע "We shall do, then we shall obey," (Exod 24:7). Here again the spiritual operation of hearing, understanding, proceeds from the doing. This thought order is also reflected in the way the Hebrews report events, proceeding from the actual event to the cause which produced it. Instead of thinking from cause to effect as Modern Western thinking tends to do, Ancient Hebrew thinking reasons from effect to cause. For example in Mic 1:10-15, the cities that mourn for the exiles are listed before the cities that gave up exiles. First the effect, then the cause.[1] Indeed the mechanism of Hebrew thinking stands at the opposite to the Cartesian *cogito*, the latter being the basic presupposition in Western methodology. Instead of stating "I think, therefore I am," Hebrew thought proclaims "I am, therefore I think." Here the thought is not initiated and controlled by the thought, but is generated and governed by the adventures of history.

B. Knowledge and Intelligence

Another incidental implication of this principle is found in the Hebrew concept of knowledge and of intelligence. Since the thought comes *a posteriori*, as a result of the event, the Hebrew comes to know something out of the existential experience with it. The Hebrew word יָרַע which expresses the idea of knowledge is also used to express the dynamics of the conjugal relationship between man and woman (Gen 4:1, 17; Gen 19:8) or even, in a figurative way between God and human beings (Ps 16:11; Jer 9:23-24; Hos 8:2). To know means "to live with." "Knowing" does not

---

[1]See especially William Shea, *Selected Studies in Prophetic Interpretation*, rev. ed. (Washington, DC, 1991), 163.

consist in observing and analyzing the object; it is the result of experience, a walk with someone (Ps 95:10), and implies a personal commitment to the object or the person to be known.

The same process may be recognized in the way Hebrew intelligence functions. In Hebrew intelligence is not as we tend to believe in Western thinking, the ability to judge and criticize something from outside. On the contrary it is in essence the ability to receive. Significantly, the Hebrew seat of intelligence lies in the ears (Isa 50:5; Job 12:11; Neh 8:3; Jer 6:10; cf. Rev 2:7; 3:22). Intelligence is the ability to listen, to be open to the experience which comes first. This process is clearly indicated in the already mentioned phrase "נַעֲשֶׂה וְנִשְׁמָע" (Exod 24:7). The operation of the intelligence which is contained in the word שָׁמַע (to listen) follows the performance of the action עָשָׂה. No wonder then that intelligence has been understood in the Bible not as a mere intellectual ability but as a gift to be received from outside, thus belonging to the category of Revelation (Ps 119:125, 144; Job 32:8). Only if we have heard, if we have received, are we able to behave as an intelligent person. This is the reason why the act of intelligence is described as the operation of distinguishing between good and evil (בִּינָה "intelligence" is derived from the root בֵּין "between"), thereby implying the information of Revelation (1 Kgs 3:9;[1] 2 Sam 14:17). Significantly the word בִּין which is one of the key words of the book of Daniel is related to the prophetic Revelation (Dan 8:15, 17, 27; 9:2, 22, 23; 11:33; 12:8-10).

C. Silence

This Hebrew emphasis on the ability of listening as the act of intelligence explains the importance of silence in Hebrew thought. Silence functions as the nerve of the relationship between God and man. It lies in the heart of Revelation on the level of God (1 Kgs 19:12)[2] and on the level of man (Deut 27:9). It also belongs to the existential experience of that relationship, on the level of God (Ps 22:2) and on the level of men (Ps 62:1, in Hebrew verse 2; 65:1, in Hebrew verse 2). Silence also plays a

---

[1]Note that the English word "understand" in the text (NKJV) is the translation of the Hebrew word שמע "to listen, to hear."

[2]The Hebrew phrase generally translated by "a still small voice" (NKJV) means literally "the voice of a thin silence" (see NRSV; cf. also A. Graeme Auld, *I, II Kings* [Philadelphia, 1986], 127).

decisive role in the relationship between human beings as an expression of fear (Amos 5:13), of indifference (2 Kgs 7:9), but also as the manifestation of respect (Job 2:13) and of love (1 Sam 18:1).[1]

D. The Totality

Knowledge and intelligence are never described as mere mental faculties, but in the totality of their function. "To know" is not only a mental process or the result of sensation, it is also the concrete act of its application in life, involving the whole person in that experience. "To understand" is not only an intellectual operation; it is also the concrete act of making the right choice, and applying that choice in life. The totality of the notion is conveyed. It is one of Pedersen's merits to have shown how fundamental the notion of totality is in Hebrew thought.[2] For the Hebrew, to think is to grasp the totality. The vocabulary as well as the grammar are indicative of that particular frame of mind. The root of the word encompasses the totality of the notion. The root דָּבַר means "to speak" and "to act." The word is the act. When God speaks, He acts (Isa 55:11). The root which designates the notion of sin חָטָא may mean the act of sin (Isa 31:7), the blame for that act (Gen 43:9), the guilt of sin (Deut 15:9), the punishment for sin (Zech 14:19), the sacrifice for sin (Lev 7:37). The same phenomenon may be observed in the terms expressing the idea of faith, justice, grace, etc. The grammar bears the same character. Regardless of the number of syllables each word is stressed with one accent and is therefore perceived in its totality. This emphasis on totality is also expressed in the genitive form (construct state). The two words which determine each other are understood as a total unity; the two words are governed by the same article and the same accent. Another token of this trend may be recognized in the frequent use of "merismus," this way of expressing totality through the association of contrary motifs: North and South (Ps 89:12), rich and poor (Prov 22:2), evening and morning (Gen 1:5), old and young (Gen 19:4).

---

[1]The text says: "and it was so, when he had finished speaking . . ." David could have reminded Saul who he was, that is the musician who used to play the harp when the king was visited by an evil spirit (1 Sam 16:23). Instead, David refrains from speaking further, and this "silence" impresses Jonathan who then started to love David "as his own soul."

[2]Johannes Pedersen, *Israel, Its Life and Culture*, 108.

Incarnated in life, Hebrew thought conveys the totality of the concepts (world, time, man, and God) even to its contradictions through the tension between opposite poles.

II. The Hebrew Concept of the World

The Hebrews had no specific word to express their idea of the space where they lived. They had therefore to resort to a paraphrase like שָׁמַיִם וָאָרֶץ, "heavens and earth," an expression which they always associated with the idea of Creation (Gen 1:1; Isa 65:17; Jer 33:25; Ps 115:15; 121:2; 124:8; 134:3; 146:6, etc). Thus the Hebrew concept of the world is fundamentally committed to the doctrine of Creation. Now the expression שָׁמַיִם וָאָרֶץ, heaven and earth, applies only to the human universe and does not refer to worlds which are beyond the human experience. The Hebrew concept of the world refers only to the created world in which man is a part. The Hebrew is not concerned with other worlds (although he does not ignore them, Job 38:7; Ps 148:2-4) nor is he with the scientific objective reality of the world. Only the created world as it relates to him interests him. Starting from there, "his created world," the Hebrew will draw all his theological implications.

A. The World is Limited and Infinite

1. The World is Limited

The concept that the world has been created implies first of all that the world is an object with no power in itself whatsoever, therefore owing its existence to an external power. The divine ownership (Ps 82:8; 1 Chr 29:11) and sovereignty (1 Chr 29:12, Job 38:23) of the world are related to the idea of Creation. In that connection it is significant that the technical term בָּרָא has only God as a subject.

It also implies that the world came out as something new. The verb בָּרָא "to create," is significantly always associated with the idea of newness (Jer 31:22; Isa 65:17; Ps 51:10). Thus, to the concept of "genesis" implying an organic (genetic) link between the "not yet" and the "being," the Bible opposes the concept of Creation implying an essential breech between the actual world and what is before. The world is not perceived as preexistent, either being God (ancient mythology) or coming from God (emanatism, pantheism). The space of the Hebrew is void of gods, it is demythologized. The sun, the moon and the trees are not gods to be worshiped but limited things to be used. This concern explains why the author of Genesis 1 is so reluctant to use the common names of שֶׁמֶשׁ and יָרֵחַ respectively for sun and moon which are also names of common pagan deities. He prefers to refer to them as to ordinary instruments, the great and the small lamps (Gen 1:16).

2. *The World is Infinite*

On the other hand because it is created, the world comes to man as something which precedes and therefore surpasses him. The world also escapes human apprehension. This ambivalent perception of the world is indicated on the linguistic level. Besides the vague expression שָׁמַיִם וָאָרֶץ (heaven and earth) the Hebrew uses two specific words when he wants to refer to the earthly world: אֶרֶץ (Ps 22:27; Isa 23:17) and עוֹלָם (Ps 73:12; Isa 64:4). אֶרֶץ connotes the idea of limitation; it may also mean the country distinct from another country (Gen 12:1; 47:27); or the dry land as it is distinct from water (Gen 1:10); or simply the earth as it is distinct from heaven (Gen 1:1). The word עוֹלָם on the other hand connotes the idea of the unseen (Job 28:21) and is commonly used to express the idea of infinity and eternity (Isa 26:4; Ezek 37:25).

3. *A Vital Tension*

These two perceptions of the world are suggested in Genesis 1 and 2, in the way man is situated in regard to the world. In Genesis 1 man is lost in the infinite of a world which has preceded him. In Genesis 2 man occupies the whole space and everything evolves around him in order to serve him. So, the Bible sometimes describes man as the lord of the world having dominion over nature (Gen 1:28; Gen 2:19-20; Gen 9:2; Ps 8:6-8), sometimes as an insignificant creature overwhelmed by the infinite grandeur of the Universe (Ps 8:3-4; Job 7:17; Job 38-41).

It is also noteworthy that these two views are often used in the same context (see especially Ps 8 and Gen 1 and 2), so as to convey the idea that both should be assumed together. In fact this tension is vital since it preserves man from two often experienced pitfalls, namely idolatry and ecological abuse.

B. The World is Good and Bad

1. The World is Good

The second original idea of the Bible is that the world has been created good (טוֹב Gen 1:4, 10, 12, 18, 21) and even very good (טוֹב מְאֹד Gen 1:31). Paradoxically, because the world is not divine, because it is created, it is not perceived as a threat (dualism) or as a degeneracy (pantheism, emanatism). Instead, it is accepted and enjoyed (Eccl 9:9; 11:7; Josh 1:15). The Hebrew assumes his space and finds his happiness within this space and does not despise the sensual pleasure of food, beauty, perfume, etc. (Song of Songs 4:10-11; Deut 14:26; Num 13:23, 27). Man has the right and even the duty to enjoy the good (Gen 1:28-29; Gen 2:16; Eccl 2:24, 26).

2. The World is Bad

On the other hand, the world is also perceived as bad, and this bad is fully recognized as such. No room here for a philosophy which would deny its existence or transform it into something good. The bad does exist and is considered something negative. Evil is an unplanned, unfair and abnormal accident, and an unavoidable reality (Gen 3:17-19; Job 2:10; 7:11; Eccl 1:14-15, 5:8). This cohabitation of good and bad makes the appreciation of the world ambiguous. The enjoyment of the good always has its counterpart of bitterness and death and is therefore to be tempered by the restriction of ethics (Eccl 11:9).

3. The Tension of Hope

Thus both good and bad are assumed as such and this tension is important because it nurtures in man his hope for something better. Within the experience of evil and death man keeps touch with good, and it is this very conflictual situation which will inspire his revolt (Gen 18:22-32; Job 3:3; 31:35-36; Ps 83:1) and his yearning for another order (Ps 6:3, 74:10; 94:1-3; 130:5-6; Job 19:27).

C. The Unity of the World

1. *In Creation*

Now, if the contradiction is assumed and the two views of the world do not exclude each other, it is essentially because the world is also perceived as one. The unity of the world is indeed another implication of the idea of Creation. The fact that the beginning of mankind is connected with the beginning of the world, and the fact that the world has been created as a whole and in relation to man, indicates an organic unity of the world within itself and as it relates to man.

2. *In History*

The nature of this relationship is such that the history of the whole world is described as dependent upon man's actions. The original "good" creation becomes bad as soon as man disobeys God. Evil and death enter the world and the ecological balance has been upset due to the sin of man. This lesson of dependence is repeated over and over again in the Scriptures. In Genesis 4, as a result of his murder, Cain had to be protected (Gen 4:15). The text does not specify from what, but it is clear that animals are implied since these are the only beings left besides his parents. The same principle underlies the Hebrew concept of the promised land which has the property of "vomiting out" its sinful inhabitants (Lev 18:25, 28). The iniquity of the Israelites who kill, steal and commit adultery (Hos 4:2) affects the character of the land which "will mourn . . . and waste away with the beasts . . . the birds and the fish" (Hos 4:3). Likewise the mere lie of the individual Achan has an incidence upon the immediate surroundings. Not only will the whole people be hurt but the space in which the sin takes place, the valley, is hit and becomes the "valley of trouble" (Josh 7:10-26). Thus the geography seems to bear witness to the iniquity. And this principle is so vivid for the prophets that they go so far as to infer the fate of the nation merely from the meaning of the names of the cities where that nation dwells (Mic 1:10-16). As a matter of fact, the world is intimately associated with its inhabitants (Isa 49:13; Jer 51:48; Ps 96:11; 1 Chr 16:31) and man's success or failure involves the failure or success of all creation (Isa 51:6; 44:23; 45:18).

3. *In the End*

This principle of Unity is one of the characteristic features of biblical eschatology. Along with the end of human conflicts, the prophet refers to a covenant with the animals which will not hurt anymore (Hos 2:18; Isa 11:6-9). And since the original Creation has been spoiled by evil, the only solution to the problem of evil is then the return to the original state of Creation; to make salvation of man possible a new Creation of the whole world will be necessary (Isa 65:17; 66:22). Thus the unity of the world is consistent from the beginning to the end.

III. The Hebrew Concept of Time

The Hebrew did not formulate an abstract concept of time as an external entity *per se*. The Hebrew concept of time is bound up with its content and even identified with it. "The precedence of the time content as opposed to the chronological statement of time can be observed in the linguistic phenomenon that the Hebrew verb does not have any real tenses. Actions are determined primarily by the content-aspect of being completed, not by the time categories past, present, and future."[1] Thus when the Hebrew will need to express the idea of past and future, he will have to do it from the perspective of this essential connection between time and man. The idea of past and future is rendered through the spatial terms "before" קֶדֶם (Ps 139:5) and "after" אַחַר (Gen 22:1). The past is then understood as something already here, before man, whereas the future is understood as something coming after him and not yet experienced. These two dimensions of time do not exist *per se*. They are only perceived subjectively in relation to the real man in space. Thus time is created along with the Universe. The light is called "day" and the darkness is called "night." God marks the time, and the luminaries are created later to hold the same function (Gen 1:4, 14). Time is then received like the Universe as a gift (Eccl 3:1) and is therefore perceived as something positive. In contrast to Greek thought where the idea of time is associated with death and is feared as a threat, in Hebrew thought time is understood as life and is therefore fully accepted as something good.

[1]E. Jenni, "Time," in *The Interpreter's Dictionary of the Bible*, IV (New York, 1962), 646.

A. Time is New and Rhythmic

1. *Time is New*

a. A Time for Everything

Since time is related to the life of the event, time implies a new and unique experience. Human life is made of a succession of several times. Therefore the Hebrew speaks of "times" "my times are in your hand" (Ps 31:15; Job 24:1). Time (עֵת) is the moment at which something happens (2 Chr 25:27; 1 Kgs 11:4; Jer 50:16). This means that every event has its time. There is a time to gather the cattle (Gen 29:7), a time when the kings go out to battle (2 Sam 11:1), a time for the tree to give its fruit (Ps 1:3), a time to be born, a time to die, etc. (Eccl 3:2ff.), a time for every purpose (Eccl 8:6).

b. The Concept of History

Another implication of this identification between time and event is the Hebrew understanding of History. Contrary to the Moira of the Greeks or to the "forces" of Hegel, the Hebrew course of events is not imposed from outside but belongs to the human experience. Hebrew language conveys this idea of history through the word דָּבָר which means both "event" (Gen 22:1) and "word" (Mic 4:2). The event is thus understood as the expression, the word of the person. The expression דִּבְרֵי שְׁלֹמֹה may either mean the events (actions) of Solomon (1 Kgs 11:41) or the words of Solomon (1 Kgs 5:7, in Hebrew verse 21). Significantly, the expression דִּבְרֵי הַיָּמִים "the actions (or words) of the days," is used as the title of the books of Chronicles. Along the same lines, when the Hebrew wants to express the idea of an unlimited time in human history he uses the expression דּוֹר וָדוֹר "generation after generation" (Isa 61:4) or מִדּוֹר לָדוֹר "from generation to generation" (Isa 34:10). This reference to "generation" again shows that the concept of time, is associated with the human beings who live in that period of time.

c. The Concept of Eternity

Undoubtedly the relation between time and life reaches its climax in the Hebrew concept of Eternity. Time does not stop there. On the contrary, the content of time that is life, will never be interrupted there. This view of Eternity is suggested by the prophets through the image of the sun which will never set (Isa 60:19ff.; Zech 14:7). This understanding of Eternity is also reflected on a linguistic level through the word עוֹלָם. This word which is also used with a spatial connotation to designate the Infinite (see above) implies on a temporal level the idea of an experience which is beyond the human apprehension. Man has only the thought (the intuition) of Eternity (Eccl 3:11). This does not mean that Eternity is beyond him. Instead, time is still there, but its "eternal" quality escapes human eyes. For instance if the word עוֹלָם is used to qualify the covenant of the rainbow (Gen 9:16), it is to say that this covenant will never set down. For us this is just a thought because this perception does not belong to the human experience. *Eternity is not the end of time, but is a time which has no end.* This means that Eternity will always be provided with new events. In essence, biblical eschatology implies the absolute new. It is the Creation of a new heavens and new earth (Isa 65:17). Eternity is characterized therefore by the intensification of "newness." Thus, in Eternity, time is more present than ever.

2. *Time is Rhythmic*

Besides this "punctual" conception of time, Hebrew thought attests also a rhythmic conception of time. Time is always new, yet it is also determined by rhythms. History is not reproducing itself, new events always occur, yet they also participate in the natural movement of regular repetitions.[1]

---

[1]This is why the word "rhythmic" is preferable over the word "cyclic" to qualify the Hebrew concept of time. The book of Ecclesiastes stating that "what has been is what will be" (Eccl 1:9) should not be understood along these lines, and so interpreted as an influence of the Greek cyclic view. The teaching of Ecclesiastes is not about the cyclic movement of history but about the continuity of what he sees as identical. What he observes is not cyclic but static. "There

a. Astrological Time

Time is indicated by the heavenly luminaries which govern the rhythms of seasons, days and years (Gen 1:14). The time of the day and the night, as well as the time of months and seasons depends on an astrological rhythm (Gen 1:16; 1 Sam 20:5, 27). Even the various times during the day are measured through the different intensities of light and warmth of the heavenly luminaries (1 Sam 11:9, 11).

b. Biological Time

The life of the body manifests itself not only through the fact that it goes on and knows new feelings and experiences, but also through the fact that it responds to rhythms. Just as continuity, rhythm is sign of life. Thus the rhythm of breathing guarantees life; if one stops breathing one stops living (1 Kgs 17:17). Another example of the dimension of rhythm in time is the way the phenomenon of menstruation is understood. The word עִדָּה "menstruation" is derived either from a root meaning "to reckon" (עדד) or from a root meaning "to repeat" (עוד). Whatever the etymological tracing of this word may be, both imply the significance of rhythm in life. It is indeed noteworthy that not only the biological life but also the social and conjugal life were determined by this rhythm (Lev 15:33; 18:19).

c. Religious Time

Likewise, the feasts for the Israelites are recurring experiences which mark the rhythm of their time. The word מוֹעֵד meaning "appointed time," "fixed times" (from the verb יעד to appoint) conveys the nuance of such a specific time with an emphasis on the sameness of the content (Gen 1:14;

---

is nothing new under the sun" (Eccl 1:9). This idea should be understood from within the framework of his thought basically dealing with the concept of vanity. His point is that history is not moving, nothing new happens and is therefore a non-sense, a vanity. It is death. Note that on the other hand the same book holds the "punctual" view of time (Eccl 3:1ff.).

Hos 9:5). These appointed times were not created by men. The ecclesiastical year and the civil year did not coincide. These were times which were appointed from outside by God himself.

B. Time is Chronological and Synchronical

In Hebrew, the capacity of representing time as a chronological line went side by side with the capacity of actualization which associated distant events and made them simultaneous.

1. *Time is Chronological*

a. Chronological Progression

Events are described in a chronological manner. The divine interventions are recorded and situated in time chronologically. History has a beginning and develops towards an end. This acute consciousness of the chronological movement of history is already reflected in the overall structure of the canonical Bible. The Bible opens with Creation (Gen 1) and closes with the end of human history in the perspective of the Kingdom of God (Mal 4; 2 Chr 36:21-23).[1] In the course of the Israelite history, salvation history is remembered in a chronological manner either from Abraham to the entry of Canaan (Deut 26:5-9; Josh 24:2-13), or from the first man to the post-exilic period (1 Chr 1 - 2 Chr 36); likewise the apocalyptic vision of History follows the same line; it starts with the first kingdom with a hint to Creation (Dan 2:37-38; 7:2) and develops chronologically up to the end of human history (Dan 2, 7 , 8). The word תּוֹלְדוֹת "genealogy" (Gen 5:1; 1 Chr 1:29) which is another word for History (Gen 2:4; Num 3:1) is another indication of that chronological concept of time. Indeed the genealogies regularly articulate the biblical record and increase thus the chronological impression and the forward progression of History.

---

[1]This principle seems also to have governed the canonical arrangement of the New Testament (see Matt 1:1-17; John 1:1-5; and Rev 22:12-21).

b. Future-Orientation

This future-orientation is actually one of the most striking particularities of Hebrew theology. As soon as the Hebrew appears in salvation history, he becomes future-oriented. Abraham is one of the greatest examples. His call "to go" (Gen 12:1; Gen 22:1), which characterizes his spiritual journey, marks from the beginning to the end his movement towards a future he did not know. The promise which points to the future lies in the heart of the patriarchal religion (Gen 13:15; 22:15-18; Exod 6:3-4). When the people of Israel are called out of Egypt, they become suddenly a people turned towards the future, with a promised land in perspective (Gen 50:22-25; Exod 3:17; 12:25; Num 10:29; Deut 6:3-23; 29:13). Even her God defines himself with a future perspective "אֶהְיֶה אֲשֶׁר אֶהְיֶה," "I will be what I will be" (Exod 3:14). The assurances given to David were both a fulfillment of earlier promises and steps towards their future fulfillment (2 Sam 3:18; 7:18-29). Later the prophets will illustrate their expectation of a new future by reference to the people wandering in the desert and not yet arrived at the promised land (Hos 2:14-15; Jer 31:2-14; Ezek 20:35-37).

This openness towards the new can be observed in the Hebrew language. The importance of the Imperfect—certainly the original verbal form—and above all the witness of the syntax which projects the subject after the verb, are even on the unconscious level of the language indicative of this openness towards the new. Finding himself in the wake of the action, the Hebrew forges his identity in the becoming of his movement towards the future.

c. The Idea of Eschatology

This concept of time bears also an incidence upon the Hebrew eschatology which is nothing but the expectation of something coming after the end, bringing along a kingdom where the future will be insured. Significantly, one of the keywords of the eschatological terminology is אַחֲרִית, "that which comes afterwards." Biblical eschatology teaches that there is an "afterwards" beyond the end, and the conviction of this future is hope (Jer 29:11; Dan 10:14).

This dynamic idea of eschatology affects the Hebrew concept of eternity. Thus the Hebrew word עַד or וָעֶד in the expression לָעַד, "forever" (Ps 111:3), or וָעֶד לְעוֹלָם, "forever" (Ps 9:6), comes from the root עָדָה, "to pass on," "to advance" (Job 28:8), pointing to the continual advance of time into the future.

2. Time is Synchronical

This linear and chronological view of time has not prevented the Hebrew from also conceiving the principle of simultaneity. The synchronic view of time is made possible precisely because the content of time prevails over chronology. Events which are distant in time can, if their content is similar, be regarded as simultaneous.

a. In the Feasts

This process of conversion is especially intense through the experience of the feasts which actualize the past or the future event. The past event of Creation is actualized in the Sabbath (Exod 20:11). The past event of the wandering in the wilderness is actualized in the feast of Tabernacles (Lev 23:43). Likewise, the future event of God's salvation may be actualized in the Sabbath, the sabbatical year or even in the institution of the Jubilee (Ps 92:4; Jer 25:9-12; Isa 61:1, 2; Dan 9:2, 24-27).

b. In Events

This phenomenon however is not unique to the feasts. The same principle is used by the prophets who may base their predictions of a future event on the reference to a past event. The past event of Creation will be reactualized in the Exodus (Exod 15:8) or in the return from the Exile (Isa 42:5-9). The past event of the Exodus will be reactualized in the return from the Exile (Jer 31:1-8). The past event of the return from the exile will be reactualized in the final salvation (Ezek 37:21-28). The more specific battle of Jezreel of the past (2 Kgs 10:11) will be reactualized in another future battle (Hos 1:4,11). This phenomenon of actualization is even attested on the linguistic level through the use of the *perfectum propheticum*. In Jer 32:37-44 for instance, the Perfect tense is used to express the certainty of the hope of the restoration. This future event is so sure that it is perceived as if it were *already* accomplished. In most versions it has significantly been rendered by a future.

> Behold I have already gathered them of all countries, . . . I have already brought them back to this place, and I have already caused them to dwell safely: . . . Yes I have already rejoiced over them to do them good, and I have assuredly planted them in this land. . . . (Jer 32:37-41)

c. In Hebrew Grammar

In addition to the regular usage of tenses which express completed or uncompleted actions, Hebrew grammar has the capacity of reversing the two categories of time by the use of the so-called "consecutive-conversive *vav*." So, the tense of the "Perfect" which is commonly used to refer to an action in the past is suddenly reversed and points instead to a future event (Jer 32:44). This capacity of synchronization may be explained through the Hebrew concept of the "corporate personality." The elected people of Israel is in solidarity with the people of past and future generations; so the past and the future event may be perceived as their own in the present (Deut 29:9-14). Indeed, the chronological reality of History is not ignored, but through his identification with the past and future events, the Hebrew places himself in the historical perspective.

IV. The Hebrew Concept of Man

Like the world and time, man is defined as the result of a creative act. The description of this operation is given in Gen 2:7: "And the Lord God formed man of the dust of the ground and breathed into his nostrils the breath of life; and man became a living being." The material of man is completely earthly. There is nothing divine in him. The etymology of אָדָם man (Gen 2:7) from אֲדָמָה, ground (Gen 2:7), has preserved on a linguistic level this understanding of man. Man is nothing but dust (Gen 3:19; Eccl 3:20; 12:7; Ps 30:9) and this earthly nature is constantly reminded through the rituals of repentance (Josh 7:6; Job 2:12; Neh 9:1). Yet the description of man's creation suggests also that to the earthly element, God has added a new element, "breath" נְשָׁמָה. Man is not only an earthly being, he is a

breathing being. This capacity is implied in the word נֶפֶשׁ which designates
the final product coming from the combination of the two elements "earth"
and "breath." The word נֶפֶשׁ is a term applied to men and animals as well
(Gen 2:7, 19). Etymologically it connotes the idea of breath (Jer 15:9).
The text however suggests that man is more than just the addition of two
elements. Man is in fact the result of two divine operations. The definition
of man is not static, referring to the analysis of the composition of man, it
is dynamic, telling about the creative action of God. Thus man is designed
to be a complex creature.

A. Alive and Spiritual

The first implication we may infer from the story of this creative act
is that man's life is directly dependent on his relationship with God. God
breathes into man's nostrils and man becomes alive. Life is then a
dimension of the "encounter" between God and man. The notion of "air"
or "breath" רוּחַ (Job 15:30; Isa 26:18) which refers to the Hebrew principle
of life (Gen 6:17; 7:15; cf. Gen 1:2; Job 33:4; Isa 38:16), refers also to the
Hebrew principle of spirituality (Num 27:18; Isa 63:10, 11). There is no
distinction between the רוּחַ of God and that of man (Ps 104:30). The
lesson of this identification is double. First it means that man owes his life
to God. God gave him the רוּחַ, the breath. God is his Creator. It also
implies a philosophy of existence. Man exists only in relationship with
God. Man is religious, or he does not exist. The religious dimension is
not simply an answer to spiritual needs, it is a biological necessity (Gen
2:17; cf. 3:17, 19). The Israelite of the Bible does not envisage life
without that dimension. This would be an absurdity (Ps 14:1). Religion
is not a choice, it is simply the observation of a fact. We cannot omit the
spiritual life as we cannot omit breathing. On the other hand, if a man
stops breathing, he stops having a spiritual life; the dead cannot worship (Ps
115:17).

B. Unique and One

1. *Man is Unique*

It has been said that Israel is the only culture so far to have conceived the idea of individuality.[1] The reason for this boldness stems perhaps in the monotheistic way of thinking. God being conceived as unique (Deut 6:4), man who was designed to reflect Him was to be unique also. The same emphasis on man's individuality recurs in Genesis 2 where the Creation of man is told in contrast to that of the animals (Gen 2:7; cf. 2:19). Man alone receives the vital breath in his nostrils directly from God, a token that only man was considered as an individual. The animals are created in conformity to species (Gen 1:24, 25). This principle of individuality is particularly vivid in Hebrew psychology. The uniqueness of the human person makes him or her impossible to remain locked in a definitive category. Man is always free to be different and can say "no" even to God (Gen 3:6; Gen 18:25; 1 Sam 15:11). Man can also be free and change his ways and repent (Jonah 3:5-10). The Hebrew method of giving names is indicative of that thought. Every man receives a name which will be specific to him, as an expression of his unique identity and history (Gen 16:11; 1 Chr 22:9; Isa 8:3; Gen 10:25). Yet no man will be "stuck" under the label of his name; if he changes his ways and shifts to another history, his name is changed accordingly. Abram becomes Abraham (Gen 17:5). Jacob becomes Israel (Gen 32:28). *Lo Ammi* becomes *Ammi* (Hos 2:1). In essence, man is different and his mystery always remains a wonder (Ps 8:4-6). It is the awareness of that difference, and the respect for that difference which underlie the Hebrew principle of love. "You shall love your neighbor as yourself" (Lev 19:18) is not a narcissist concept of love, but on the contrary the recognition that my neighbor deserves the same respect as myself. For love implies the right for difference. It is the ability to notice the other in spite of myself. One of the implications of this principle is the so often misunderstood "eye for eye, tooth for tooth . . ." (Exod 21:24). This law has nothing to do with some idea of revenge. It is simply the practical application of the respect for the difference. The Israelite had to learn in his flesh that his neighbor needed the same space as he

[1]See Bernard-Henri Lévy, *Le testament de Dieu* (Paris, 1979), 75-92.

himself. This very idea is in fact suggested in the preposition פַּחַת "under" translated "for." Concretely it means that the neighbor's eye or tooth is supposed to occupy the same space as mine: eye *under* eye, tooth *under* tooth.   More than just the passive tolerance for the difference, the active openness to that difference is the prerequisite for love.   The recognition of that difference is actually defined as the prevention for murder.   The very reason why man shall not kill his neighbor is related to the fact that man has been created in the image of God (Gen 9:5-6).   Killing a man means the destruction of what is unique in space and time—a kind of deicide.   Thus killing stands as the contrary of love: as much as love is the affirmation of the difference, murder is its negation (Gen 4:4-8).

2. *Man is One*

Another implication of the creation of man in Gen 2:7 is that man is conceived as a whole.   Man became a living נֶפֶשׁ (soul).   Thus it would be inappropriate to say that man has a soul; man *is* a soul.   The Hebrew conception of man makes no room for a dualistic theory of man.   The word נֶפֶשׁ which is commonly translated by "soul" implies in fact all the functions of man, spiritual, mental, emotional, as well as physical.   The נֶפֶשׁ can be hungry (Ps 107:9; Deut 12:20), thirsty (Ps 143:6), satisfied (Jer 31:14), enjoy good food (Isa 55:2); it can also love (Gen 34:3; Song of Songs 1:7), be troubled (Ps 31:9), cry (Ps 119:20), make research (Lam 3:25), know (Ps 139:14), be wise (Prov 3:22), worship and praise God (Ps 103:1; Ps 146:1).   The same principle applies for the human organs.   Guts רַחַם have compassion (Gen 43:30); kidneys כְּלָיוֹת convey instruction (Ps 16:7); the heart thinks לֵב (Ezek 38:10), feels (Ps 39:4) or understands (1 Kgs 3:9); the ears אָזְנַיִם understand (Prov 18:15).   The flesh בָּשָׂר which is supposed to contain all the physical functions of man has also spiritual functions. The flesh is troubled (Jer 12:12), knows (Ezek 21:10), is spiritual (Joel 3:1), worships (Isa 66:23; Ps 145:21).

Thus, man may think with his body and eat with his soul, just as he may think with his soul and eat with his body.   Actually the two words נֶפֶשׁ (soul) and בָּשָׂר (flesh) are often interchangeable (Num 31:35; cf. Ps 145:21).   The reason for that confusion is that soul and body do not exist separately.   Man is conceived in totality.   If the physical mechanism stops working, the spiritual mechanism does the same (Eccl 9:5).   Death is total just as life.

C. Set Apart and Social

1. *Man is Set Apart*

The process of "being set apart" follows the biblical man through-out salvation history. In the beginning, man is set apart out of his environment for a special relationship with the Creator. In fact, he begins his life with this experience of a time which is set apart (Gen 2:3). Then history unfolds a series of separations from the rest of mankind. Seth (Gen 4:25), Noah (Gen 7:1), Abraham (Gen 12:1), Jacob (Gen 25:23), the people of Israel (Amos 3:2) and finally the eschatological remnant (Zeph 3:13) are separated from the rest of the family or of the nations. The reason for this separation is that they are designed to be holy (Lev 21:6). Holiness implies separation. Israel must leave Egypt and experience the lonely wanderings in the desert in order to learn to be holy (Num 23:9, Ezek 20:8-12). As soon as they intend to relate to the others and to behave like them, they loose their vocation for holiness (Deut 12:27-30; 1 Sam 8:7, 8, 20). Even in exile they must remain apart from the rest (Dan 3:12). This requirement is not simply a faithfulness to a political entity. It is not just the remembrance of a belonging. "To be set apart" implies a perpetual choice in daily life, a special choice of food (Gen 1:29; 9:4; Lev 11; Dan 1:8), of the spouse (Gen 27:46; Judg 3:6), days (Lev 23), and places (Deut 12:5). Man is not only set apart in space, he is set apart in his existence by what he does and what he is.

2. *Man is Social*

Man is also defined in relationship with the outside. When Gen 2 describes the creation of man, the accent is put on his sociability (Gen 2:18). The Hebrew word אִישׁ which is used in that context (it is absent in Gen 1) may well have been chosen because of the particular "social" dimension it connotes. The etymology of the word suggests this basic idea since the word אִישׁ is derived from the root אנשׁ which conveys the idea of weakness, of sociability, of dependence and need. No wonder then that the word אִישׁ appears only at the last step of the chapter when the social dimension of man is finally realized in the couple (Gen 2:22-25). Likewise, in Gen 1 man is presented as male and female (Gen 1:27); not that the text suggests that the original man was androgynous, but on account of this total view of man. The story of the creation of the woman out of man's side makes men and women a part of the same totality and has its counterpart on a linguistic level since the two words for woman and man אִשָּׁה and אִישׁ are related (Gen 2:23).

Beyond the couple, man belongs also to another body such as the family, the tribe and ultimately the people. The son בֵּן or the daughter בָּת belong to the larger group בַּיִת which means family (2 Sam 3:1), tribe (1 Kgs 11:28), the people (Amos 5:1). The words are etymologically related, pointing to the Hebrew concept of corporate personality. The same concept accounts for the identification between the forebear and his descendants (Gen 10). Abraham contains in himself all the nations he is supposed to engender (Gen 12:3). Jacob designates the patriarch and those descended from him (Gen 25:26; cf. Isa 43:1). Adam, the name of the first man, will become the generic name for man. The organic link between the group and its members is such that the slightest mistake of a member will affect the totality of the group, the present and the future (Gen 3:19; 9:25-27; Josh 7). The covenant made with one man concerns his family and his descendants as well (Gen 9:9-10, 16; Isa 61:9). The blessing and the curse function in the same way (Deut 5:9-10). This identification of the individual and his group is even reflected in Hebrew grammar, for instance in the usage of the so called "collective singular." Instead of saying the Assyrians, the Canaanites, the Arabians (in plural), the Hebrew will rather use the singular and say the Assyrian (Num 24:22), the Canaanite (Hos 12:7), the Arabian (Isa 13:20), etc.

3. Holy and Human

The biblical man has the double duty as Abraham Heschel puts it, "to be holy and human."[1] The tension between the two requirements is difficult to bear, but it is vital because it prevents the excesses of fanaticism and the seduction of liberalism, the pride of isolationism and the compromises with sin.

---

[1]Abraham Heschel, *God in Search of Man* (New York, 1955), 238.

V. The Hebrew Concept of God

Like the concepts of the world, time and man, the Hebrew concept of God is also very much indebted to the idea of Creation. God is the Creator. The reality of God imposes itself beyond all demonstration. He exists before the world, time and man (Ps 90:2). He is therefore not a concept which has germinated from below. The Hebrew does not try to define or analyze this concept. In fact, God is unconceivable. It is impossible to represent Him (Exod 20:4). The only certainty is that He is living. The expression "God (or the Lord) is living" is one of the most frequent phrases about God (Josh 3:10; Judg 3:19; 1 Sam 14:39; 25:34; Ezek 5:11; Ps 84:3, etc.). God's existence is never questioned. Only the fool says "There is no God" (Ps 14:1; Job 2:10). On the other hand, God's reality is experienced in space (Deut 26:15), in time (Exod 20:8-11) and among men (Gen 18). These two evidences seem in tension with each other. God is unconceivable, unseen, yet He is a concrete and living reality. The Hebrew concept of God reflects the complexity of this tension and accounts for the fact that God can never be apprehended.

A. God is Far and Near

1. *God is Far*

This concept is implicit in the idea of Creation (Job 38:4). In Genesis 1 God is depicted as the great God who transcends the Universe (Gen 1:1). The name אֱלֹהִים which designates Him in that context confirms this view. The root אלה conveys the idea of strength and preeminence which is reinforced by the plural form, expression of intensity or of majesty. God is far away in space. He dwells in a place very far away in heaven (Ps 113:5; Isa 14:13-14), a place localized: "above the stars . . . on the farthest sides of the North" (Isa 14:13-14), a way of saying that God is as far away as one could be. God is also far in time. He is eternal (Jer 10:10). He is very far in the past and very far in the future. "He is the first and the last" (Isa 41:4). This expression does not mean that He has a beginning and an end. God is not described in Himself, from an ontological standpoint. He is described from the human point of view. Thus, God's eternity is not described as an atemporal quality. God's eternity has a time quality since it parallels human time. "The Lord shall endure for ever . . ." and His "years are throughout all generations" (Ps 102:12, 24).

His being in time does not mean however that He is determined by time, as if time were an outside power. God still controls time which means that He is able to fix time (Gen 1:4-5; Ps 75:2), to change time (Dan 2:21). He is even able to push time beyond its borders (Josh 10:12; Isa 38:8). This "motion" of time may be observed in the Hebrew verbs whose reference to past and future may be reversed through the phenomenon of the conversive *vav*. God is far from man.

This means that God escapes any control; He does whatever He pleases (Ps 115:3). God's distance is also the most painful experience man endures. It is associated with suffering (Job 13:24; Ps 13:1-2), death (Deut 32:20; Ps 89:46-48), and sin (Isa 57:17; 59:2).

2. *God is Near*

The idea that God is near is also implicit in the event of Creation. In order to create, God had to come down (Ps 113:6; Ps 8:4). In Genesis 2, the second Creation story, God is depicted as a God who is near. The contact between God and man is even physical (Gen 2:7). The whole text is concerned with this relationship. The name *YHWH* which designates God in that context confirms that emphasis. The etymology of the name *YHWH* which seems to be alluded to in Exod 3:13-14 conveys the idea of a God who is with man (Exod 3:17), the God of Abraham, Isaac, and Jacob (Exod 3:15). The God of the Bible is not an abstract principle or an ethereal power. He is described as a concrete and physical being with hands (Gen 49:24; Ps 75:8), a nose (Isa 65:5), a mouth (Deut 8:3), and bowels (Isa 63:15). The principle of the *Imago Dei* which is generally interpreted rather on the plane of man, has its implication also on the plane of God. The fact that man has been created in the image of God implies a reciprocal resemblance. Moreover the image of God should not be limited to the spiritual dimension. The Hebrew concept of man as a totality where the physical dimension is considered as important as the spiritual one, confirms this perception. God is as concrete and physical as man is. He walks (Deut 20:4; Gen 3:8), speaks (Gen 17:22; Isa 65:12), fights (Gen 32:22-32; Exod 14:14, 25) and even touches physically (Gen 32:25; Ps 23:5). God even dwells among the people (Num 5:3; 1 Kgs 6:13; Ps 22:3; Zech 2:11), more precisely in Jerusalem (Ps 135:21), in the Sanctuary (Exod 15:17; 29:43-46). God is in time. The Israelite calendar is saturated with times in which God is particularly present. The feasts, the Sabbaths, are appointments in time where God and man meet together (Lev 23:2). The most obvious presence of God in time is in History. God reveals Himself through events. Creation, Exodus, personal experiences, eschatological salvation, are God's insertions in the time of man. History is controlled from above (Dan 4:35) and follows a line which is predicted by God Himself (Isa 46:10). God is with man. God's relationship with man is therefore fulfilled on the level of existence and History. This experience is described as a covenant בְּרִית where God and man engage like partners in the same action. Indeed the experience of covenant carries implications on both levels. On the level of God it implies an act of grace. God has taken the initiative to make a covenant with man (Exod 6:4; Jer 31:31). He has come down to man (2 Sam 22:10; Exod 34:5). Indeed, grace חֶסֶד is an inherent part of the event of covenant (Deut 7:9; Dan 9:4; Exod 15:13; 1 Kgs 8:23; Ps 89:49). It means specifically a powerful action through which God expresses his strong loving relationship to man (Gen 32:10; Ps 17:7). On the level of man it implies a life according to the prescriptions of the תּוֹרָה, the law graciously granted to man (Exod 24:12; Deut 33;4; Neh 9:34; Ps 119:29). The word תּוֹרָה usually translated "law," means more, indeed, than just the legalistic observance, it means a way to walk in, a direction in life (Neh 10:29; Ps 119:105). The way of תּוֹרָה is actually the human response to the divine חֶסֶד (Ps 119:41-45).

3. Universal and Particular

This presence of God in space, in time, and with man, is one of the most difficult ideas of Hebrew thought. The Universal God of gods (Deut 10:17), who has all power and wisdom (2 Sam 14:20; Job 15:8; Dan 2:20-23), who is everywhere (Ps 139:7-12), is also known as the God who is "one" (Deut 4:35; 6:4; 32:39), to be met only in one specific place (Deut 12:5; Neh 1:9). This paradox lies in the heart of the mystery of Revelation. It simply means that the Great God has revealed Himself to human beings. Then, to know God, one has to pass by the reference to man.[1] The phenomenon of prophecy illustrates the requirement. The נָבִיא (prophet) is the man who communicates God's message in his own articulated words (Exod 7:1; Hos

[1]This concept will reach its climax in the New Testament idea of incarnation (John 1:1-5; Heb 1:1-2).

12:10). The universal salvation passes by the reference to a particular
people (Ps 67:1-2; cf. John 4:22), a particular man (Gen 12:3; cf. John
14:6), a particular history (Ps 98:1-3).

B. The Tension of Religion

The biblical man has assumed the contradiction. For him the God who
is far away is also very close (Jer 23:23). The God of justice is also the
God of grace (Ps 112:4; 116:5). The Hebrew word צֶדֶק conveys both the
connotation of grace and justice (Mal 4:2; Ps 5:8; Joel 2:23). The God
who is everywhere is also the God who is particularly here. The unique
God is also the God who holds all power. It is the same God. The
tensions of that religion are preserved ritually in the gestures of worship
and psychologically in the sacred fear.

1. Worship

Whether the Israelite prays or performs a sacrifice, he expresses
his awareness of that tension. In his prayers he addresses the God of
heaven (Neh 1:4; Ps 136:26) as a Shepherd (Ps 23), or a Father (Ps
89:26; Matt 6:9) who draws close to man. It is noteworthy that the act
of sacrifice carries the same tension; while it reminds the Israelite that
he could not approach God by himself (Jer 30:21), it is also used as a
sign of God's proximity (Exod 29:42). The root of the word קָרְבָּן
sacrifice (Lev 1:2) derived from the root קרב meaning "near," may
well have preserved this dynamics. Significantly, the biblical idea of
worship is often associated with the idea of Creation (Ps 95:6; 102:18;
Neh 9:6; cf. Rev 14:7). Only the Creator deserves worship. For
through the act of Creation, God has shown both His power and His
grace. He is great enough to be awed and near enough to be loved;
worship necessarily implies that tension between the sense of the
distance of God and yet the intimate experience of His proximity.

2. The Fear of God

The Hebrew concept of the fear of God יִרְאַת יְהֹוָה is an important
element of Hebrew religion (Ps 111:10; Prov 1:7; Josh 4:24; Isa 11:3).
It expresses the consciousness of God's eye upon us wherever we are
(Ps 33:18; Job 28:24-28). In this concept, God's justice and love are
intertwined. God is everywhere and therefore He is able to watch upon

us: He is the Judge (Ps 139; 50:1-6; Ps 33:13-15; Prov 24:12; Ezek 8:12). He is everywhere and therefore He is able to protect us from any harm: He is the Savior (Exod 3:7-8; Ps 106:43-44; 138:6-7). The "fear of God" associates both dimensions of justice and love (Deut 10:12-13). Thus, the Hebrew concept of "fear of God" assumes a real tension between joy and trembling (Ps 2:11), fear and trust (Exod 14:31), and between fear and love (Neh 1:5).

Conclusion

The study of Hebrew thought is a relevant concern indeed. First, because the thought of the Hebrews did exist in reality. The influence of Hebrew language and civilization, in addition to the unique experience of prophecy have certainly played a role in the shaping of Hebrew mentality. If we recognize the validity of this principle, we shall expect that the Bible as a whole, in spite of its diversity, displays a specific way of thinking.

Second, because we cannot have access to the *universal* Truth, that is God's Revelation, without passing through the humble references to its historical witness that is the *particular* people of Israel. Those who claim to hold to the divine Truth while despising its human witness, stumble on this basic requirement. As a matter of fact, this view, sometimes expressed by Old Testament scholars, not only falls in the dualistic trap which dissociates the spirit from the flesh, but also betrays the old anti-Semitic bias.

This principle does not mean, however, that we have to think exactly the same way as did the ancient Hebrews; our own languages and cultures as well as our historical adventures with God today are different than theirs. But this "subjective" experience with Israel will at least help us to understand the biblical message the way it was understood by the men who conveyed it. This sympathetic approach will draw the person of the Bible close to us on a spiritual level; and the intimacy thus created may well affect our lives and even our civilization.

This is actually the *raison d'être* of the biblical truth: not necessarily to teach us how to think, but rather to teach us how to commit ourselves to the same God. This is what makes the influence of the Bible essentially different from any other cultural product. As Abraham Heschel observes: "Socrates taught us that a life without thinking is not worth living. . . . The Bible taught us that life without commitment is not worth living; that

thinking without roots will bear flowers but no fruits. Our commitment is
to God, and our roots are in the prophetic events of Israel."[1]

VI. Exercises (Hebrew Thought)

56. Give one linguistic example in Gen 22 which would illustrate the
     principle that in Hebrew action precedes thought.

57. What are the words expressing the Hebrew concept of knowledge and
     of intelligence?

58. How is the emphasis on totality (synthesis) expressed in Hebrew
     vocabulary and grammar (give examples)?

59. What are the words expressing the Hebrew idea of the world?
     Indicate their basic meaning, their etymology and their diverse
     applications.

60. Same question for the Hebrew idea of time, history and eternity.

61. How does Hebrew grammar and vocabulary express the idea of past
     and future?

62. What are the two main words expressing the Hebrew idea of man?
     Indicate their basic meaning and their etymology.

63. Indicate several Hebrew words for human organs and indicate their
     "spiritual" function.

64. What are the two main words expressing the Hebrew idea of God?
     Indicate their basic meaning and their etymology?

*65. Indicate several Hebrew words expressing the Hebrew concept of
     religion (law, covenant, prophet, grace, justice, holiness, sacrifice,
     fear of God), and explain them on the basis of their etymology.

---

[1]Heschel, *God in Search of Man*, 216.

HEBREW IN A NUTSHELL

1. The Letters

A. 22 Consonants

ו	ה	ד	דּ	ג	גּ	ב	בּ	א
w	h	d̲	d	g̲	g	b̲	b	ᵓ

ל	(ך)	כ	כּ	י	ט	ח	ז
l	k̲	k̲	k	y	ṭ	ḥ	z

(ף)	פ	פּ	ע	ס	(ן)	נ	(ם)	מ
p̲	p̲	p	ᶜ	s	n	n	m	m

ת	תּ	שׂ	שׁ	ר	ק	(ץ)	צ
t̲	t	š	ś	r	q	ṣ	ṣ

B. The Vowels

＿ *patah* (*a*); ＿ː *hatef patah* (*a*)

ˍ *qametz* (*ā*); ˍː *hatef qametz* (*o*); ˍ short *qametz* (*o*)

וֹ, ◌ *holem* (*ô*); וּ *shureq* (*û*); ˌ *qibbutz* (*u*)

219

ָ *segol* (e); ֱ *hatef segol* (e); ְ *sheva* (e); ֵ *tsere* (ē)

ִ *hireq* (i); ִי *long hireq* (î)

Note: The long vowels are transcribed with a hat on them. Long vowels come generally in open syllables (ending with the sound of the vowel "ba"), while short vowels generally come in closed syllables (ending with the sound of the consonant "ab").

C. Two *Shevas* and Two *Dageshes*

□ְ□   *Sheva nah* (quiet) = silent *e*, at the end of a syllable
□□ְ□   *Sheva na^c* (mobile) = pronounced *e*, at the beginning of a syllable
בּ   *Dagesh qal* (weak) = explosive letter, in *begedkefet* (beginning of syllable)
בּ   *Dagesh hazaq* (strong) = doubling letter in other letters (not gutturals)

2. Particles

The article (the), הַ□; before guttural, הָ or הֶ
The interrogative, הֲ; before guttural, הַ or הֶ
The *vav* (and), וְ; before *(bumpf)* or *sheva*, וּ

3. Prepositions

עַל (on)

from מִן, מֵ□ | בְּ (in) | אֶל, לְ (to)

תַּחַת (under); כְּ (like)

4. Nouns

A. Gender and Number

חֲמוֹר, donkey (M.S.) → חֲמוֹרִים, donkeys (M.P.)
חֲמוֹרָה, donkey (F.S.) → חֲמוֹרוֹת, donkeys (F.P.)

B. With Adjective

חֲמוֹר טוֹב, a good donkey (adjective after the noun)
הַחֲמוֹר הַטּוֹב, the good donkey (adjective has an article like the noun)
הַחֲמוֹר טוֹב, the donkey is good (adjective has no article)

C. Construct

חֲמוֹר הַמֶּלֶךְ, the donkey of the king (the article before the second noun)

Vocal changes of the construct:
(words of) דִּבְרֵי ← (words) דְּבָרִים; (word of) דְּבַר ← (word) דָּבָר
(kings of) מַלְכֵי ← (kings) מְלָכִים; (king of) מֶלֶךְ ← (king) מֶלֶךְ

5. Pronouns

Personal Pronoun		Pronoun Suffix	
אֲנִי	I	כּוֹסִי	my cup
אַתָּה	you (M.S.)	*כּוֹסְךָ	your cup (M.S.)
אַתְּ	you (F.S.)	*כּוֹסֵךְ	your cup (F.S.)
הוּא	he	*כּוֹסוֹ	his cup
הִיא	she	*כּוֹסָהּ	her cup
אֲנַחְנוּ	we	*כּוֹסֵנוּ	our cup
אַתֶּם	you (M.P.)	*כּוֹסְכֶם	your cup (M.P.)
אַתֶּן	you (F.P.)	*כּוֹסְכֶן	your cup (F.P.)
הֵם	they (M.P.)	*כּוֹסָם	their cup (M.P.)
הֵן	they (F.P.)	*כּוֹסָן	their cup (F.P.)

*(Plural: י before the suffix)

6. Verbs

Perfect		Imperfect (אתינתי = *Atynty* before the root)	
כָּתַבְתִּי	I wrote	אֶכְתֹּב	I shall write
כָּתַבְתָּ	you wrote (M.S.)	תִּכְתֹּב	you will write (M.S.)
כָּתַבְתְּ	you wrote (F.S.)	תִּכְתְּבִי	you will write (F.S.)
כָּתַב	he wrote	יִכְתֹּב	he will write
כָּתְבָה	she wrote	תִּכְתֹּב	she will write
כָּתַבְנוּ	we wrote	נִכְתֹּב	we shall write
כְּתַבְתֶּם	you wrote (M.P.)	תִּכְתְּבוּ	you will write (M.P.)
כְּתַבְתֶּן	you wrote (S.P.)	תִּכְתֹּבְנָה	you will write (S.P.)
כָּתְבוּ	they wrote (M.P.)	יִכְתְּבוּ	they will write (M.P.)
כָּתְבוּ	they wrote (F.P.)	תִּכְתֹּבְנָה	they will write (F.P.)

A. Forms

Names: *Paal-Niphal*; *Piel-Pual*; *Hiphil-Hophal*; *Hitpael*
Imperfect: the *Atynty* carries **Hireq** in *Paal, Niphal, Hitpael*
                        Sheva in *Piel, Pual*
                        Patah in *Hiphil*
                        Short Qametz in *Hophal*

Participle: prefixed by מ in every form (except *paal* and *niphal*), with the vowel of the *atynty*.

B. Irregular Verbs

פ"ן, פ"ו, פ"י = the ן, ו, י remain in the Perfect, but drops out in the Imperfect (in פ"ן conpensated by *dagesh*).

ע"ו = the ו remains in the Imperfect, but drops out in the Perfect.

ל"ה = the ה remains in the Imperfect, but changes into *yod* in the Perfect.

7. Vocabulary (The 28 Most Important Hebrew Words in Theology)

1.	אֱלֹהִים	God	15.	יָשַׁע	save
2.	אָמַר	say	16.	צַדִּיק	righteous
3.	דָּבָר	word	17.	תּוֹרָה	law
4.	יְהֹוָה	The Lord	18.	בְּרִית	covenant
5.	הָיָה	to be	19.	נָבִיא	prophet
6.	שׁוּב	return	20.	הַר	mountain
7.	מַלְאָךְ	angel	21.	נֶפֶשׁ	self, being
8.	רוּחַ	Spirit	22.	עָבַד	serve
9.	חֶסֶד	grace, piety	23.	דָּם	blood
10.	יָרֵא	fear (of God)	24.	עוֹלָם	eternity
11.	קֹדֶשׁ	holy	25.	זָכַר	remember
12.	חַטָּאת	sin	26.	בָּרָא	create
13.	יָדַע	know	27.	אֱמֶת	truth
14.	שָׁלוֹם	peace	28.	שָׁמַע	listen, obey

8. Syntax

A. Order of Words

Verb, subject, object

B. Articulations of the *Vav*

Vav of addition (connection, explanation, consequence, etc.), before a verb

Vav of opposition (distinction, contrast, etc.), before a non verb

C. Accents

Disjunctive: *Silluq* (: ˌ); *Athnah* (ˌ); etc.

Conjunctive: *Munah* (ˌ); *Merka* (ˌ); etc.

9. The Main Principles of Hebrew Thought

1. The action precedes the thought ("I am therefore I think").
2. Knowing is experiencing with; subjective rather than objective (synthesis rather than analysis).
3. The world is created one (limitation and unity).
4. The Hebrew concept of time is bound up with its content (emphasis on history).
5. Man is "human and holy" (social and special).
6. God is near and far (worship implies fear and love).

APPENDIX: FURTHER STEPS

At this stage, the student may pursue his effort in four directions, depending on his own skills or interests: 1) improve his knowledge of the Hebrew language (Advanced Hebrew), 2) focus on specific texts (Exegesis), 3) focus on specific words (Word study), 4) apply his knowledge for practical purposes (Sermon). We shall propose here guidelines for each of these four basic assignments.

Advanced Hebrew

For further study of the Hebrew language, it is enough after this introduction to keep working on a variety of selected texts (different in regard to difficulty, literary genre, books, historical period). For each text we suggest the following guidelines:

1. Analyze all the nouns and adjectives (etymology, grammatical function) with the help of dictionaries (*A Hebrew and English Lexicon of the Old Testament* by F. Brown, S. Driver, and C. Briggs; *Lexicon in Veteris Testamenti Libros* by L. Koehler and W. Baumgartner).

2. Parse all the verbs.

3. Learn the vocabulary of the text.

4. Translate.

5. Recognize the accents of the text (names, grades, disjunctives, conjunctives).

6. Decipher the Apparatus at the bottom of the page of BHS with the help of William R. Scott's *A Simplified Guide to BHS* (Berkeley, CA, 1987).

7. Study the sections in grammars (*An Introduction to Biblical Hebrew Syntax* by B. Waltke and M. O'Connor; *Gesenius' Hebrew Grammar* by E. Kautzsch and A. Cowley; *Grammaire de l'Hebreu Biblique* by J. Jouon) where your text is used as an illustration to the grammatical points thereby treated (proceed from the index of Scripture references).

8. Learn to read the text fluently (practice reading it without vowels).

Exegesis

A. General Remarks

Definition: The word "exegesis" comes from the Greek word *exege-omai*, which basically means "to lead out, to bring out" the meaning of a specific text.

Necessity: As applied to the biblical text, exegesis becomes a religious necessity, not only because it concerns the word of God; but also because it implies a gap between the source which originated the "word," and the receiver, i.e., ourselves: 1) a gap between the text and the reader of today; 2) a gap between the biblical author and the reader of today; 3) a gap between the God who inspired this word and the religious interpretation of today. Exegesis consists essentially in narrowing these gaps as much as possible.

Methodology: Thus, exegetical work pertains to Science, to Art, but also to Faith.

It is a *Science*: it must proceed rigorously under the control of as much information as possible, for the data are historically remote.

It is an *Art*: it implies intuition, literary sensitivity, and even poetic creativity for it is first of all an experience with a text.

It is a *Faith*: it concerns a prophetic word that is a word which has been inspired by a God with whom the exegete entertains a special relationship.

B. Specific Remarks

Presupposition: The text which is the only actual data we have so far will be considered as such, in its "finished state," as the fundamental presupposition of our exegetical enterprise. A basic knowledge and understanding of the vocabulary of the text, and its grammatical structure is then implied before engaging in the exegetical work (for this preliminary work, see our guidelines above in "Advanced Hebrew").

A Basic Principle: Read the text repeatedly in its original language with great attention (close reading) and fresh eyes (forget what you know about that text), and ask at every step, at every word, the key question"why?" (Why does the author/the text, say what he/it says? Why does the author/ the text say it that way?).

Strategy: The exegetical work will be described through seven assignments leading ultimately to the exegetical paper (the eighth assignment). These eight assignments cover 35 exercises; they are by no means chronological steps, but may be integrated according to a different organization.

I. Textual

1. Note the most important textual variants. Compare independent sources (eg. MT, LXX, Qumran; see especially Apparatus BHS). Try to translate them back into Hebrew and explain them. Choose the best version and justify (textual criticism).

2. Write down (without vowels) the consonantal text and try different possibilities of reading. Compare with the Masoretic version. Make your best choice and justify it.

3. Master the meaning of all the accents of the text (learn their name and their grade). Put the punctuation on the text following the indications of the hierarchy of the accents. Compare this punctuation with the one suggested in the other ancient versions. Make your best choice and justify it.

4. Write a first literal translation recording your choices.

II. Linguistic

5. Note the grammatical difficulties. Explain them with the help of technical tools (grammars, articles, etc.).

6. Note and explain the grammatical and syntactical irregularities (because of the history of the language, of the specific language of the author, or of an intention of the author).

7. Note and explain the rare words and expressions (less than 5 occurrences including *hapax legomena*).

8. Analyze the syntactical relations between clauses; indicate the specific nuances expressed by the articulating *vavs* and particles.

9. Render your observations in your translation.

III. Literary

10. Situate your text within the literary structure of the whole book. Explain the logic of this sequence and the position of the text.

11. Indicate the delimitations of the text (beginning and end). Indicate the clues (Masoretic, structural) which justify this delimitation.

12. Depending on the literary nature of the text, prepare a poetic analysis of the passage. Point out the parallelisms, play on words, alliterations and other poetic devices. Analyze the meter of the passage (accents, syllables).

13. Note the words which occur most frequently in the text, or (and) those which are distributed according to a regular pattern; detect the key word(s) of the text.

14. Establish the literary structure of the text; show how some clues (key words, poetic devices) serve that structure.

15. Do a word study of the most crucial key word(s) of the text (see below).

16. Show how the literary structure, the key word(s) and other poetic devices serve the specific meaning of the text. Copy the text according to its literary structure (bring out parallelisms, stanzas, etc.).

17. Detect the literary genre of the text (narrative, hymns, laments, poetry, genealogy, etc.), and compare with other texts of the same genre, in order to establish the validity of the genre you are referring to. Show how the literary genre serves the meaning of the text.

18. Detect and examine the discrepancies and the repetitions in the text and explain them in regard to its historical composition or (and) its literary construction. Address the question of the literary unity and the authorship of the passage.

IV. Historical

19. Pinpoint the words and forms which betray its historical setting. As far as possible, justify your choice by reference to the evolution of the language.

20. Pinpoint the words, expressions, ideas, etc., which allude to specific events, situations, persons, places or times.

21. Situate the text in its historical context; establish, if possible, the events which may have generated what the text says and the events which may have been generated by what the text says.

22. Evaluate critically the diverse opinions concerning the date of the book to which the text belongs.

V. Theological

23. On the basis of your observation of the text *as a whole*, its literary structure and its key words, its literary genre, etc., establish the central idea of the passage. Indicate why this idea is central in the passage, and how (on the stylistic level) the author makes it central.

24. Situate this idea within the theology of the book, of the Hebrew Scriptures, and of the whole Bible. Relate this idea to the classical theological concepts (God, man, salvation, eschatology, etc.), to the system of Hebrew thinking, and to the doctrine of your religious community.

25. Detect other secondary ideas of the passage. Show how they are related to the central idea, and how they are themselves interrelated. Write a short statement exposing the coherent unity between all these ideas.

26. Courageously, but prudently, point out the theological problems this passage may arouse, in relation to biblical theology in general or to

your doctrines in particular. Discuss the nature of these problems, and if possible propose a solution.

VI. Interpretation

27.   Prophetic interpretation: Examine the use of this passage throughout the Scriptures. Using a Hebrew and an English concordance, find the biblical passages which refer or allude to your text. Establish how your passage is transmitted, and interpreted in those new contexts. Show how those texts allude to your passage through the use of echoes, repetitions of unique associations of words or of ideas, the same key words, etc. Indicate the exegetical method used in the new passage (hermeneutics), and show to what extent this new "reading" fits, confirms, enlightens, enriches, or even differs from the original one. Explain the new meaning in relation to the new context. Indicate the elements of interpretation you decided to adopt in your own interpretation and translation. Justify your choice.

28.   Traditional interpretation: Investigate the interpretation of the passage in Jewish (especially Mishna, Talmud, Midrash), Christian (especially the Church Fathers and the Reformers), and even Moslem (especially the Koran and the Hadith) classical traditions. Gather all the passages which quote and interpret your passage. Compare them within the different traditions. For each tradition, write a statement which capsulizes the characteristics of its interpretation(s). Compare with the original meaning and with its "prophetic" interpretation. Indicate the exegetical method used in each tradition (hermeneutics), and show to what extent this interpretation fits, confirms, enlightens, enriches, or even differs from the original one. Explain the new applications in relation to the theological setting of these traditions. Indicate the elements of interpretation you decided to adopt in your own interpretation and translation. Justify your choice.

29.   Critical interpretation: Consult modern biblical commentaries, dissertations, articles, etc., dealing with your passage and being representative of modern schools of interpretation (historical-critical, structuralist, materialistic, psycho-analytical, rhetorical, etc.). Describe their respective interpretations of the passage. Indicate in each case the exegetical method (hermeneutics), and show to what extent this interpretation fits, confirms, enlightens, enriches, or even differs from the original one. Explain the new interpretation in relation to the philosophical presupposition inspiring each

method. Indicate the elements of interpretation you decided to adopt in your own interpretation and translation. Justify your choice.

30. Write your final translation in good English while integrating the results of your research. Try to be both communicative, and faithful to the intentions of the original text. Compare your translation with modern English translations, and justify your choice when you differ significantly from them.

VII. Relevance

31. Infer from your "total" exegesis of the text, lessons which are relevant for the church in regard to doctrine, as well as in regard to the religious life of the community.

32. Interpret the text from an existential point of view, under the control of your exegesis. Note the lesson(s) of the text which speak to man in general, and to you personally in your situation now.

33. Investigate the possibilities of exploiting your exegesis for one or several sermons (see below).

VIII. The Exegetical Paper

34. Organize your material depending on the form of paper you choose. There are several options: 1) the technical paper: you follow the seven steps of your research as indicated above; 2) the commentary paper: you follow the text verse by verse, from the beginning to the end; 3) the issue related paper: you address one or several issues of the text and follow the logical order of the arguments; 4) the topical paper: you organize your paper around theological motifs and follow the logical order of these motifs; 5) the essay paper: you discuss the passage in a free-flowing fashion. Whatever form of writing you may choose, integrate your research and the scholarly discussion covered in the seven assignments in your paper. Make a clear distinction between your contribution and what you have found elsewhere (refer diligently to your sources and discuss critically).

35. Write your Introduction where you justify the choice of your research, and raise the issues in regard to the scholarly discussion. Write your Conclusion where you summarize your research, and remind of the

issues raised in the Introduction; indicate the solutions you propose and your contribution as well as the problems which are still to be addressed.

Note: Five main qualities make a good paper: 1) well informed, 2) original, 3) rigorously argued, 4) well written, 5) well presented (see Kate L. Turabian, *A Manual for Writers of Term Papers, Theses, and Dissertations*, 5th ed., rev. and expan. [Chicago, 1987]).

The Word Study

Definition: The *word study* is a systematic analysis of the meaning(s) of one particular word.

Goals and Limits: To arrive at its specific meaning in a particular biblical text (exegesis), or to indicate the direction(s) of Hebrew thinking (theology). We should keep in mind, however, that the meaning of the word depends ultimately on the context in which it is used; the word study provides just an orientation within which we have to seek the specific meaning. The absolute meaning of the word does not exist as such. Besides the rigor which the systematic analysis requires from the researcher, this dynamic implies for him great flexibility, intuition, and serious consideration of the living context of the word (see Moisés Silva, *Biblical Words and Their Meaning: An Introduction to Lexical Semantics* [Grand Rapids, 1983]).

Methodology: The methodology of this study varies, depending on the frequency of the word; if the number of its occurrences is very little (less than 10), or if it is an *hapax legomenon*, the statistical and historical argument is not significant (see especially 2 and 3). As the data are not the same for every word, the 15 steps we propose here are therefore theoretical and will not work the same way for every word. To safeguard the specificity of the biblical meaning, and allow a fresh approach to it, we suggest the following process from the center (information from the Hebrew word itself and its translations) to the periphery (information from its cognates and the technical studies).

I. The Hebrew Word

1. Use a *Hebrew lexicon*: find the basic meaning, and its secondary meaning, in the Bible; write them down with one or two references as an illustration for each meaning. See Francis Brown, S. R. Driver, and Charles A. Briggs, *A Hebrew and English Lexicon of the Old Testament*

(Oxford, 1966); Ludwig Koehler and Walter Baumgartner, *Lexicon in Veteris Testamenti Libros* (Leiden, 1958).

2. Use a *Hebrew concordance*: write down the total frequency of the word; its distribution in the biblical books (a diagram recording this data is recommended). See Solomon Mandelkern, *Veteris Testamenti Concordantiae Hebraicae atque Chaldaicae* (Jerusalem, 1969); Abraham Even-Shoshan, ed., *A New Concordance of the Old Testament* (Grand Rapids, 1984).

3. Use a *Hebrew concordance* and a *Hebrew grammar*: analyze the syntax of the word (grammatical form, place in the sentence) according to its distribution in the biblical books (a diagram recording this data is recommended).

4. Use a *Hebrew concordance* and a *Hebrew lexicon*: find the various words with which this word is usually associated; indicate the frequency of the respective associations and give the respective basic meanings of the associated words. Find idiomatic expressions in which the word may be used. Find synonyms and antonyms of the word (with the help of topical concordances such as Orville J. Nave, *Nave's Topical Bible* (Chicago, 1974). See also Robert B. Girdlestone, *Synonyms of the Old Testament*.

5. Use a *Hebrew concordance* and a *Bible* (Hebrew and English): find biblical texts where this word plays the role of a keyword; indicate the connection between the word and this context.

6. Use a general *Hebrew thesaurus* and other *lexicons*: find if possible the non-Old Testament usages of the word (inscriptions, Rabbinic literature); indicate their respective meaning and describe the history of their evolution. See Charles-Francois Jean and Jacob Hoftijzer, *Dictionnaire des inscriptions semitiques de l'ouest* (Leiden, 1965); Marcus Jastrow, *A Dictionary of the Targumim, the Talmud Babli and Yherushalmi, and the Midrashic Literature*, 2 vols. (New York, 1962).

II. Translations

7. Find and write down the diverse renderings of the word in ancient versions (the Greek *Septuagint*, the *New Testament*, the Latin *Vulgate*); for each meaning, give a dictionary definition of the Greek and the Latin word,

and as far as possible provide with an example of a sentence (with reference) in which the word is used.

8. Find and write down the diverse renderings of the word in modern English translations (such as the *Jerusalem Bible*, the *New International Version*, the *New King James Version*); for each meaning provide one or two references.

III. Cognates

9. Use a *Hebrew Lexicon*: find the Hebrew words of the same root; indicate their respective basic and secondary meaning(s).

10. Use a *Hebrew Lexicon*: find the Hebrew words which belong to the same phonetic family (at least two common letters); indicate their respective basic and secondary meaning(s).

11. Use a *Hebrew Lexicon* and other *Language Dictionaries*: find words of the same root and indicate their respective basic and secondary meaning(s) in other Semitic languages (such as Akkadian, Ugaritic, Aramaic, Arabic), unless this word is derived from a non-Semitic language (see then in the corresponding family of languages). Trace the etymology of the word (attested or reconstructed), and write a statement summarizing the common basic idea of these words.

IV. Technical Studies

12. Use a bibliographic aid such as *Elenchus* (since 1988 in *Ephemerides Theologicae Lovanienses*) or *Old Testament Abstracts*, etc.: set up a bibliography of articles in journals and biblicaltheological dictionaries, dissertations, and books on this word or on related words (synonyms, antonyms). See G. Johannes Botterweck and Helmer Ringgren, eds., *Theological Dictionary of the Old Testament*, vols. 1-6 (Grand Rapids, 1974-1990), in progress; R. Laird Harris, ed., *Theological Wordbook of the Old Testament*, 2 vols. (Chicago, 1980).

13. Read through these works and write a summary of the state of the question; compare critically with your own observations and conclusions.

V. Synthesis and Conclusion

14. Write a nuanced synthesis of your research: delineate the wide range of meanings and directions of thought which are attested while indicating those which are mostly represented.

15. Apply your findings to understand the specific meaning of the word in the given text (for exegesis), or to grasp the Hebrew category of thinking (for theology).

The Sermon

Here are some guidelines to make your study of Hebrew language and thought relevant and practical in your "present ministry of the word."

I. The Three Qualities of a Good "Biblical Sermon"

In order to be faithful to the biblical message, and also to be efficient, this sermon should be creative, communicative, and true.

1. Creative

Seek out *new* ground (texts, words, ideas, stories, etc.).
Do not echo others; do not repeat yourself.
Be open to surprises.

2. Communicative

Be committed: be intellectually convinced of what you say; be existentially committed to your message; integrate this message in your life, in your thought.

Be clear: be modest (focus on few ideas); be organized (plan); be simple (do not be technical).

Be relevant: meet the needs, the interests, and the sensitivity of your people where they are.

3. True

Focus on the sacred word.

Be interested in the truth rather than in the reflection of, or support for your concerns and opinions.

Preach from the text and not through the text.

Avoid shallowness (you are dealing with sacred material).

II. Two Categories of Sermons

Your study of Hebrew will inspire you and will more or less affect several of your sermons. We shall concentrate here only on the two categories of sermons which are directly generated by the Hebrew information, namely the sermon on the biblical text and the sermon on the Hebrew word.

1. On the Text

a) Choice

From your studies (the Bible, courses, books, discussions, etc.).

From yourself (biblical texts you like or even dislike, texts that speak to you personally).

From a definite program (liturgical: the text of the week; didactic: key-text in doctrine; circumstantial: text related to a similar occasion).

b) Preparation (See above "Exegesis")

Read the text in your version repeatedly over a long period of time (one to two weeks to allow maturation and saturation).

Consult the Hebrew original and one or two English translations.

Detect words which are repeated, the key word(s), other important words (names of places, of persons); with the use of a Hebrew lexicon indicate their respective basic and secondary meanings.

Outline the literary structure of the text, note the parallelisms, the play on words, and other stylistic devices.

Situate the text in its literary, historical, and theological context.

Look at the text as a whole: deduce the main idea(s) of the text.

Read some literature (especially commentaries) about this text (only *after* your personal work, to safeguard your creativity).

Write down all the ideas or situations in the text which appear significant to us today.

Write down other ideas, historical or personal experiences which cross your mind by way of association.

c) Exposition (Plan)

1) Introduction: situate the text in *its* context and in *your* context (its significance then and now).

2) Development, several options:

Progress according to the chronological order of the text (from beginning to end).

Section 1 → Idea A
Section 2 → Idea B
Section 3 → Idea C, etc.

Progress according to the literary structure of the text; e.g., if the text displays the parallelisms A B C / A1 B1 C1, treat A with A1, B with B1, and C with C1.

Progress according to the ideas of the text (follow a logical order: Idea A → B → C).

Idea A → Verses 1, 2
Idea B → Verses 12, 15, 16
Idea C → Verses 4, 6, 7

3) Conclusion: summarize, apply to life.

2. On the Hebrew Word

a) Choice

From your studies (Hebrew vocabulary, biblical dictionaries, courses, etc.).

From yourself (the word which struck you, names of biblical persons, or places, etc.).

From a definite program (didactical: theological words; existential: related to life; circumstantial: word or name related to a special occasion).

b) Preparation (See above "The Word Study")

Write down all the various meanings of the word in relation to their respective context; find a practical application, and an illustration (story, experience) for each meaning.

c) Exposition (Outline)

1) Introduction: Justify the choice of your word; situate the word (its importance in the Bible and for us). Indicate the basic meaning.

2) Development, several options:

If this word has several meanings, one section for each meaning.

Derived words from the same root: one section for each word.

Focus on the basic meaning of the word and develop this basic idea deductively.

3) Conclusion: Synthesis of the diverse meanings and applications; show the connection between them; apply to life.

ANALYTICAL INDEX

COMPANION TAPE

TO *HEBREW FOR THEOLOGIANS*

(Length: 60 minutes)

Contents:

Side one: The signs (accompanies pp. 3-11 of the book)

- Alphabet (consonants and vowels)
- Reading exercises (letter by letter)

Side two: The texts: Genesis 22:1-19, Psalm 23, Micah 4:1-4
(accompanies pp. 3-11 of the book)

- Reading (verse by verse)
- Chanting (Sephardic Masoretic cantillation)

Ordering Information:

Address: Dr. Jacques Doukhan, Andrews University Theological
Seminary, Old Testament Department, Berrien Springs, MI
49104-1500; Telephone No. (616) 471-2861

Price: $7.00 (shipping and handling included; Michigan residents
please add 4% for Michigan sales tax; this price is subject to
change)